Sustainable Software Architecture

Carola Lilienthal is managing director of WPS – Workplace Solutions GmbH and is responsible for the department of software architecture. Since 2003, Dr. Carola Lilienthal has been analyzing over 300 architectures in Java, TypeScript, C #, C ++, ABAP and PHP, and advising development teams on how to improve the sustainability of their software systems. She is particularly interested in the education of software architects, which is why she regularly passes on her knowledge at conferences, in articles and training courses.

Carola Lilienthal

Sustainable Software Architecture

Analyze and Reduce Technical Debt

dpunkt.verlag

Carola Lilienthal
carola.lilienthal@wps.de

Editor: Michael Barabas / Christa Preisendanz
Copyeditor: Jeremy Cloot
Layout and type: Josef Hegele
Cover design: Helmut Kraus, *www.exclam.de*

Bibliographic information published by the Deutsche Nationalbibliothek (DNB)
The Deutsche Nationalbibliothek lists this publication in the Deutsche Nationalbibliografie;
detailed bibliographic data can be found on the internet at *http://dnb.dnb.de*

Copyright © 2019 dpunkt.verlag GmbH
Wieblinger Weg 17
69123 Heidelberg

ISBN:
Print (dt.)   978-3-86490-673-2
Print (engl.) 978-1-68198-569-5
PDF   978-3-96088-780-5
epub   978-3-96088-781-2
mobi   978-3-96088-782-9

Title of the German original: Langlebige Software-Architekturen.
Technische Schulden analysieren, begrenzen und abbauen
2., überarbeitete und erweiterte Auflage 2017
ISBN 978-3-86490-494-3

Distributed in the UK and Europe by Publishers Group UK and dpunkt.verlag GmbH.
Distributed in the U.S. and all other territories by Ingram Publisher.

Foreword

The first time I met Dr. Carola Lilienthal was at a conference on Domain-Driven Design where we were both presenting. As she went through her slides and discussed many of the concepts in this book, two things became clear.

First, her understanding of software architecture is simultaneously deep and broad. The advice she gives comes from decades of hands-on experience working with hundreds of legacy systems. She works in the trenches, far removed from the ivory tower that so many software architects move into. Yet, technical as she is, her expertise transcends a single specialty. Her stories, examples, and advice apply to a wide range of domains, languages, and technical stacks. While it might be rare to find an individual with equal breadth and depth, it's exactly the skill set that's required for a book on making software architecture sustainable.

The second thing I noticed was the way she lit up when she talked. For her, making software systems more modular, extensible, and sustainable isn't simply an intellectual or academic pursuit. It's a passion. The joy, hope, and optimism she exudes when talking about improving software architecture is contagious. While this might seem trivial on the surface, make no mistake—that mentality is a crucial asset when you're wading through the mire and chaos of a system bogged down with technical debt. So many systems are abandoned because their maintainers lacked not just the skill to make a change, but the hope that a change was even possible.

For these reasons, I'm thrilled that Dr. Lilienthal has decided to share her experience with the world through her book, *Sustainable Software Architecture*. Legacy code is notoriously difficult to work with for a variety of reasons, not the least of which is the amount of interdependency that exists within a system. Throughout the book, Dr. Lilienthal has provided sound advice on diagnosing, understanding, disentangling, and ultimately preventing the issues that make software systems brittle and subject to breakage. In addition to the technical examples that you'd expect in a book on software architecture, she takes the time to dive into the behavioral and human aspects that impact sustainability and, in my experience, are inextricably linked to the health of a codebase. She also expertly zooms out, exploring architecture concepts such as domains and layers, and then zooms in to the class level where your typical developer works day-to-day. This holistic approach is crucial for implementing long-lasting change.

There is an immense amount of gratification to be found in making a system sustainable. Too often in our society, "makers" (people who get the most joy during the initial phases of a project) are the ones who enjoy all the glory. However, it's important to recognize the tremendous value that already resides within existing software systems, along with the value of "menders" like Dr. Lilienthal who are eager to dive in and make these systems better. Legacy code runs our world. While it might be tempting to bulldoze a system and start over, doing so, especially if done in haste, rarely accomplishes the goal that we ultimately want—software systems that are easier to modify, extend, grow, and maintain. The better path, the path that ultimately uses fewer resources, causes less frustration, and gets better results, is the path of committed sustainability, and taking the first step down that path is just a few page turns away.

Andrea Goulet
CEO, Corgibytes
Founder, Legacy Code Rocks

Preface

Dear Reader,

Welcome to this book on sustainable software architecture. In the following chapters I invite you to explore the inner life of software systems with me and admire the beauty and cruelty that can be found within.

In recent years, I have been fortunate enough to be allowed to look deeply into many software systems. In doing so, I have pondered and discussed with many architects, debating which structures are more sustainable than others and why. In this book you will find many recommendations on all aspects of developing sustainable systems. There are also real-world case studies, screenshots of real systems to help my observations come to life, and a little theory too, to help you quickly grasp the principles involved and retain what you learn.

I would be delighted if you could give me feedback on my experiences. Perhaps you have seen similar things, or perhaps you have a completely different view of software architecture. I hope you will find the following pages interesting, informative, discussion-worthy, and perhaps even amusing.

I would like to thank everyone who accompanied me on the journey that led to the creation of this book. Thanks go to my family who always support me in all my projects, even with an idea as crazy as writing a book. You are wonderful! Merci beaucoup!

Thanks go to everyone who reviewed the German version of the text: Eberhard Wolff, Gernot Starke, Johannes Rost, Stefan Sarstedt, Stefan Tilkov, Stefan Zörner, Tobias Zepter, Ulf Fildebrandt, and my anonymous reviewers. Your comments have made me think, rethink, and then think even further—thank you!

Thanks to all my colleagues at *WPS Workplace Solution* for the many discussions about software architecture, without which this book could never have been written: Holger Breitling, Kai Bühner, Guido Gryczan, Stefan Hofer, Bettina Koch, Jörn Koch, Michael Kowalczyk, Kai Rüstmann, Arne Scharping, Lasse Schneider, Henning Schwentner, and Heinz Züllighoven.

Thanks also to everyone who covered for me so that I could write in peace, especially Martina Bracht-Kopp, Inge Fontaine, Petra Gramß, Silja Heitmann, and Doris Nied.

Many thanks to Norman Wenzel, Heinrich Rust, and Alexander von Zitzewitz who worked with me for such a long time on the architectural review. It's a privilege to work with you.

My thanks also go to everyone at my publisher. You have all been so kind and constructive while this book was taking shape.

And, of course, many thanks to all the customers who allowed me to tell you about their systems—you have made a really valuable contribution to this book. And finally, many thanks to my colleague Ben McDougall, who corrects my English texts with a lot of patience and humor.

Hamburg, June 2019
Carola Lilienthal
@cairolali
www.sustainable-software-architecture.com

Table of Contents

1 Introduction

Software systems are certainly among the most complex constructions that human beings have ever conceived and built, so it's not surprising that some software projects fail, and legacy systems often remain unmodified for fear they will simply stop working. In spite of this complexity, I still encounter project teams that are in control of their software systems, regardless of their industry, technology stack, size, or age. Adding functionality and fixing bugs in such legacy systems involves much less effort than I would have imagined, and new employees can be trained with reasonable effort. What do these project teams do differently? "How do they manage their software so effectively in the long run?"

The main reasons for long-term success or failure in software development and maintenance can be found on many different levels. These include the industry, the technology used, the quality of the software system, and the qualifications of the users and developers. This book focuses on the **sustainability of software architecture**. I will show you which factors are most important for maintaining and expanding a software architecture over many years without making significant changes to your staffing, budget, or delivery schedule.

Sustainability of software architectures

1.1 Software Architecture

Computer science has not been able to commit itself to a single definition of software architecture. In fact, there are more than 50 different definitions, each highlighting specific aspects of architecture. In this book we will stick to two of the most prominent definitions:

50 definitions

> **Definition #1:**
>
> "Software architecture is the structure of a software product. This includes elements, the externally visible properties of the elements, and the relationships between the elements." [Bass et al. 2012]

Architecture Views This definition deliberately talks about elements and relationships in very general terms. These two basic materials can be used to describe a wide variety of architecture views. The static (module) view contains the following elements: classes, packages, namespaces, directories, and projects—in other words, all the containers you can use for programming code in that particular programming language. In the distribution view, the following elements can be found: archives (JARs, WARs, assemblies), computers, processes, communication protocols and channels, and so on. In the dynamic (runtime) view we are interested in the runtime objects and their interactions. In this book we will deal with the structures in the module (static)[1] view and show why some are more durable than others.

The second definition is one that is very close to my heart. It doesn't define architecture by way of its structure, but rather the decisions made.

> **Definition #2:**
>
> "Software architecture = the sum of all important decisions
>
> Important decisions are all decisions that are difficult to change in the course of further development." [Kruchten 2004]

Structure vs. decisions These two definitions are very different. The first defines what the structure of a software system consists of on an abstract level, whereas the second refers to decisions that the developers or architects make regarding the system as a whole. The second definition defines the space for all overarching aspects of architecture, such as technology selection, architectural style selection, integration, security, performance, and much, much more. These aspects are just as

---

1   The structures of the module view usually also influence the distribution view. Section 7.2 contains a proposal for displaying the distribution view in the module view.

important to an architecture as the chosen structure, but are not the subject of this book.

This book deals with the decisions that influence the structure of a software system. Once a development team and its architects decide on the structure of a system, they have defined **guardrails for the architecture**.

Decisions create guardrails

> **Guardrails for your architecture**
>
> Create an architecture that restricts the design space during the development of the software system and gives you direction in your work.

Guardrails allow developers and architects to orient themselves. The decisions are all channeled in a uniform direction and can be understood and traced, giving the software system a homogeneous structure. When solving maintenance tasks, guardrails guide all participants in a uniform direction, and lead to faster and more consistent results during adaptation or extension of the system.

Guardrails for development

This book will answer questions regarding which guardrails lead to durable architectures and extend the life of a software system.

1.2 Sustainability

Software that is only used for a short period of time shouldn't have an architecture that is designed for sustainability. An example of such a piece of software is a program that migrates data from a legacy system into the database of a new application. This software is used once and then hopefully discarded. We say "hopefully" because experience has shown that program parts that are no longer used can be still found in many software systems. They are not discarded because the developers assume that they might need them again later. Also, to delete lines of working code that were created with a lot of effort isn't done lightly. There is hardly a developer or architect who likes to do this.[2]

Short-lived software

---

2   In order to perceive discarding software as something positive, the clean code movement has introduced "Code Kata" workshops in which the same problem is solved several times and the code is discarded after each step.

The "Year 2000" problem

Most of the software we program today lives much longer than expected. It is often edited and adapted. In many cases software is used for many more years than anyone could have imagined at the coding stage. Think, for example, of the Cobol developers who wrote the first major Cobol systems for banks and insurance companies in the 1960s and 1970s. Storage space was expensive at the time, so programmers thought hard about preserving storage space for every field saved on the database. For the Cobol developers at the time, it seemed a reasonable decision to implement years as two-digit fields only. Nobody imagined back then that these Cobol programs would still exist in the year 2000. During the years prior to the turn of the millennium, a lot of effort had to be made to convert all the old programs to four-digit year fields. If the Cobol developers in the 1960s and 1970s had known that their software would be in service for such a long time, they would have used four-digit fields to represent years.

Our software will get old

Such a long lifetime is still realistic for a large number of the software systems that we build today. Many companies shy away from investing in new development, which generates significant costs that are often higher than planned. The outcome of new developments is also unknown, and users too have to be taken into consideration. In addition, the organization is slowed down during the development process and an investment backlog arises for urgently needed extensions. At the end of the day, it is better to stick with the software you have and expand it if necessary. Perhaps a new front end on top of an old server will suffice.

Old and cheap?

This book is rooted in the expectation that an investment in software should pay for itself for as long as possible. New software should incur the lowest possible maintenance and expansion costs in the course of its lifetime—in other words, the technical debt must be kept as low as possible.

1.3 Technical Debt

The term "technical debt" is a metaphor coined by Ward Cunningham in 1992 [Cunningham 1992]. Technical debt arises when false or suboptimal technical decisions are made, whether consciously or unconsciously. Such decisions lead to additional effort at a later point in time, which delays maintenance and expansion.

If there are capable developers and architects on the team at the beginning of a software development project, they will contribute their best experience and accumulated design know-how to creating a long-lasting architecture with no technical debt. However, this goal cannot be ticked off at the beginning of the project according to the principle "First we will design a long-lasting architecture and everything else will be fine from then on."

Good intentions

In truth, you can only achieve a long-lasting architecture if you constantly keep an eye on technical debt. In figure 1-1 we see what happens when technical debt grows over time in comparison to what happens when it is reduced regularly.

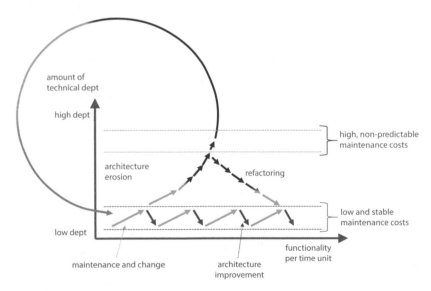

Figure 1-1

Technical debt and architectural erosion

Imagine a team that is continuously developing a system using releases or iterations: if the team focuses on quality it will knowingly pile on new technical debt with each add-on (the yellow arrows in fig. 1-1). During the development of an expansion, the team will already be

A quality-oriented team

thinking about what needs to be done to improve the architecture. Meanwhile (or after the expansion), technical debt will be reduced again (indicated by the green arrows in fig. 1-1). A constant sequence of expansion and improvement occurs. If the team works this way, the system remains in a corridor of low technical debt with a predictable maintenance effort (see green bracket in fig. 1-1).

A chaotic team

If the team doesn't aim to constantly preserve the architecture, the architecture of the system is slowly lost, and maintainability deteriorates. Sooner or later, the software system leaves the corridor of minor technical debt (indicated by the ascending red arrows in fig. 1-1).

Architectural erosion

The architecture erodes further and further. Maintenance and the extension of the software become increasingly expensive until you reach the point where every change becomes a painful effort. In figure 1-1 this case is made clear by the red arrows becoming shorter and shorter. As the erosion of the architecture increases, less and less functionality can be implemented, fewer bugs can be fixed, and fewer adaptations to other quality requirements can be achieved per unit of time. The development team becomes frustrated and demotivated and sends desperate signals to the project's management. Such warnings are usually registered far too late.

Too expensive!

If you are on the path depicted by the ascending red arrows, the sustainability of your software system will continuously decrease. The software system becomes error-prone, the development team gets a reputation for being sluggish, and changes that used to be possible within two person-days now take up to twice or three times as long. All in all, everything happens much too slowly. In the IT industry, "slow" is a synonym for "too expensive". That's right, technical debt has accumulated and with every change you have to pay interest on the technical debt principal plus the cost of the expansion.

Returning to good quality

The way out of this technical debt dilemma is to retroactively improve architectural quality. As a result, the system can be pulled back into the corridor of low technical debt step by step (see the red descending arrows in fig. 1-1). This path requires significant resources (both time and money) but still represents a reasonable investment in the future. After all, future maintenance will involve less effort and will be cheaper. For software systems that once had good architecture, this procedure usually leads to rapid success.

The CRAP cycle

The situation is completely different if the corridor of high technical debt is reached and the maintenance effort becomes disproportionately high and unpredictable (see the red bracket in fig. 1-1). I am frequently asked what "disproportionately high maintenance" means. A general answer that is valid for all projects is of course difficult to provide. However, in various systems with good architecture I have noticed that for every 500,000 lines of code (LOC), one or two full-time developers are required for maintenance. In other words, 40-80 hours per week per 500,000 LOC is a good starting point for determining the time needed to fix bugs and make small adjustments. If new functionality is to be integrated into the system, you will of course require even more capacity.

When I visit a company to evaluate an architecture, the first question I ask is about the size of the system(s). Secondly, I ask about the size and efficiency of the development department. If the answer is, "We employ 30 developers for our Java system of 3 million LOC, but they are all busy with maintenance and we can hardly get any new features implemented ..." I immediately assume that it is an indebted system. Naturally, setting such an expectation is harsh, but it has usually proved helpful as an initial hunch.

If the system has too much debt to be maintainable and extensible, companies often decide to replace the system with a new one (see the colored circle in fig. 1-1). In 2015, to my great delight, Peter Vogel described the typical lifecycle of a system with technical debt as a "CRAP cycle". The acronym CRAP stands for C(reate) R(epair) A(bandon) (re)P(lace)[3]. If repairing a system seems fruitless or too expensive, the system is left to die and eventually replaced.

However, this last step should be approached cautiously. As early as the beginning of the 2000s, many legacy systems written in COBOL and PL/1 were declared unmaintainable and replaced by Java systems. Everything was supposed to get better with this new programming language, and this promise was made to the managers who were tasked with funding the new implementation. Today, a number of these eagerly built Java systems are full of technical debt and generate immense maintenance costs.

---

3 *https://visualstudiomagazine.com/articles/2015/07/01/domain-driven-design.aspx*

Causes of technical debt   In the course of my professional life to date, I have repeatedly encountered four major causes of technical debt:

1. No knowledge of software architecture

2. Complexity and size of software systems

3. Architectural erosion arises unnoticed

4. A lack of understanding of custom software development processes on the part of managers and customers

These four factors usually occur in combination and often influence each other.

1.3.1   No Knowledge of Software Architecture

Programming ≠ Software Architecture   When a development team starts a new project, I always try to include an experienced developer-architect in the team. Every developer can program, but knowledge of sustainable software architecture only comes with experience.

Unusable software   If nobody in the team cares about sustainable architecture, the resulting system is likely to be maintenance-intensive. The architecture of these systems evolves over a period without any planning. Each developer fulfills her own personal ideas on architecture and/ or design for her part of the software. "It's a legacy system!" is often heard in the latter case.

Starting with technical debt   In this case, technical debt is accumulated right from the beginning of and increases continuously. The usual attitude to such software systems is that they somehow grew up under a bad influence. Systems like this can often no longer be maintained after a relatively short period of time. I have even seen systems that have become unmaintainable after just three years.

Significant refactoring   The architectural and design ideas of architects and developers must initially be questioned and their quality standardized in order to move these systems closer to the corridor of low technical debt using whatever possible means. Overall, this is much more complex than getting a system with previously good architecture back on track. However, large-scale quality refactoring can be broken down into manageable sub-steps. After some initial small improvements (quick wins) the quality gain becomes noticeable through faster maintenance. Such quality-improving work often costs less than a new implementation, even if many development teams understandably enjoy new development projects much more. This positive attitude to a new development project is often accompanied by underestimation of the complexity of the task.

1.3.2 Complexity and Size

The complexity of a software system is fed by two different sources: the use case for which the software system was built and the solution (the program code, the database, and so on).

An appropriate solution for the problem must be found within its specialized domain—a solution that allows the user to carry out the planned business processes using the software system. These factors are known as "problem-inherent" and "solution-dependent" complexity. The greater the complexity of the problem, the greater the solution-dependent complexity will be[4].

Problem-inherent complexity

This correlation is the reason why cost predictions and software development duration are often estimated too low. The actual complexity of the problem cannot be determined at the beginning of the project, so the complexity of the solution is underestimated many times over[5].

This is where agile methods apply. Agile methods only estimate the functionality that is to be implemented up to the end of each iteration. The complexity of the problem and the resulting complexity of the solution are rechecked time and again.

Solution-dependent complexity

Not only the complexity inherent to the problem is difficult to determine. The solution, too, contributes to the complexity. Depending on the experience and methodical strength of the developers, the design and implementation of a problem will vary in complexity. Ideally, a solution will only be as complex as the problem. In this case, we can say that it is a good solution.

Essential or accidental?

If the solution is more complex than the actual problem, the solution is not a good one and a corresponding redesign is necessary. The difference between better and worse is called the *essential*

---

4   see [Ebert 1995], [Glass 2002] and [Woodfield 1979]
5   see [Booch 2004] and [McBride 2007]

and *accidental* complexity. Table 1-1 summarizes the relationship between these four complexity terms.

Table 1-1

Complexity

	Essential	**Accidental**
Problem-inherent	■ Complexity of the domain	■ Misunderstandings about the domain
Solution-dependent	■ Complexity of technology and architecture	■ Misunderstandings about technology ■ Superfluous solution elements

Essential = inevitable

Essential complexity is the kind of complexity that is inherent in the nature of a project. When analyzing the domain, developers try to identify the essential complexity of the problem. The essential complexity inherent to a domain leads to a correspondingly complex solution and can never be resolved or avoided just by using a particularly good design. The essential complexity of the problem has thus become the essential complexity of the solution.

Accidental = superfluous

In contrast, the term "accidental complexity" is used to refer to the elements of complexity that are not necessary and can therefore be eliminated or reduced. Accidental complexity can arise from misunderstandings during analysis of the domain as well as during implementation by the development team.

If no simple solution is found during development due to incomprehension or lack of an overview, the software system is already unnecessarily complex. Examples of unnecessary complexity are multiple implementations, integration of unneeded functionality, and disregard of software design principles. However, developers sometimes risk additional accidental complexity if, for example, they want to try out new but unnecessary technology during development.

Software is complex

Even if a team manages to incorporate only essential complexity into its software, the immense number of elements involved makes software difficult to master. In my experience, an intelligent developer can retain an overview of about 30,000 lines of code and anticipate the effects of code changes in the other places. Software systems in productive use today tend to be considerably larger than this. We are more likely talking about a range of 200,000 to 100 million lines of code.

All these arguments make it clear that developers require software architecture that gives them the greatest possible overview. Only then can they navigate their way around the existing complexity. If developers have an overview of the architecture, the probability of appropriate software changes being made increases. When they make changes, they can take all of the affected areas into account and leave the functionality of the unaltered lines of code untouched. Of course, additional techniques are very helpful, such as automated testing, high test coverage, architectural education/ training, and a supportive project and enterprise organization.

Architecture reduces complexity

1.3.3 Architectural Erosion Takes Place Unnoticed

Even with a capable development team, architectural erosion occurs unnoticed. How does this happen? Well, it's often a long, drawn-out process. During implementation, developers increasingly deviate from the architecture. In some cases, they do this consciously because the planned architecture does not meet the increasingly evident requirements. The complexity of the problem and the solution were underestimated and demands changed within the architecture, but there is no time to consistently follow these changes through for the entire system. In other cases, time and cost issues arise and must be solved so quickly that there is no time to develop a suitable design and rethink the architecture. Some developers are not even aware of the planned architecture, so they unintentionally violate it. For example, relationships are built between components that disregard prescribed public interfaces or run contrary to the modularization and layering of the software system. By the time you notice this creeping decay, it is high time to intervene!

A drawn-out process

Once you have reached the nadir of architectural erosion, every change becomes unbearable. No-one wants to continue working on such a system. In his article *Design Principles and Design Pattern*, Robert C. Martin summed up these symptoms of a rotten system [Martin 2000]:

Symptoms of severe architectural erosion

- **Rigidity:** The system is inflexible to modification. Each modification leads to a cascade of further adjustments in dependent modules. Developers are often unaware of what is happening in

Rigidity

the system and are uncomfortable with changes. What starts as a small adjustment or a small refactoring leads to an ever-increasing marathon of repairs in ever more modules. The developers chase the effects of their modifications in the source code and hope to have reached the end of the chain with every new realization.

Fragility   ■ **Fragility:** Changes to the system result in errors that have no obvious relationship to the modifications made. Each adjustment increases the probability of new subsequent errors in surprising locations. The fear of modification grows, and the impression is that the developers are no longer in control of the software.

Immobility   ■ **Immobility:** There are design and construction units that already solve a similar task as the one that is currently being implemented. However, these solutions cannot be reused because there is too much "baggage" surrounding the unit in question. A generic implementation or separation is also not possible because reconstructing the old units would be too complex and error-prone. Usually the required code is copied, as this requires less effort.

Viscosity   ■ **Viscosity:** If developers need to make an adjustment, there are usually several options. Some of these options preserve the design, while others break it. If such "hacks" are easier to implement than the design-preserving solution, the system is described as viscous.

Development teams must constantly fight these symptoms to keep their systems durable and make customizing and maintenance fun in the long run. If only the costs didn't exist ...

1.3.4 We Don't Pay Extra For Quality!

Architecture costs   Many customers are surprised when their service providers—either
extra money   external or in-house—tell them that they need more money to improve the architecture and thus the quality of the software system. Customers often say things like, "It already works! What do I gain if I spend money on quality?" or, "You got the contract because you promised you would deliver good quality. You can't demand more money for quality now". These are very unpleasant situations. As software developers and architects, our goal is to write software

with sustainable architecture and high quality. At this point, it is not easy to explain that an evolving architecture is an investment in the future and saves money in the long run.

These situations often arise because the customer/management doesn't realize (or doesn't want to know) that custom software development is an unplannable process. If new, unprecedented software is developed, the essential complexity is difficult to master. The software itself, its use, and its integration into the context of work organization and changing business processes are unpredictable. Possible extensions or new forms of use cannot be foreseen. These are essential characteristics of custom software development!

Custom software development = unplannable

Today, every software system is custom-developed software and integration into the customer's IT landscape is different every time. The technological and economic developments are so rapid that a software architecture and the resulting system that represents the ideal solution for today will reach its limits by tomorrow. These constraints lead to the conclusion that software is not an industrially manufactured product. Instead, it is a custom solution that makes sense at a given point in time, with an architecture that will hopefully endure for a long time but that must continue to evolve. This includes both functional and non-functional aspects, such as internal and external quality.

Software ≠ industrially produced goods

Fortunately, increasing numbers of customers are beginning to understand the terms "technical debt" and "sustainability.

1.3.5 Types of Technical Debt

Many types of technical debt and their variants are mentioned in discussions about technical debt. Four of these are relevant to this book:

- **Implementation debt:** The source code contains "code smells", such as long methods, code duplicates, and similar.

Code Smell

- **Design and architecture debt:** The design of classes, packages, subsystems, layers, and modules is inconsistent or complex and does not fit the planned architecture.

Structural Smell

- **Test debt:** Tests are missing or only the positive case is tested. The test coverage with automated unit tests is low.

Unit Tests

Documentation   ■ **Documentation debt:** There is no documentation, or the documentation that exists is incomplete or outdated. The overview of the architecture is not supported by the documents. Design decisions are not documented.

Basic requirement: Most of the hints, suggestions, and good and bad examples you
low test debt   will find in this book relate to the first two types of technical debt. You will see how such debt arises and how it can be reduced. However, this debt can only be reduced safely if the level of test debt is low or is reduced while you work. In this respect, low test debt is a basic requirement. On the one hand, documentation of the architecture is a good basis for the architectural analysis and improvements dealt with in this book (i.e., low documentation debt helps with the analysis). On the other hand, architectural analysis also produces documentation for the analyzed system, thus also reducing documentation debt.

1.4   The Systems I Have Seen

After completing my computer science studies in 1995 I worked as a software developer, before moving on to software architecture, project management, and consultancy. Since 2002 I have often been invited to examine the quality of software systems. In the beginning I was only able to look at the source code, but this aspect has been tool-supported since 2004. Architectural analysis and improvement developed with thorough, tool-assisted checks of the source code according to certain criteria. In Chapters 2 and 4 you will see how analysis and improvement take place technically and organizationally.

Sizes and languages   In the course of time, I have reviewed systems written in Java (130), C++ (30), C# (70), ABAP (5), PHP (20), and PLSQL (10). TypeScript and JavaScript will soon be added to this list. Each of these programming languages has its own peculiarities, as we will see in Chapter 3. The size of a system (see fig. 1-2) also influences how the software architecture is (or should be) designed.

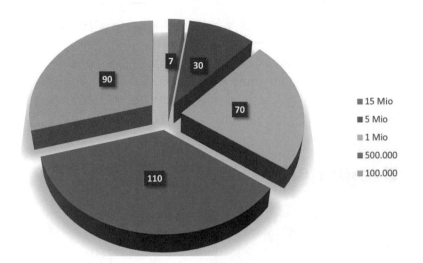

Figure 1-2

Sizes of analyzed systems in lines of code (LOC)

■ 15 Mio
■ 5 Mio
■ 1 Mio
■ 500.000
■ 100.000

The "lines of code" (LOC) specification in figure 1-2 includes the lines of executable code, blank lines, and comments. If you exclude comments and blank lines, you need to subtract an average of 50 per cent of the LOC. Typically, the ratio between executable and non-executable code is between 40 and 60 per cent, depending on whether the development team placed begin and end markers ({}) on separate lines. The sizes of systems analyzed in this book are quoted for code written in Java/C#, C++, and PHP. These languages all have a similar "sentence length". ABAP programming is much more wordy and generates two or three times as much source code.

Lines of code

All these analysis have sharpened and deepened my understanding of software architecture and my expectations of how software systems should be built.

1.5 Who Is This Book For?

This book is written for architects and developers who work with source code on a daily basis. They will benefit most from this book because it points out potential problems in large and small systems as well as offering solutions.

Programming

Consultants with development experience, practicing architects, and development teams who want to methodically improve exist-

Improving existing systems

ing software solutions will find many references to large and small improvements in this book.

Learning for the future

Inexperienced developers will probably have trouble understanding the content in some places due to the complexity of the issues involved. However, they will still be able to learn the basics of how to build sustainable software architectures.

1.6   How To Use This Book?

The book consists of twelve chapters, some of which follow on from one another, but that can also be read separately.

Main contents

Figure 1-3 shows a schematic of the book's chapters. The two white chapters provide the basic framework of introduction and summary. The turquoise chapters are the theoretical parts of the book, and the dark blue chapter deals with organizational aspects. The light blue chapters contain many small and large practical examples.

Different Paths

Ideally, you will read the entire book from start to finish. However, if your time is limited, I recommend you read Chapters 1 and 2 first to give you a good foundation. You can then skip to Chapters 5 and/or 6 followed by Chapters 7, 8, 9, or 10. You can also jump

Figure 1-3

Structure of the book

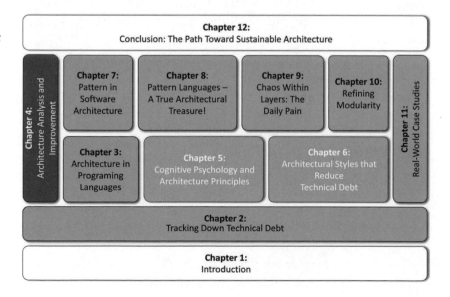

directly from Chapter 2 to Chapters 4 or 8, and dive right into the procedure of architectural analysis or the case studies.

Chapter 1 lays the foundation for understanding sustainable architectures and technical debt. *Chapter 2* shows how to find and reduce technical debt in existing architectures. *Chapter 3* explains the specialties of programming languages in architectural analysis. *Chapter 4* explains which roles in architectural analysis and improvement have to work together to achieve a valuable result, and how architectures can be compared using the Modularity Maturity Index (MMI). *Chapter 5* deals with the question of how large structures must be designed so that people can quickly navigate their way around them. Cognitive psychology gives us clues as to which specifications lead to architectures that can be quickly grasped and understood. *Chapter 6* presents the architectural styles commonly used today. With their rules, they provide guardrails for software architectures. *Chapters 7, 8, 9,* and *10* describe the findings from various practical, real-world analysis and consultations. *Chapter 11* contains seven exemplary (anonymized) case studies that I find particularly interesting. To conclude, *Chapter 12* contains a brief summary of how architects, development teams, and management should proceed to improve the quality of their architecture. The appendix presents a range of analysis tools that I have enjoyed using in the course of my everyday work.

2 Tracking Down Technical Debt

The analysis of technical debt is a broad field. It can be a matter of questioning the architecture of a system that had previously been planned on paper, or you can work out quality assurance goals for an architecture with the customer and fine-tune them using scenarios as detailed in the ATAM[1] architecture analysis method. However, this book takes a different approach, analyzing the source code of multiple systems in a search for sustainability and technical debt.

The best way to build sustainable software is covered in Chapter 5. This chapter begins with a look at the practical side of things. This will help you get an idea of the options available when investigating today's source code. Once we have introduced the terms involved (such as "building blocks", "target architecture" , and "actual architecture") we will analyze the architecture of a dummy system. We will also dive into the typical boundary conditions of an architectural analysis. Last but not least we will look into the peculiarities of some of the programming languages involved.

2.1 Building Block Terminology

Metamodel for building blocks

Unfortunately, the terms used in our discipline are not consistent. For the purposes of this book we will stick to the terminology defined in [iSAQB 2019]: All software or implementation elements that can be found in the module view are called building blocks, although some of the terms included in the metamodel (script and layout definitions) are not used in this book and therefore don't appear in figure 2-1. A new category, "Modeling Construct", has been included to provide a home for terms such as "layer", "module" and "subsystem".

---

1 ATAM = Architecture Tradeoff Analysis Methode: *https://en.wikipedia.org/wiki/Architecture_tradeoff_analysis_method.*

Figure 2-1

*"Building block" as a
generic term for software
and implementation
elements*

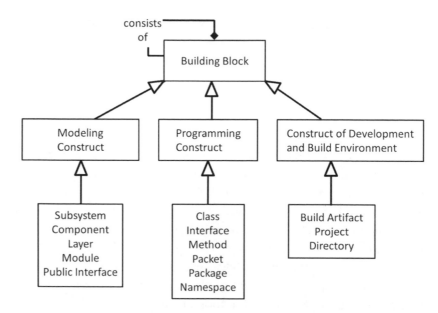

Figure 2-1

*"Building block" as a
generic term for software
and implementation
elements*

Except for the term "package", the programming constructs in figure 2-1 are defined within their respective programming languages. The other terms in figure 2-1 need a definition in order for them to stay clearly defined for the remainder of the book[2]:

Programming Constructs

■ **Packet:** Used as a generic term for packages and namespaces, but also for the programming construct that combines classes and programs in ABAP.

Modeling Constructs

■ **Subsystem:** A uniquely named unit for a set of classes/interfaces, packets, and/or subsystems of a software system. An individual public interface is often defined for a subsystem (see below).

■ **Component:** In the context of this book, a component is the same as a subsystem.

■ **Layer:** A subsystem for which rules are defined regarding which other subsystems it may and may not access. These rules create a hierarchy of layers (see Section 6.3).

---

2   Since this book examines the inner workings of customer software systems, all terms are defined on this level. The terms need to be defined more thoroughly for the analysis of multiple systems.

- **Module:** In this book, a module is defined as a domain-oriented slice that runs through all technical layers of a software system (see Section 6.3.2). In other contexts, "module" is synonymous with "component" or "subsystem".

- **Public interface[3]:** A subset of the building blocks contained within a building block that can be accessed from outside. For example, the public interface for a subsystem could consist of a set of classes and interfaces, or a set of packets.

- **Build artifact:** Units created by the build system that are usually executable and invokable (for example: JARs, WARs, DLLs, EXEs, OSGi bundles, or Maven modules).

  Constructs in the development and build environments

- **Project:** A way of organizing source code made available by development environments. A project often corresponds to a build artifact.

- **Directory:** Folders in a file system that can be used to organize source code.

We will need these modeling constructs to describe the target architecture in the next section. In contrast, the other terms are usually part of the actual architecture and are used by many development teams to make the target architecture visible within the source code.

2.2   Target and Actual Architecture

There are several sources we could use in order to investigate the architecture of a software system. Ideally, the development team planned the architecture and documented it or discussed it informally. If this is not the case, the plan can be reconstructed during the analysis using a process known as "software archaeology". The architecture planned by the development team is called the "target architecture" and the architecture represented by the source code is the "actual architecture" (see fig. 2-2).

Documentation or archaeology?

---

3   In this book I use "interface" for the technical interface construct that exists in many programming languages and "public interface" for the concept of a public interface of a building block.

Figure 2-2

Target and actual architecture

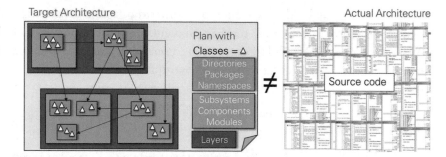

Source code = actual architecture

The source code itself is referred to as the actual architecture (see fig. 2-2). Large parts of the complexity of a software system—both essential and accidental —can be found in the source code and the implemented structures (see Section 1.3.2). This book gets to the nub of the accidental complexity that hides within the source code and the target architecture.

Plan = target architecture

The target architecture is an abstraction and simplification of the actually implemented system. It is important that the target architecture defines the components (see Section 2.1) that are not found within the source code—for example, components, subsystems, modules, and layers.

Actual architecture ≠ Target architecture

In all cases known to me, the actual architecture deviates from the target architecture. The reasons for this are manifold (see Section 1.3):

- The development team misunderstands or is ignorant of the target architecture. The implementation therefore violates the specifications of the target architecture.

- Business and technical details were overlooked while planning the target architecture and it wasn't adapted accordingly. In such a case, the target architecture may be superfluous or should be developed further.

- Competing quality goals, such as performance and loose coupling, only become apparent during later development. Furthermore, they are often implemented differently in different areas of the source code.

The difference between actual and target architecture creates complexity for the development team. To some extent, this complexity is essential if the target architecture was not clearly defined, making adaptation necessary. In some cases, it is superfluous because the development team violated the specifications of the target architecture, although a different implementation could still have been possible. Depending on the relationship between the target and actual architectures, the analysis is either about finding deviations or about developing a new and improved target architecture.

Divergence = complexity

Today, analysis tools are used to compare actual and target architecture. The analysis tool must be fed with both. The analysis tool extracts the actual architecture from the source and/or byte code of the system. It identifies the existing programming constructs (such as classes, methods, variables, packages, and namespaces) but also directories, build artifacts, and projects. The tool analyzes all the various elements and checks which elements contains which others. It also extracts the usage and inheritance relationships between all classes and builds a model of the structures within the source code (see fig. 2-3). This extraction step is automated and can take a few minutes or up to several hours, depending on the size of the parsed system.

Extraction

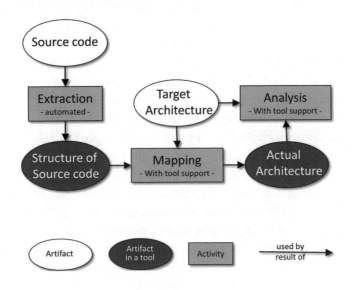

Figure 2-3

Architecture analysis methodology

The comparison between the target and actual architecture (i.e., the architecture analysis) consists of two further steps: mapping the target architecture to the source code and analyzing the structures that the mapping reveals.

Mapping the target architecture

Consider the target architecture of a system that consists of five subsystems (Proxy, Organizer, Client, Transport and Config on the left in fig. 2-4). These subsystems are arranged in three layers (purple, yellow, green) that make only top-down relationships between these layers acceptable. From the start, the architects defined the permitted relationships between the five subsystems (once again, see the target architecture on the left in fig. 2-4).

Figure 2-4

Sample mapping of target architecture to actual architecture

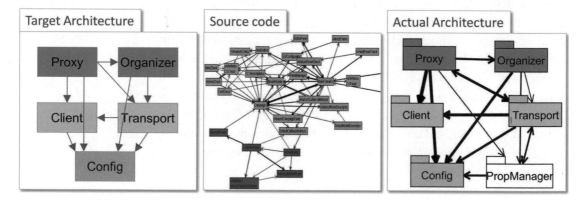

Extraction

We can now extract the structure of the source code using an analysis tool. The result is a depiction of the structure of the various classes and the relationships between them, as well as the packages that contain them. The illustration in the center of figure 2-4 shows such a structure. The classes are represented as rectangles and the relationships between them as arrows. The assignment of the classes to two different packages is indicated by the colors yellow and purple.

Mapping

The illustration on the right in figure 2-4 shows what the mapping of the target architecture does to the source code. The classes from the center illustration are no longer visible and have instead become part of the subsystems to which they were assigned during mapping. The relationships between the classes are summarized on the right at the subsystem level. The first surprise provided by this analysis was the addition of a sixth subsystem PropManager to the previously planned five subsystems.

This sixth subsystem emerged while discussing the mapping with the development team. It was not included in the original plan. However, while mapping packages to subsystems, some packages were left over. The software developer responsible for this part of the project told us he wanted to introduce the `PropManager` subsystem. In the future we will have to discuss with the development team whether this subsystem is necessary and, if it is, how it should interact with the other subsystems.

Evaluation

The illustration on the right in figure 2-4 shows all the relationships implemented almost exactly as planned. Only the relationship between `Proxy` and `Transport` goes against the planned layering. This reverse relationship (i.e., from bottom to top) was not planned in the original architectural design.

Reverse relationship

Two things usually happen during discussions with the development team: violations are discovered and lined up for refactoring, and revision of the target architecture is initiated.

2.3   Improvements to a Running System

What does a tool-assisted analysis look like on a real system? I selected the open source system *Infoglue* to demonstrate the possibilities that are nowadays available for tool-based analysis and architecture improvement. We selected this system because we can inspect it without the risk of unwanted legal issues, and because its architecture looks pretty good too. Moreover, the documentation is freely available on the Internet, so you can simulate architectural improvements without having the actual architects around.

Sample system

The first step is to feed the *Infoglue* source and byte code into the analysis tool. Once the tool has finished parsing, it displays the project's structure. Each analysis tool has its own visualization methods (see the appendix for more details). Since most of the graphics in this book originate from Sotograph[4] I will use this program's look and feel for most of the illustrations that follow.

---

4 If you would like to see the use of the Sotograph in action, a video is available on the book's website *www.sustainable-software-architecture.com*

Circles and triangles   Sotograph shows structural information that it extracts from the source code as a tree diagram (see fig. 2-5). The source code of a Java system provides structural information in the form of the packages and classes contained within it. Packages are represented as circles and files or classes as triangles. In the illustration, packages are displayed in the upper area and the display is expanded to show the first level of packages within `org.infoglue.cms`. The lower part of the illustration shows some classes. The display is adjusted so you can see four classes in the package `com.frovi.ss.Tree`. The plus signs in front of the packages indicate that they can be expanded to show the additional packages or classes they contain. The number of sub-elements a package contains is indicated by its color. The darker the color, the more sub-elements it has. For example, `applications` contains more sub-elements than `io` or `net`.

Figure 2-5

Infoglue *package tree and classes shown in the Sotograph user interface*

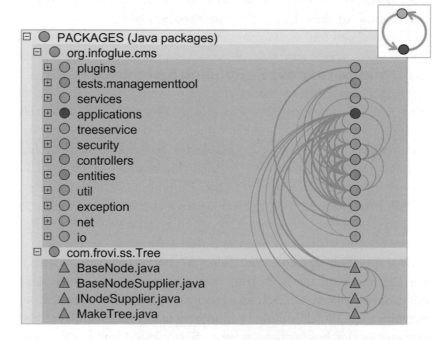

Arcs   The right-hand side of figure 2-5 shows a series of arcs connecting the packages and classes. These arcs represent the relationships that exist between the system's classes. The arcs on the left lead from top to bottom, while those on the right lead from bottom to top (see the smaller graphic at top right).

The graphic shows that the classes in the package com.frovi.
ss.Tree are used by the classes from org.infoglue.cms. There is no
bottom-up relationship, and this is probably the intention of the
Infoglue development team. Since these four classes are part of their
own package tree com.frovi.ss.Tree (next to the actual package
tree for the system org.infoglue.cms) we can assume that they form
the basis for a company-owned framework. In a case like this it is a
fine thing that only these classes are used. Positive also is that they
don't use classes from other *Infoglue* packages.

If a package is not expanded, the relationships of the classes
within are displayed as arcs with the package as the starting point.
For example, consider the arcs in figure 2-5 that emanate from
package applications. The arc leading from applications to the
MakeTree.java class means that somewhere in the applications
package there are one or more classes using MakeTree.java.

Now for the second step. The target architecture has to be
mapped to the source code to make the actual architecture visible. In our *Infoglue* example, we modeled the technical layering.
Later we will get to know very different types of models that depict
domain-specific principles and patterns.

Rectangles, diamonds, and squares

Sotograph provides three modeling concepts to create this mapping: layers (represented by rectangles), independent subsystems
(represented by diamonds), and unrestricted subsystems (represented by squares). These modeling concepts are shown schematically in figure 2-6, and can be created in Sotograph while assigning
packages and/or classes to them.

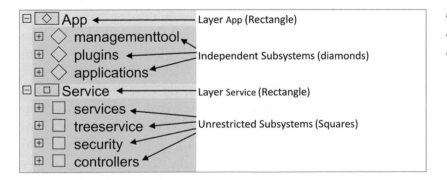

Figure 2-6

Modeling concepts in Sotograph

Figure 2-7 shows the result of mapping *Infoglue*.

Figure 2-7

Infoglue *following*

mapping in Sotograph

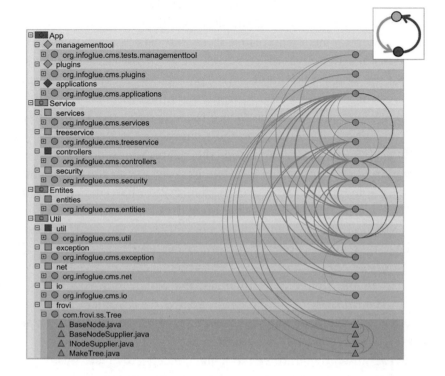

Mapping for Infoglue   The package trees in `org.infoglue.cms` and the package `com.frovi.ss.Tree` have become unrestricted subsystems (squares) and independent subsystems (diamonds). These subsystems are assigned to a total of four layers (App, Service, Entities, and Util). The subsystems in the app layer are not meant to know of each other and are therefore shown as independent subsystems (diamonds). All subsystems in the other layers are allowed to access each other within their layers and are therefore modeled as unrestricted subsystems (squares).

With the package nodes collapsed, the result is a somewhat clearer picture, as shown in figure 2-8:

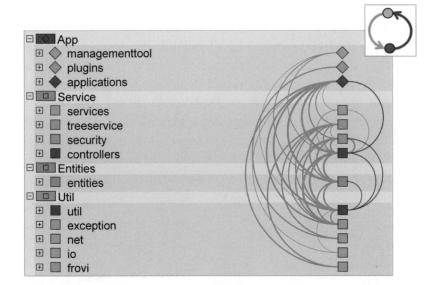

Figure 2-8

Infoglue's *actual*
architecture

By modeling four layers for *Infoglue*, the relationships that lead   *Red arcs = layer violations*
from a lower to a higher element between the layers are displayed
as red violations. *Infoglue* show a total of four violations. The Util
subsystem in the Util layer alone causes three of these (in Entities
and Service). The fourth layer violation is caused by the `controllers`
subsystem. Classes in `controllers` require functionality that is in the
`applications` subsystem on the app layer.

The modeling concepts Layer and Subsystem can be nested arbi-
trarily, enabling us to create a deep tree of subsystems and layers.
Since *Infoglue* is a relatively small system with only 83,000 LOC,
an architectural modeling consisting of just two levels suffices. Later
examples will show that the combination of layers and subsystems
can be quite different depending on the type and scope of the system.

Following the initial modeling of the architecture, we can   *Analyzing violations*
now turn to the second phase: analyzing the violations. First, we
will investigate the violation between the service and app layers
(see fig. 2-8). In order to investigate this violation, we will use a
Sotograph feature that reduces the displayed system parts to the
classes, packages, subsystems, and layers that are involved in the
violation.

Focus on what is involved

Figure 2-9 shows the seven classes involved in this violation: five `controller` classes, one class called `CreateContentWizardInfoBean`, and one called `VisualFormatter`. If not all the elements in a layer (classes, packages, and subsystems) are shown, Sotograph displays a black triangle—i.e., each element depicted using a black triangle has more sub-elements than are displayed in the selection.

In figure 2-9 all classes that don't play a role in the red violations (`wizards.actions`, `common`, and `kernel.impl.simple`) are filtered out. Their relationships are also ignored, and we only see the relationships that exist between the classes involved in the violation.

Figure 2-9

Layer violation between
Service and App

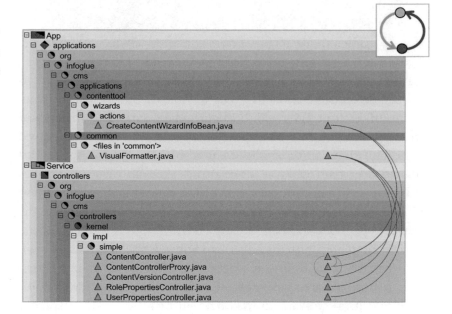

The layer violation between Service and App is triggered by two different groups of classes. `VisualFormatter` is required by three Controllers and the `ContentController` and `ContentControllerProxy` classes use `CreateContentWizardInfoBean`. Let's look first at the violation in `VisualFormatter` (see fig. 2-10).

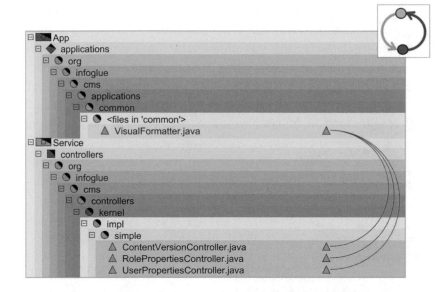

Figure 2-10

Violation with VisualFormatter

A look at the source code of the three controllers shows that they all use the VisualFormatter functionality. They all contain a method that includes the following line of code:

```
value = new VisualFormatter().escapeHTML(value);
```

The first question the developers would surely be asked about this line of code is whether the method should instead be static. Of course, this doesn't solve the underlying problem—a static call from a method of the VisualFormatter class would also contravene the existing layering. In order to resolve the layer violation, the escapeHTML method must either be moved to a class further down the layer. Or the incorrectly-sorted VisualFormatter class has been sorted into the wrong layer. We will look into this second consideration in order to discover one way to improve the architecture.

To determine what VisualFormatter's job is within the overall system, we extend the filter in figure 2-10 to all classes on which VisualFormatter operates. Figure 2-11 shows that VisualFormatter is used by different classes on the App layer and has a relationship with the Util layer.

Focus on the context

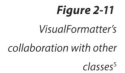

Figure 2-11

VisualFormatter's collaboration with other classes[5]

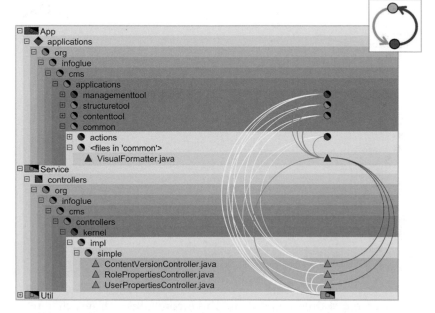

Looking at figure 2-11, we can assume that VisualFormatter has to be moved further down (away) from the App layer. The name Formatter indicates that this class is a utility class. It may have ended up in the common package node in the App layer because it was created during the development of the various applications. However, because it is used by the Service layer it cannot remain in the App layer.

Refactoring of the first violation

Sotograph enables us to move classes into other packages. In figure 2-12 you can see the effect this has. The layer damage caused by VisualFormatter has been eliminated. In addition, the VisualFormatter class now shows a small "r" (for "refactoring") to indicate that it has been moved.

---

5 Some relationships (arcs) in this figure are shown in white because the VisualFormatter class is selected. The relationships of all other nodes are displayed in white for better clarity.

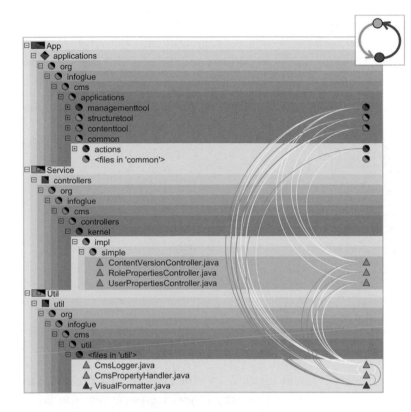

Figure 2-12

Resolving the violation by moving VisualFormatter

The second layer violation between the Service layer and the App layer remains (see fig. 2-13).

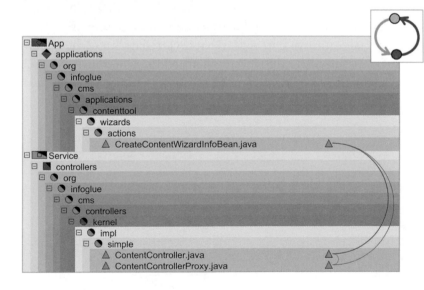

Figure 2-13

Layering violation caused by CreateContent-WizardInfoBean

Refactoring of the second violation

Again, the question arises whether `CreateContentWizardInfoBean` was sorted into the wrong package and into the wrong layer like `VisualFormatter`. Let's have a look at `CreateContentWizardInfoBean`'s relationships.

Figure 2-14
CreateContentWizard-InfoBean's relationships

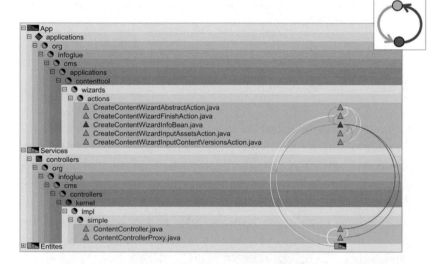

Special features within the architecture

If you look closely at figure 2-14 you will see that `CreateContent-WizardInfoBean` does not use any other classes on the App layer, so it can easily be moved down to `ContentController` and `Content-ControllerProxy`. Further research within the source code shows that `CreateContentWizardInfoBean` is the only bean class in *Infoglue*.

The other controllers and actions do not cooperate using beans. This special feature of the `ContentController` classes and their actions must be discussed by the development team. To remove the architecture violation, we have to move the `CreateContentWizardInfoBean` onto the Service layer (see fig. 2-15).

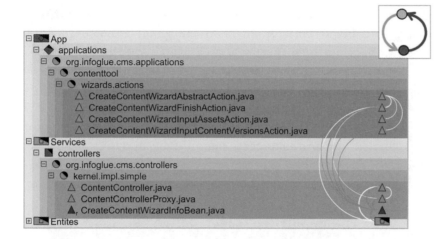

Figure 2-15

Resolving the violation by moving Create-ContentWizardInfoBean

By applying these two changes, we have resolved a violation in *Infoglue*'s layered architecture. The actual architecture now looks like this:

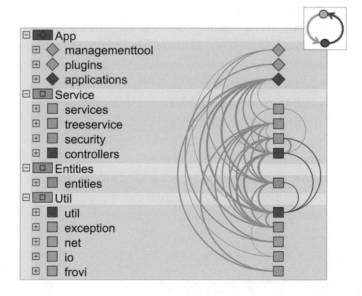

Figure 2-16

First step towards improving the Infoglue architecture

The next step is to examine the violations between the Util layer and Entities and Service. There are a few interesting steps involved in resolving the relationship between Util and Service. First, we will look at the classes that cause this violation. Figure 2-17 is adjusted so that the packages that don't contain classes are shown as dot-notated one-liners. This further condenses the display.

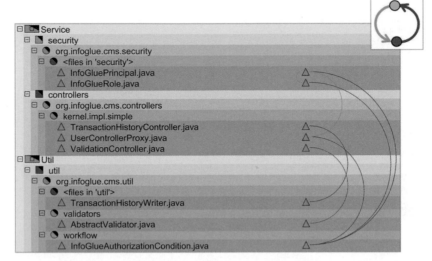

Three classes from Util are causing the violation: `TransactionHistoryWriter`, `AbstractValidator`, and `InfoGlueAuthorizationCondition`. If the filter in figure 2-17 is expanded to include all classes that `InfoGlueAuthorizationCondition` uses, it becomes apparent that `InfoGlueAuthorizationCondition` actually belongs to the security subsystem (see fig. 2-18), which is where most other classes that utilize `InfoGlueAuthorizationCondition` are located.

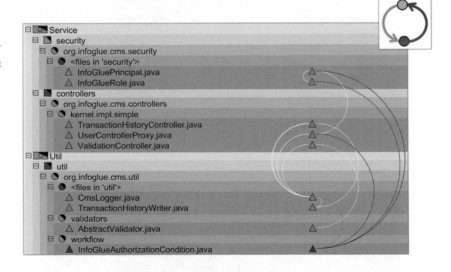

If we move `InfoGlueAuthorizationCondition`, two violations involving `AbstractValidator` and `TransactionHistoryWriter` remain. Let's start with `TransactionHistoryWriter`.

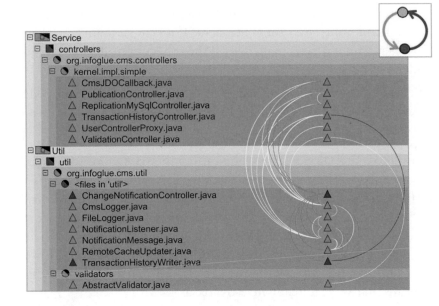

Figure 2-19

TransactionHistory-

Writer's relationships

Figure 2-19 shows that `TransactionHistoryWriter` is used in Util by `ChangeNotificationController` and that it uses `TransactionHistoryController`.

Violation without

a simple solution

This relationship leads to the (red) violation. If you look at the source code of these classes, you will find suspicious comments like the following:

```
/**
 * This method is a bit different from other creates
 * as it does not use the common base-class-method.
 * Using it would result in a recursive loop of
 * new notificationMessages.
 */
```

Two more hints of bad design are:

1. The class `TransactionHistoryWriter` uses the `TransactionHistory-Controller` and is used by the `ChangeNotificationController`. The relationship between the controllers and this writer is unclear. Is a writer a utility class for controllers? If it is, it shouldn't use controllers. If it is a class that controls the other controllers, it should definitely not be used by controllers.

2. There is no other class called `XYWriter` in the whole source code base, making this a similar case to the `CreateContentWizard-InfoBean` case described above.

In order to find an adequate solution for this violation, we would have to talk to the developers and architects. A fundamental redesign of the classes may be necessary to achieve design and layer clarity. If the *Infoglue* development team were on site, we would export figure 2-19 from the tool and save it for a later design session. Since we don't have the *Infoglue* development team at our disposal, we won't resolve this violation now, but instead mark it in yellow to indicate that we've already investigated it.

Figure 2-20

Refactoring accomplished and the remaining violations

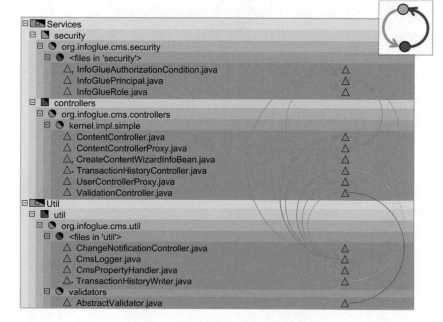

Figure 2-20 shows the current system state. Two classes were moved (indicated by the refactoring "r" next to their names). We could not resolve the `TransactionHistoryWriter` violation, which is marked in yellow to indicate this. The only thing left is the `AbstractValidator` violation (see fig. 2-21).

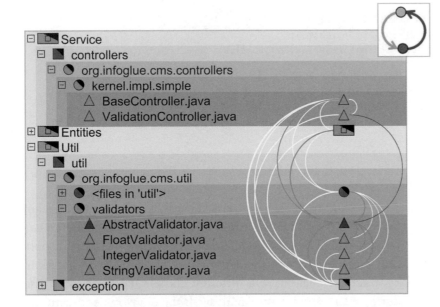

Figure 2-21

AbstractValidator's relationships

The `AbstractValidator` class cannot simply be moved like the classes in our other examples. If you move `AbstractValidator` into the Service layer, a number of new violations occur between `Abstract-Validator` and the other validators. Additionally, this would cause a violation between Entities and Service. This is because classes from Entities use `AbstractValidator` (shown by the green arc connecting Entities to `AbstractValidator`). Moving `ValidatorController` in the opposite direction (i.e., from Service to the Util layer) would be architecturally wrong, as all controller classes are collected within the Service layer.

Tricky Violation

ValidatorController is called from only one method in Abstract-Validator:

```
protected void validateUniqueness(String value) throws ConstraintException,
                                                             SystemException {
   if (this.mustBeUnique){
      Pattern p = Pattern.compile("[.\\s]+");
      String[] arrString = p.split(fieldName);
      String cleanField = arrString[arrString.length-1];

      If (ValidationController.fieldValueExists(
         objectClass, cleanField, value, excludeId, excludeObject)) {
            throw createConstraintException(NOTUNIQUE_FIELD_ERROR_CODE);
         }
      }
   }
}
```

Design discussion This design also needs to be discussed with the development team in order to improve the structure of the classes. Can the Valida-tionController call be made outside of AbstractValidator and only the result passed to it? Is this functionality correct at this location, or does it actually belong to a different class? Questions like these arise during every architecture analysis. If the development team has a clear understanding of the architecture, this is the point at which you will hear things like: "But that's not nice! We'll have to do it differently. I already know how ... ". This is the right moment to export the corresponding image from the tool and give it a meaningful name so you can recognize the problem in the future.

Improving the Architecture The result of this step is an architecture with one remaining violation between Util and Entities, and two design tasks for the development team. Figure 2-22 shows the remaining red relationship between Util and Entities. We already marked the violation between Util and the controller's subsystem in yellow to indicate that we have investigated it but were unable to resolve it.

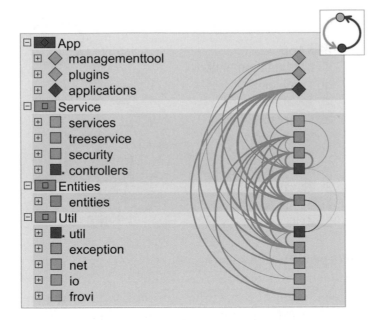

Figure 2-22

The cleaned up Infoglue

architecture

We will resolve the last remaining violation between Util and Entities in Section 9.1.3 as an example for how to resolve a cycle.

There are still two possible architecture analyses and improvements that we have not yet considered, namely: the effects of independent subsystems and subsystem public interfaces. The following Sections illustrate these two options using the *Infoglue* code, even if the application's small size and unique architecture may cause a number of violations during modeling.

There are no violating relationships between the independent subsystems in the app layer of the *Infoglue* source code (see the top portion of fig. 2-23). This is why we have to try the modeling constructs on a different part of the system. To illustrate the effect of independent subsystems (diamonds), the unrestricted subsystems (squares) are converted from the Service layer into independent subsystems (diamonds). This results in many new violations. All relationships between the subsystems in the Service layer are shown as red violations in figure 2-23. In our earlier representations (see fig. 2-8), these relationships were depicted in green (i.e., without violations).

Independent subsystems

Figure 2-23

Independent subsystems
(diamonds) on the
Service layer

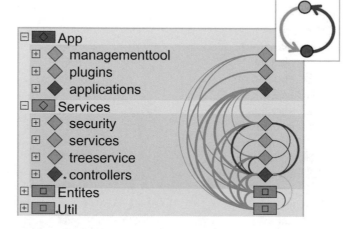

Using independent subsystems is one way to express such a restriction within the architecture. For example, if a developer were to include relationships between the subsystems in the App layer in a later version of *Infoglue*, red arcs like those currently visible on the Service layer would appear. However, this restriction appears too strict for the *Infoglue* Service layer. The four subsystems have various relationships with each other, as depicted in figure 2-23.

Public interfaces   Public interfaces can be defined for all three modeling constructs (layers, unrestricted subsystems, and independent subsystems). Anything that does not belong to a public interface cannot be accessed from the outside (i.e., it is declared as private). Violations of defined public interfaces are also displayed in red. As an example, figure 2-24 shows the expanded subsystem controllers. In the package tree, this subsystem contains a package with the name impl. A package name like this is often used to show that this package should not be accessible from the outside.

Red arcs = public   To visualize the effects of public interfaces, we converted the
interface violations   impl package to private (see fig. 2-24). It now has a small "p" in front of its name and all relationships that go from outside the controller's subsystem to impl are shown in red. This usage is only permitted from within controllers. The classes in the package use cases are allowed to access kernel.impl, and their relationships to kernel.impl are therefore shown in green.

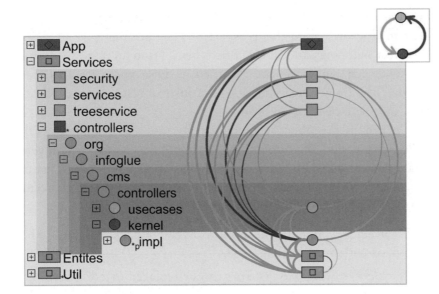

Figure 2-24

Public interface violations between sub-system controllers and the impl package

Unfortunately, there are several relationships with the impl package in *Infoglue*, so we have to assume that the application's developers didn't want to define a public interface or a private section in this area. Despite its name, the impl package belongs to the public interface of *Infoglue*'s controller subsystem. Given the small size of the application, it would be possible and also useful to create some public interfaces. It would then be necessary to discuss with the architects and developers when they plan to introduce public interfaces and where to put them.

This concludes our sample analysis, and you should now be familiar with the basic possibilities of tool-supported architecture analysis. Real-world architecture analysis involves several other aspects that need to be examined too, including modularity via metrics, strongly coupled structures on all levels, the use of design patterns, and much more. Chapter 5 introduces and explains these aspects in more detail.

2.4 False Positives and Generated Code

During the analysis detailed in the previous section, there were several cases in which we corrected the assignment of individual classes to their packages. Such corrections are typical during the initial

Cleanup

analysis of a system. Because developers and architects have never seen their system from this perspective, they are unaware of these incorrect mappings and don't notice them. From an analyst's point of view, such violations are regarded as false positives. In other words, they are not real violations but instead result from carelessness and the lack of an overview.

Such finds are often accompanied by utterances such as, "Oh hello, what's this? That doesn't seem right!" or, "Mind if we investigate that, please?" or, "Aha, someone has gone and done … again. That's easy to repair!" The following types of false positives occur in practically all case studies:

- *Incorrect assignment:* One or more classes or packages have to be moved within the package tree.
- *Incorrect copying:* Copy errors can be replaced by correct calls.
- *Calls of constants:* The constants have to be moved to a different class.
- *Incomplete public interface:* Missing classes or interfaces have to be added to the public interface.

Influence of generated code

In addition to false positives, we have to consider how to deal with parts of the system that have been generated when preparing an analysis. In reality, analysis focuses on the structures within the system that the developers program and edit themselves—hence, it makes no sense to analyze generated system parts. The generated source code should never be edited by the developers. Analyzing generated code would only verify the quality of the generator but would distort the view of the actual complexity, at least as far as the metrics are concerned.

Generated code and architecture

The generated parts of the system can be important on the architectural level in cases where a central component of the application is generated. Examples of this are:

- Classes that are generated based on custom XML schemata and which form an essential part of the domain model within the application.
- Generated glue code that performs model transformations and thus creates connections within the application that would not

otherwise be visible. For example, an application generates "assembler" classes that copy values from entities to JAX-B objects and vice versa.

If you omit these parts of the application, you would not be able to see that certain classes access data from completely different parts of the application. This kind of access is often handled exclusively by generated classes.

Due to these different views of architecture (i.e., generated code is important to the architecture but pollutes the metrics) it is worth parsing the system's source code multiple times. This enables the examination of both aspects, depending on which angle you are approaching the task from.

2.5   Cheat Sheet for Sotograph

Figure 2-25

Sotograph modeling and visualization elements

Sotograph screenshots play an important role in the following sections. Figure 2-25 summarizes all the elements you are likely to encounter.

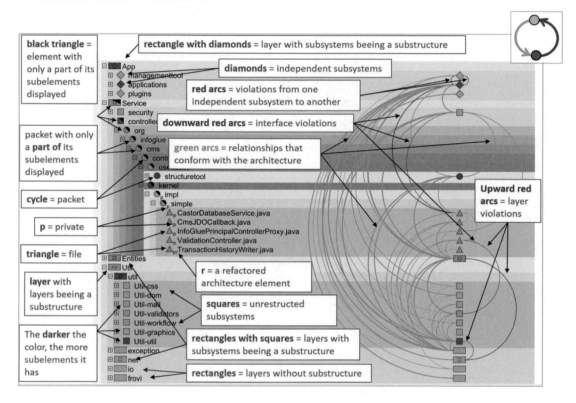

If you want to see Sotograph in action, visit

www.sustainable-software-architecture.com.

3 Architecture in Programming Languages

Different programming languages have their own peculiarities at the keyword level and in their development environments, and they also function differently on the architectural and structural levels. This chapter contains statements on Java, C#, C++, PHP and ABAP. We are currently analyzing TypeScript and JavaScript. As soon as there are findings for these languages, we will publish them as well.

The following sections explain what can be found within a system's source code and how the resulting structures can be mapped from an architectural perspective.

3.1 Java Systems

In Java systems, the architecture is found in the package tree and in the way the various build artifacts are partitioned. It is really useful if we can glean architectural data directly while parsing the source code, which we can then include in our analysis.

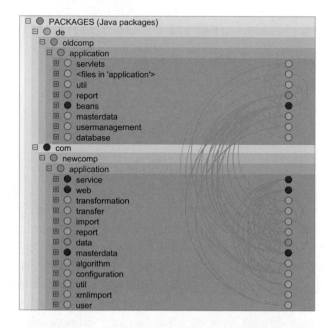

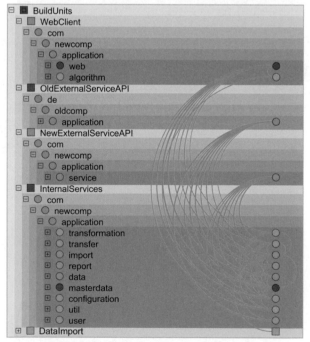

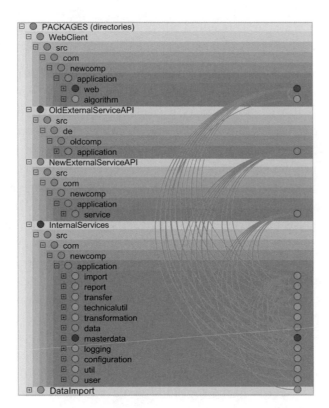

Figure 3-3

Directory tree view of a Java system

Figure 3-1, figure 3-2, and figure 3-3 show the same system viewed as its package tree, as its defined build artifacts, and as its directory tree:

Different structures

■ Figure 3-1 shows that this particular system has two package trees: de.oldcomp.application and com.newcomp.application. The first development of this system started with the typical root node in German software systems "de". Later they changed to "com" to become more international.

■ If we view the structure formed by the build artifacts (see fig. 3-2) the package trees will be visible below the build artifacts (WebClient, OldExter-nalServiceAPI, NewExternalServiceAPI, InternalServices, DataImport). Figure 3-2 shows how the package com.newcomp.application is distributed over the first four of the five build artifacts (WebClient, OldExternalServiceAPI, NewExternalServiceAPI, InternalServices).

■ If we use the directory tree as the basis for our analysis (see fig. 3-3), the picture is very similar to that provided by the build artifacts. This view of a system is required when performing specialized analysis that relates to pattern languages (see Chapter 8 for more detail).

Where's the architecture? During architecture analysis we use the representation of the system that comes closest to the architectural vision of the development team. If there are build artifacts, we usually use them as a foundation.

Split packages The developers of the system shown in figure 3-2 structured the system so that each node of a package maps exactly to one build artifact. Hence, the same package node can never exist in two different build artifacts. In my analysis, however, identical package paths can very often be found within the different build artifacts. If we look at the analysis based on build artifacts, this duplication doesn't seem too serious at a first glance. However, the difficulties begin as soon as we start talking about classes within the packages whose paths appear in two different build artifacts. You have to specify which build artifact you are currently in at every step of the way.

Example for split Figure 3-4 shows a Java system's package tree, and figure 3-5 *packages* shows the same system sorted by its build artifacts. When comparing the two structures you can see that almost all package nodes of the top JAR einbeispiel_extra_jar also exist in the JAR below. Only taglib exists in the top build artifact alone. The third build artifact clustermanager_jar also shares its cluster package with the JAR above it.

Figure 3-4

Package tree composed of several JARs

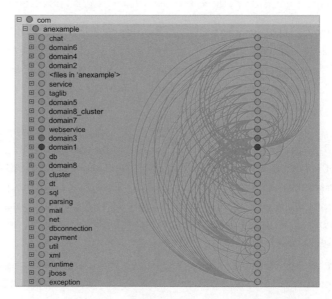

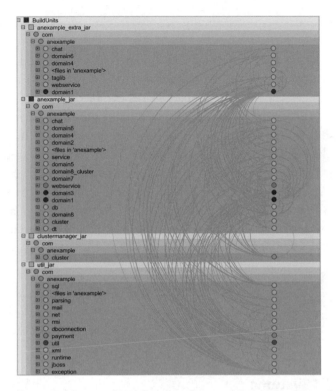

Figure 3-5

Packages split across

multiple JARs

Split packages indicate that the developers have not cleaned up. In a good hierarchical structure, no node should belong to two parent nodes. The technical effect also seems strange: the classes from one JAR can access the classes defined as package-protected from another JAR if they are part of the same package. If you work with OSGi, split packages across bundle boundaries cause conceptual and technical problems at runtime.

Therefore, our recommendation for every development team is:

Naming packages in build artifacts

Use a separate root package for each build artifact.

Java 9 introduces a real system of modules called Jigsaw. Jigsaw finally extends Java to include a real encapsulation mechanism above the class level. Package trees can be combined into a named module. The module also declares which packages are externally accessible and which other modules it requires. All classes that are not contained in the externally accessible packages remain hidden from the outside.

Neither the package constructs available in the original Java nor the later option to package classes in JARs was able to achieve a comparable encapsulation effect. Classes can be defined in packages with two different views (public and package-private), although this visibility only refers to the corresponding package but not to sub-packages. This leads to having either large, unstructured packages or packages consisting of public classes only. On the other hand, JARs are just a set of compressed class files plus data. They have no influence on the visibility of the classes contained within them and therefore have no public interface. Java 9 finally fixes this problem.

> **Using the Java module system**
>
> Use the module system as soon as it is available. It will contribute significantly to the clarity of your architecture because it will become explicit.

3.2   C# Systems

In a similar way to Java, C# offers different levels for expressing architecture in source code. Visual Studio as a development environment for C# offers projects that are managed together in a single solution. This level of build artifacts is useful in an architectural analysis. Additionally, C# source code is stored in directories and you can specify a namespace for each class.

Namespaces ≠ Directories   Unlike packages, Java namespaces do not have to be synchronized with corresponding directories. This means that projects can have a second, independent structure in addition to the directory trees.

The architects of the C# system shown in figure 3-6 and figure 3-7 were surprised when they saw how different these structures looked, as they had expected both to look the same. They gave their development team the specification that directories and namespaces should always be the same. The reason they drifted apart is because Visual Studio supports the refactoring of directories, while namespaces are not refactored.

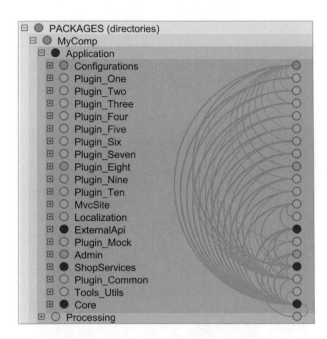

Figure 3-6

A C# system's directories

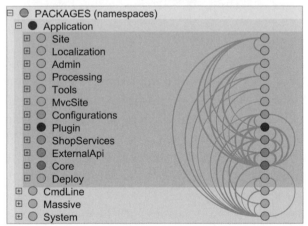

Figure 3-7

A C# system's namespaces

In such cases I inquire the architects to find out which view of the system contains more information about the architecture. For the system depicted in figure 3-6 and figure 3-7 we analyzed the architecture based on its directories.

I haven't yet fond a good reason to use namespaces to build a second structure in a system that doesn't run parallel to the directory structure. This results in two competing hierarchies that only increase the complexity of the architecture. For developers and

Two competing hierarchies

architects, each class raises the question of why it belongs to a certain directory and to a different namespace. The result is additional complexity that reduces development speed and increases costs. Every development team should therefore consider the following advice:

> **Use namespaces and directories synchronously**
>
> Create parallel hierarchies in your C# source code using namespaces and directories.

Visual Studio vs. assemblies

What makes the C# development situation even more complicated is the fact that developers using Visual Studio see the directory path, so their natural way of thinking is to build substructures using directories. When using a C# assembly, the directory structures are no longer available. The classes contained in the assembly are now addressed via the namespace.

3.3   C++ Systems

Namespaces ≠ Directories

Like C#, C++ offers directories and namespaces as sorting mechanisms for classes. As with C#, directories and namespaces are not automatically kept synchronous. Here, we also recommended that the development team take care of synchronicity. In addition, the source code in C++ can be distributed over several projects that are relevant to the architecture. We use this information from the build artifacts during our analysis.

In addition to these similarities with Java and C# projects, C++ has two special features:

Separation of declaration and implementation

In C++, declaration (*.h, *.hpp, *.hxx) and implementation (*.cpp) are often stored in separate files. In many cases there is only one declaration and one implementation file, and these two files form a class. In some cases, there are several .cpp files for a declaration file. Depending on your needs, you can either view declaration and implementation files as separate artifacts or merge files that belong together (see fig. 3-8).

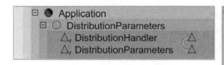
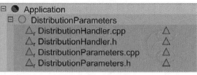

Figure 3-8

Separate and merged .h and .cpp files in C++

Depending on how the development team looks at its architecture and distributes .h and .cpp files in its directories, one of these views will make more sense than the other. For example, if the .h files and their .cpp files are stored in separate directories, merging them would also merge relationships that previously led to two files in two directories into a single directory. In this case, the .h and .cpp files should remain separate. If the files are as close to each other as the ones shown in figure 3-8, merging them makes the analysis clearer.

Declarations

In addition to the usual include, C++ allows you to work with "forward declarations". A forward declaration is necessary in C++ if you only need the type of a class without calling its methods. Sotograph represents these relationships as dashed arcs, (see fig. 3-9) so that they can be distinguished from normal relationships (shown as solid arcs).

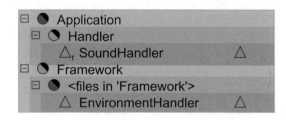

Figure 3-9

Representation of a forward declaration in C++

Forward declarations are part of the language definition in C++ and can be used to make types known before they are used. Other object-oriented languages, such as Java and C#, don't have a similar restriction.

3.4   ABAP Systems

ABAP has some unique features compared to the other programming languages considered here.

Hybrid Language

ABAP is a hybrid language that has had its own object-oriented extension for a while now. In addition to classes and interfaces, there are various non-object-oriented artifacts, such as function groups with their function modules, programs with their Dynpros and dialog modules, and reports. These artifacts make investigating ABAP systems really interesting because certain properties and locations in the architecture are linked to the different artifact types (see Section 11.6). Basically, this is a kind of pattern language on a programming language artifact level (see Section 6.6 and Chapter 8).

Packages without namespaces

ABAP uses packages as a means of structuring. However, unlike in other programming languages, these packages do not have their own namespace. Instead, ABAP has a global namespace that is managed in a repository. This means that the names of the individual artifacts are available globally, in turn making it impossible to locate artifacts with the same name in different packages. It is more common in ABAP to include the package names in the names of the artifacts, since the number of characters is limited to 30. This often leads to cryptic names and flat package hierarchies. An additional naming restriction is that the ABAP code developed by the user must be contained in packages that begin with a "Y" or a "Z". All other packages are reserved for SAP coding and test ("T").

Package interfaces

In SAP, you can define package interfaces and enforce them using global system settings. However, hardly any ABAP development teams actually activate package interfaces.

Database access

Database access is directly integrated into the ABAP language. An ABAP developer can access the database tables and objects directly without using a mapper or other technology. This means you should consider the database tables as sort of "first-class citizens" in ABAP and include them in your analysis.

SAP base system

Programming in ABAP is done from within the SAP System. The SAP base system—which is basically a framework—offers many technical and business functions that can be called from within your own ABAP code. As with database tables, the use of SAP functionality is very interesting for ABAP architects. Since the global SAP repository contains not only the names of the artifacts that you have developed yourself, but also all the SAP coding names, displaying the relationships during parsing is very easy to do (see the EXTERNAL_LIBRARY node in figure 3-10).

The packages in the SAP base system are subdivided and named according to functional criteria (see the package names in fig. 3-10). This basic functional structure is usually adopted in ABAP code that is developed in-house. In ABAP coding, you often find domain-oriented packages on the first level of a structure.

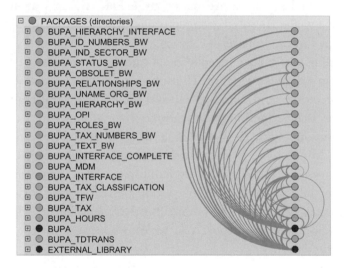

Figure 3-10

A package tree from

BUPA's SAP coding

To analyze ABAP code with one of the tools described here (see also the appendix at the end of the book), you have to export the code from the SAP System. Such exports are easy to create using ABAP reports.

3.5 PHP Systems

Unlike the other languages described here, PHP is dynamically typed. Only during runtime does the interpreter determine whether a call to an artifact (variable, class) can be executed or not. This means that PHP source code contains different options for how a call can be interpreted. If you find a call $v \to m()$ within your PHP source code, you can only be sure what object the variable $v har-

A dynamically typed language

bors at the moment it is called at runtime. Theoretically, you can only determine at runtime which relationships to other classes exist.

This makes it difficult to find unique relationships when extracting structures from PHP source code. For example, if the method m() only exists for a single class K, you can assume that there is a relationship to class K. If the method m() exists more than once you may be able to use a data flow analysis (and a little luck) to decide which class is meant. As you can see, there are a various imponderables involved when parsing PHP source code.

Nevertheless, there are many large PHP systems around that require a well-structured architecture in order to be maintained and developed in the long term.

Namespaces ≠ Directories

PHP uses similar concepts to C# and C++ to make architecture visible in system's structure. The source code files need to be sorted into directories and namespaces, and there are several conventions that the PHP community has adopted for doing this (see *http:// www.php-fig.org/*). As with C# and C++, directories and namespaces do not have to run synchronously, so the architecture can be expressed via directories or namespaces. The same difficulties await us here as with C#/C++ systems. Are the directories or the namespaces critical to the architecture? Depending on which path the development team took, you have to select one or the other as your foundation.

Figure 3-11 shows the structure of the *Magento* platform based on its directory tree. *Magento* is an open source e-commerce platform written in PHP. It doesn't use namespaces, so using the directory tree is the only way we can analyze its architecture.

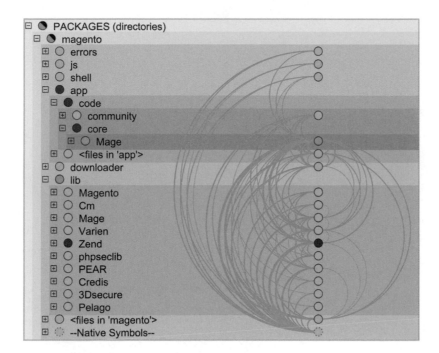

Figure 3-11

The Magento

directory tree

Some PHP environments use other structuring artifacts that lie above namespaces and directories. *Symfony* (an MVC framework for PHP) has a concept of bundles for modules. Some teams use *Composer*, a PHP dependency management tool comparable with Maven that describes dependencies using a JSON file.

Build artifacts from frameworks

4 Architecture Analysis and Improvement

Architecture analysis and improvement is a process created by people for people. Various things need to be considered if this task is to lead to positive results that help all of those involved. Who has which role? What is our goal? How do we reach our goal within the group?

This chapter begins by looking into architectural work and the relationships between developers and architects. We will then present the individual steps that make up an architecture workshop. We will explain how to deal with the creators (or "parents") of a system and how to keep architecture up and running and in good condition for a long time to come.

4.1 Developers and Architects

The ideal image in the minds of many developers and architects is a democratic team in which everyone can do, know, and decide everything. I like this image because I prefer cooperative working environments to dictatorial ones. At the same time, you shouldn't ignore the varied talents and life experiences of the different people involved.

My understanding of the roles "developer" and "architect" is that architects are experienced developers. Architects have participated in the development of many different software systems and are constantly involved in the latest changes and innovations in the field of software development. Due to their experience they know about many pitfalls and meaningful solutions. They can use their experience to advise their younger team colleagues and help them find the best way forward.

However, this approach can only succeed if architects make sure they don't live in an "ivory tower" of exclusivity. Architects must work in teams with younger developers if they are to create, maintain, and develop a common image of system architecture. This is the whole point—architecture changes in the course of development.

4.2   Working on Architecture is a "Holschuld"[1]

In some organizations, the software development department is so large that the architecture is specified by a group of architects. Difficulties arise if the architects have no time or opportunity to do development work with their teams.

Who's going to tell the architect? Let's imagine that a developer is tasked with creating a customization and an extension. Once the developer has given some thought to the customization, she realizes that it will lead to a layer violation. She now needs a forum where she can discuss the issue with the system's architects. If such a forum is not available, the developer will look for a workaround. After all, she wants to do her work and implement the feature. The quickest and, from her point of view, possibly correct solution is to install a layer violation. However, if the development or build environment doesn't allow this, she will look for an alternative solution. If it is faster and simpler to program a workaround than consult the architects, the developer will opt to implement the workaround (most likely under time pressure), unless she is particularly interested in quality or the architects can be contacted quickly and at short notice. But this is exactly where the problem often lies. In large projects, architects are not physically close to the developers, they are usually very busy, and you rarely find them at the office.

Architecture is evolutionary When I work with teams of this size, I advise the architects to meet regularly with the developers and ask about architecture issues. The architecture evolves gradually the same way a system does in the course of a project. I simply cannot imagine a complete up-front architecture design that doesn't change during the

---

1   "Holschuld" is a German word that has two meanings condensed into one. It means a debt and an obligation to collect. The German word is ideal for our purposes, so we will continue to use it throughout the book.

project—perhaps because I have never experienced it. In this sense, architectural development is a "Holschuld". The architect has to make the effort to collect the information regarding necessary changes to the planned architecture from the teams, as they will surely not be communicated automatically.

> **Architectural development is a "Holschuld"**
>
> As an architect, make sure you meet regularly with your development teams. If possible, take time to program with the team members. This will help you to recognize the need for adaptation early on. Maintaining a low offer threshold ensures that you receive as much feedback as possible.

Some companies are outstanding in this area, with architectural retrospectives firmly embedded in every iteration. Architectural discussions are held in teams, departments, and across team boundaries. Internal training on new architectural concepts and innovations is offered on a regular basis, and external speakers are invited to lead discussions and give lectures. I hope you are lucky enough to work in such an organization.

4.3　Live Architecture Improvement Workshop

It is precisely this aspect of regular, iterative architectural discussion that is supported by the kinds of architectural analysis and improvement presented in this book. A complete architecture analysis and improvement process consists of a total of five steps. These are illustrated in figure 4-1.

During step (1) I gather as much documented information about the system as I can (see fig. 4-1). From an architectural point of view, the following are most interesting: the architecture documentation, coding guidelines, any existing agreements on important quality criteria, and the coverage of the source code with automated tests. The more meaningful documentation exists and the greater the level of test coverage, the higher my expectations of the quality of the system will be. These documents are usually sent to me by the architects and developers before a workshop begins.

Documentation

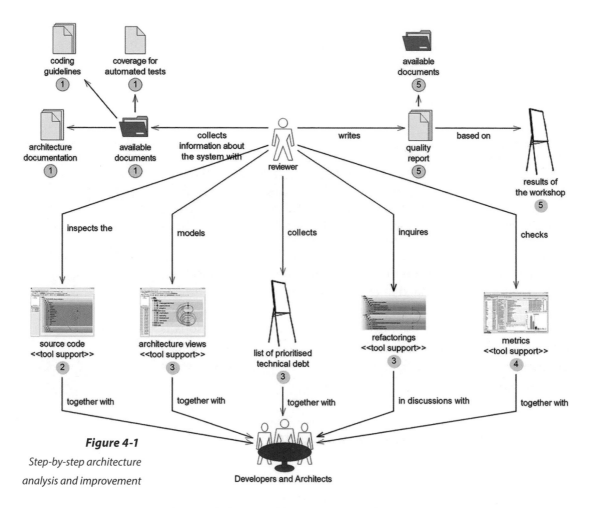

Figure 4-1

Step-by-step architecture analysis and improvement

Live workshop

The workshop itself (steps 2-4 in fig. 4-1) takes place in a meeting room with a projector and a flipchart, and all the steps are carried out together with the teams.

I usually use the time the analysis tool takes to parse the system (step 2 in fig. 4-1) to have the architects and developers explain the business task of the system and its interactions with other systems. I also introduce the participants to the basic concepts of creating sustainable software architectures (see Chapter 5).

Collect technical debt and refactoring

Then the actual work begins. Together, we use the source code to model the target architecture and make the actual architecture visible. Since the actual architecture always has deviations from the target architecture, this is the best place to begin an analysis.

We search for architecture violations and discuss possible solutions for them. This discussion leads to a series of results, which we document using tool-based diagrams (see step 3, Refactoring) or as entries in our list of technical debt (see step 3, List of technical debt). The following questions are never far from the surface of the discussion:

- How sustainable is the target architecture? Has the development team developed a plan that fits this type of application? — *Sustainable target architecture*

- How well can the plan be mapped to the actual architecture? Can the building blocks modeled in the target architecture be found as units in the source code? — *Mapping target → actual*

- How much does the actual architecture deviate from the plan? How many relationships and elements exist that were not planned in the target architecture? — *Deviation target → actual*

Towards the end of the workshop we also look at the common metrics (see step 4). We will investigate which metrics are important in Chapters 9 and 10. — *Metrics*

Following the analysis workshop, a quality report on the architecture and its existing technical debt is prepared (see step 5 in fig. 4-1). It is important that we prioritize technical debt during the work-shop. — *Quality report as result*

It is crucial to the success of architectural analysis and improvement that all participants experience the workshop as an opportunity to discuss the design. If the participants perceive the workshop as an instrument of control in which mistakes are sought and denounced, the result will be negative. It is very important to get the creators (the "parents") of the system on board. — *Success and failure*

4.4   Dealing with Mothers and Fathers

If you have a developer who has been involved since the beginning of the project and who has made important, path-setting decisions, the analysis workshop is sure to be both exciting and exhausting. On the one hand, you have someone who knows the system inside out, while on the other hand, the "parents" of a system defend their baby against all attacks and naturally view their system in a — *Defensive attitudes* positive light. I bet everyone has experienced a situation like this before.

Open for criticism?

I can relate to this attitude very well! I feel the same way when my company, my project, my apartment, my family, or anything else I'm involved in is criticized. What can an external reviewer do in this situation?

Appreciation

The first thing I try to do is honor the system's parents and everyone else involved for what they have achieved. I ask them to show me the software and explain its technical context. What business processes can be evaluated by the system? Which user roles exist? How is the architecture conceived and structured? Of course, I will also need this information for the analysis. There is enough space during this phase of the analysis process to acknowledge the performance of the development team. All too often the development teams suffer under project managers and customers who don't want to pay for quality (see Section 1.3.4)—and then a hired expert turns up and starts picking over the issues the development team has been aware of all the time!

Reflection

At this point I often tell a story that the chief developer of Sotograph told me years ago. When Sotograph reached its first executable state, the chief developer used it to analyze its own source and byte code. He expected highly balanced results with no red arcs and a wonderful visual structure. That's what he and his development team did right? Build software that analyze structures in source code. Unfortunately, he found several red arcs and bad structures. This wasn't because he had a bad development team, but rather because his developers had never seen the system from this point of view before. They couldn't see where they were violating the planned architecture. Additionally, mistakes always creep in somewhere, however careful you are. This story often eases the tension during an analysis session.

Good instincts

The rest of the analysis session involves weighing and balancing so that I can address critical points while retaining an open-minded atmosphere. Depending on the setting, things can turn out better or worse. If an IT manager invites me to work with a team on its systems' architecture, the emphasis is less on external evaluation and the situation is usually pretty relaxed. However, as an expert reviewer you always walk a fine line between assessing too harshly and taking the easier, friendly route. This is not an easy undertaking and I would like to take this opportunity to apologize to all the system parents who have perhaps suffered from my perceived lack of sensitivity.

4.5 Modularity Maturity Index (MMI)

In recent years, customers have often asked me how their system would score in relation to other systems. Since the analysis procedure has been standardized since 2008 (see Section 4.3), there are several comparable values and evaluations available for about 300 systems. On this basis, it was possible to create a uniform evaluation scheme to compare the states of multiple systems. We called this the "Modularity Maturity Index (MMI)" . We chose the name Modularity Maturity Index because modularity plays a decisive role in sustainability at all levels (see Section 5.4).

Standardized procedure

The state of the analyzed systems is mapped by the MMI on a scale from 0 to 10 on the Y-axis. Figure 4-2 shows a selection of 22 software systems that were analyzed over a period of several years. The size of the systems measured in Lines of Code (LOC) is indicated below each circle. System 2 is a 14.7-million LOC Java system. System 16 is a C# system with almost 10 million LOC. Overall, the diagram covers systems written in Java, C#, C++, and PHP.

MMI from 1 to 10

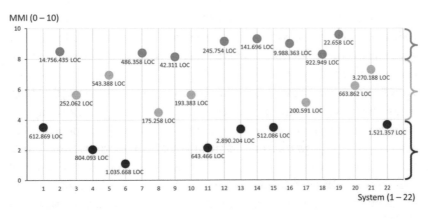

Green and yellow areas If the MMI of a system is between 8 and 10 (i.e., in the green range), the proportion of technical debt is low. The system is in the corridor of "constant maintenance effort" shown in figure 1.2 in Section 1.3. Systems with an MMI between 4 and 8 have already collected some technical debt, and the resulting architectural erosion is slowing down the speed of maintenance and development, making refactoring necessary to get the project back into the green zone. In this case, the team and the reviewer need to define and prioritize refactoring measures that reduce the technical debt. These refactoring measures have to be included step by step in the maintenance and expansion of the system, and the results need to be checked regularly too. This way, a system can be moved gradually back into the "constant maintenance effort" area.

Red area Systems with an MMI below 4 can only be maintained and expanded with a great deal of effort. Such systems are in the corridor of "high, unplannable maintenance effort" shown in figure 1-2 in Section 1.3. You have to consider carefully whether a system in this kind of state is worth renewing via refactoring, or if it should simply be replaced. As an example, let's look at system #13 with its 2.8 million LOC. This system was very expensive to maintain and expand, and our analysis was able to clearly show the bad state it had reached by revealing clear facts from inside the system. With an MMI of 3.5, the system was squarely in the red area. The company using the software had already looked for a replacement some time ago and found an off-the-shelf product to fit the bill. To avoid the same trap of constantly increasing maintenance costs, this product was examined too (see system #18 in fig. 4-2). With an MMI of 8.6, the replacement system is in good condition and the potential for improvement identified by the analysis can be implemented at reasonable cost.

MMI measures sustainability Chapters 7-10 describe the factors that are included in the MMI. These include measurable values such as size ratios and coupling between components, as well as quality evaluation by the reviewer, which covers things like the partitioning of the modules, their public interfaces, and their names. Generally, the impression we gain of the systems examined during a live workshop are always reflected in the MMI, so we are confident that we have found a reliable way to achieve sustainability through system comparisons.

4.6 Technical Debt in the Lifecycle

If you want to protect your architecture permanently against technical debt, you should implement the following steps from the start of every project:

Permanent protection

- *Architecture discussions within the team:* During the current iteration, the team members collect architectural topics that they would like to discuss. At a regular architecture retrospective meeting, these topics and other issues that are important to more experienced developers and architects are discussed.

Architectural discussions

- *Monitoring:* Various key metrics are collected automatically using appropriate tools (see the appendix for more details), so that the team can detect deviations and anomalies at an early stage and deal with them before small problems turn into large issues.

Monitoring

- *Pair Programming:* Programming is performed exclusively in teams of two, which are regularly switched. This way, knowledge of the architecture is distributed and simultaneously discussed within the team.

Pair programming

- *Mob Programming:* Important refactoring is carried out by the entire team on a large screen with just one person operating the computer. This gives all members of the team a deeper understanding of the refactoring process.

Mob programming

- *Mob Architecting:* Analog to mob programming, I often refer to the live architecture improvement workshops (see Section 4.3) as "mob architecting". The whole team gets together at regular intervals and revises its architecture. External help should be offered at the early stages and later using a suitable tool. This is a great way to counter the architectural erosion that otherwise creeps in unnoticed (see Section 1.3.3).

Mob architecting

Some companies have already established these processes. Metric tools (see the appendix for more details) are used for daily monitoring and regular architectural discussions take place within the team. Other companies already have a code base for which they would like to see long-term support for architecture improvement in the future.

Regular analysis   Long-term support should consist of regular architectural analysis, usually accompanied by architectural advice. When I am involved in this type of process, I walk through the three phases of the architectural analysis shown in figure 4-3 with the client. These phases are: Cleanup, Improvement, and Preservation.

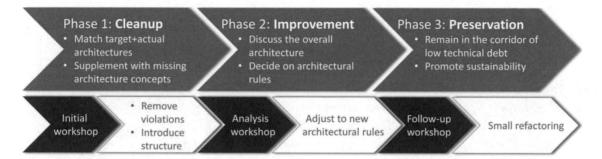

Figure 4-3   During the cleanup phase we look for deviations between the target and actual architectures—an exercise that often harbors some surprises for the development team. Such deviations must be repaired if the source code is to match the target architecture at all. However, part of this phase also involves specifying the target architecture *Cleanup* more precisely and supplementing it with missing concepts. We discuss a lot of different architectural styles and design principles that might be useful for the system in question (see Chapter 6). The cleanup phase usually requires a two-day workshop for systems with up to 500,000 LOC. If you are dealing with a larger system, you should plan a longer workshop of three to five days' duration. Systems with less than 100,000 LOC can be cleaned up in one day. The depth of the required analysis very much depends on the existing architecture and the participants' depth of architectural understanding. In addition, the presence of the system's parents has an influence on the speed at which the analysis can progress.

Improvement   The second (improvement) phase is the most enjoyable for architects and development teams. At this stage, the architecture is already cleaned up, the initial architecture discussions are already done, and global improvement is the main goal. This success of this phase depends on the time limitations the architects and developers are subject to. If they are under time pressure during the workshops, not much can be achieved. I was very impressed by the *Eclipse*

The three phases of architecture analysis

development teams, whose custom it is to build no new features for the first four weeks after a release. The team's task during this period is to clean up the source code and improve the architecture.

The third and final phase involves preserving the architecture *Preservation* so that the system remains easily maintainable and can be further developed until a completely new system becomes unavoidable. If they have appropriate analysis tools and time available, development teams can usually manage this phase on their own. As an architect or project manager, you should be careful not to make major changes to the software system during this phase. Larger changes often influence the architecture of the system. It often makes sense to go back to phase 2 (improvement) at this point so that the architecture remains viable following the change.

One of the most pleasurable aspects of my live workshops usu- *Finding allies* ally occurs on the second day when one of the participants comes to the computer and says, "May I have a go, too?" When this happens, I am only too happy to hand over the mouse and let them play with and alter their own architecture. When this happens, I have won an ally at the company. Here is someone who is interested in architectural analysis and improvement, and is happy to join in. This is where long-term architectural improvement takes seed!

5 Cognitive Psychology and Architectural Principles

The goal of durable architecture is to reduce development and maintenance costs. Software should be easily modifiable. The software development team should be able to quickly navigate the source code and its structures during their work. This is particularly important because developers and architects spend most of their time reading and understanding code (see fig. 5-1).

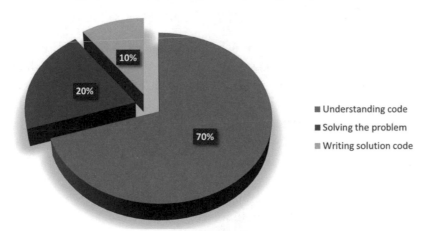

Figure 5-1

Typical code reading and writing ratio

■ Understanding code
■ Solving the problem
■ Writing solution code

Analyzability

If you have to spend a lot of time reading and understanding source code, it is extremely important that the source code has a structure that is easy to navigate. The reasoning behind the structure should remain clear and comprehensible for many years to come.

Problem solving in complex contexts

So how do we find out which structures help the development team to do its job efficiently? Cognitive psychology can help answer this question. Among other things, cognitive psychology deals with human approaches to understanding, acquiring knowledge, and solving problems—all tasks that developers are confronted with when dealing with software systems. The findings presented here summarize what people do while structuring complex relationships in everyday life. With their help, we can present arguments for the types of structure that are easier to understand than others. Admittedly, the essential complexity of an architecture cannot be resolved based on these findings, but they do make it possible to make recommendations on how technical debt can be significantly reduced.

Structure-forming processes

Cognitive psychology describes three structure-building processes that are of great importance to the understanding software architecture, namely: *chunking* smaller units into a large unit, the construction of *outline plans* for depicting general categories, and the formation of *hierarchies*. The following sections describe these processes in the context of the corresponding architectural principles.

5.1 Modularity

Modularity is an older principle introduced by David Parnas in the 1970s. His writings give no hints that he knew anything about cognitive psychology, but he nevertheless intuitively created a concept that transfers the concept of chunking directly into the computer science arena.

5.1.1 Chunking

In order to cope with the huge amounts of information they are constantly confronted with, humans need to select partial information and group it into larger units. This process of creating increasingly high-quality abstractions (i.e., ever more summarization) is called *chunking*[1].

Chunks = knowledge units

Chunking creates new units of knowledge (chunks) from several other units that were previously stored separately in memory. An example is a person working with a telegraph machine for the first time. She hears the transmitted Morse code signals as short and long tones and, in the beginning, processes these tones as separate units of knowledge. Once she has had some practice, she will

---

1   see [Davis 1984], [Henderson-Sellers 1996] and [Miller 1956]

be able to combine the sounds into letters (i.e., into new units of knowledge) so that she can understand what is being transmitted faster. Later still, individual letters become words and words build sentences, representing ever-larger units of knowledge.

This process is also known as *recoding*[2]. During recoding, existing knowledge units are condensed and stored as a new unit that contains more information per unit than each of its parts. The simplest way to recode is to group several knowledge units, give the group a name, and save the new unit under this name. The resulting (new) knowledge unit is seen as a single element, and the knowledge units combined within it are activated and processed together by the brain. Since short-term memory capacity is limited (7±2 units are usually assumed to be the upper limit) chunking is an important capacity relief process.

Condensing knowledge units

However, recoding is not a discrete process consisting of individual steps, but rather a continuous learning process. The degree of recoding achieved in each case is variable and overlaps between the existing knowledge units.

Continuous learning process

Developers automatically apply chunking whenever they need to understand a previously unknown program. The program text is read in detail, and the lines that are read are grouped and memorized as knowledge units. These knowledge units are further condensed and combined until an understanding of the required program text is achieved. This is known as a "bottom-up" approach and is usually applied by developers who need to gain an understanding of a previously unknown software system and its domain.

Understanding programs from the bottom up

If the domain and the software system are already known, developers tend to use a "top-down" approach, which mainly makes use of the hierarchical and schemata creation processes. These are introduced in more detail in the following sections[3].

Understanding programs from the top down

You can get to know a very different approach to chunking by watching experts at work. In this case, new knowledge units are not individually stored in short-term memory before they are compressed but are instead summarized directly by activating previously stored knowledge units. Experts' knowledge units condense significantly more information than those of inexperienced prob-

Expert speed

---

2 see [Boisot & Child 1999]
3 see [Mayrhauser & Vans 1997], [Storey et al. 1999] and [Wallnau et al. 1996]

lem-solvers. However, knowledge units can only be built from other knowledge units that already make sense to a test person. In experiments conducted with experts and beginners, groups of words from the expert's field of knowledge were presented to both groups. The experts were able to remember five times as many terms as the beginners, but only if the groups of words contained related terms that made sense.

Meaningful coherence   These findings can also be demonstrated for developers. In corresponding studies, it became clear that the more the programming language and the structure of a software system offer meaningfully connected units, the easier it is for developers to understand the parts of the software they examine—these connected units are then combined by the developers on a higher level of abstraction. In chunking, the connectedness of the individual components is less important than if they make sense as a unit. Program components that contain arbitrary unrelated operations[4] cannot be coded into meaningful knowledge units if the developer is unable to see why they belong together.

5.1.2 Transfer to Design Principles

In 1972, David Parnas was the first programmer to demand that a module should contain only one design decision. The data structure for this design decision should be encapsulated in the module (encapsulation and locality). Parnas called this principle *Information Hiding* [Parnas 1972].

Chunking and modularity   What does modularity have to do with chunking? Chunking is already supported at the lowest level in programming languages. We can already implement a longer calculation in a method or function, thus allowing us to save the individual instructions as higher-level knowledge units. This way, we achieve a significant capacity gain in short-term memory. Short-term memory is relieved and further information can be processed. Classes and packets give us more options for constructing increasingly large knowledge units. On the architectural level, larger building blocks are added as chunks such as components, modules, layers, but also projects (see fig. 5-2).

---

4   see [Mayrhauser & Vans 1997] and [Wallnau et al. 1996]

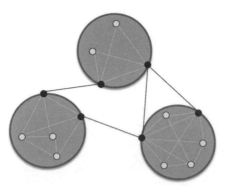

Figure 5-2

*Building blocks in a
modular architecture*

The crucial point here is that chunking can only be applied if coherent units already exist. Arbitrary grouping of operations to or from classes to packets does not facilitate chunking. In such cases, developers have to form multiple knowledge units from the various compounded partial aspects.

Meaningful coherence

The following rules therefore apply to modularity based on chunking:

Rules for modular architecture
The building blocks of a modular architecture must:
1) Internally form a consistent, coherent unit that is responsible for precisely one task (unit as chunk)
2) Outwardly form an explicit, minimal, and delegating capsule (public interface as chunk)
3) Be minimally and loosely coupled to other components (coupling to keep chunks separate)

Modular architecture

In the following sections we will look into these individual modularity rules in more detail. If you are familiar with the principle of modularity, you can skip the following pages and go directly to Section 5.2 on page page 82.

5.1.2.1 Units

Principles for units   In computer science, there are a number of established design principles that aim to meet the demand for coherent units[5] (see fig. 5-3):

Figure 5-3

Cohesive units

for chunking

■ *Separation of Concerns:* Edsger W. Dijkstra wrote in his article *A Discipline of Programming* [Dijkstra 1976], which is still worth reading today, that different parts of a larger task should be represented in different elements of the solution. This is all about the decomposition of knowledge units that are too large into several tasks. In the refactoring movement, such units with too many responsibilities reappeared as a *code smell*[6] under the name *God Class.*

Meaningful decomposition

Cohesion   ■ *Cohesion:* In the 1970s, Myers fleshed out his ideas about design and introduced the measure of cohesion to evaluate coherence within modules. Coad and Yourdon expanded the concept for object orientation.

Responsibility   ■ *Responsibility-driven Design:* This design heuristic points in a similar direction to the principles of information hiding and cohesion, and aims to design classes according to responsibilities.

5   see [Riel 1996], [Myers 1978], [Coad & Yourdon 1994], [Wirfs-Brock & Mc-Kean 2002], [Martin 2013], [Hunts & Thomas 2003], [Myers 1978] and [Coad & Yourdon 1994]

6   Wikipedia defines code smell as follows: "Code smell [...] is working program code that is badly structured. The biggest problem is that the code is difficult for the programmer to understand, so corrections and enhancements are often accompanied by new errors."

According to Rebecca Wirfs-Brock, a class is a design unit that fulfills precisely one responsibility and should therefore perform only one role.

■ *Single Responsibility Principle (SRP)*: Robert Martin defined in his SOLID principles that each class should fulfill only one defined task. A class should only contain functions that directly contribute to the fulfillment of this task. The effect of this concentration on a single task is that there should never be more than one reason to change a class. Robert Martin therefore supplements the Common Closure Principle (CCP) at the architectural level. Classes should be local in their higher-level building blocks, so that changes always affect all or no classes.

Responsibility for a task

■ *Locality of changes*: The definition provided by the IEEE *Standard Glossary of Software Engineering Terminology* especially emphasizes the aspect of changeability: "Modularity is the degree to which a system or computer program is composed of discrete components such that a change to one component has minimal impact on other components" [IEEE 1990]. The DRY (Don't Repeat Yourself) and SPOT (Single Point Of Truth) principles point in the same direction.

Local change

All these principles promote chunking via the inner cohesion of the units involved.

But modularity has more to offer. According to Parnas, a module and its public interface should form a capsule for internal implementation.

5.1.2.2 Public Interface

Public interfaces offer considerable support for chunking if—surprise, surprise—they form meaningful units. If the knowledge unit to be chunked is prepared well enough in a module's public interface, the developer won't actually have to analyze the element in order to see the chunk.

Public interface as chunk

A good coherent public interface is created (see fig. 5-4) if the principles described in the previous section are applied not only to the design of the module's interior but also to its public interface.

Principles for public interfaces

Figure 5-4

Interconnected units
with public interfaces

At this point, we need to add some further principles that relate exclusively to module public interface[7]:

Separate public interface

■ *Explicit public interface* and *separation of public interface and implementation:* Building blocks should make their public interface explicit—i.e., keep them as a separate piece of source code (see Section 7.4).

Minimum services

■ *Minimal public interface* and the *Interface Segregation Principle:* public interfaces should offer the minimal possible set of functionalities. If a client only needs a part of the public interface, then the public interface should be split into several client-specific public interfaces, as specified by Robert Martin in the Interface Segregation Principle (SOLID principle #4).

Injected dependencies

■ *Explicit dependencies:* The public interface of a module should show directly which other modules it communicates with. If this requirement is met, the developer knows which other building blocks she has to understand or create in order to work with the first building block, but without having to look into the implementation. Dependency injection fits directly with this basic principle because it leads to all dependencies being injected into a building block via the public interface.

Concluded services

■ *Delegating public interfaces* and the *Law of Demeter:* Since public interfaces are capsules, the services they offer should be designed to enable delegation. Real delegation occurs when the services of a public interface take over tasks completely. Services

---

7   see [Bass et al. 2012], [Horstmann 2006], [Jacobson 1992], [Martin 2013], [Parnas 1972], [Züllighoven 2005] and en.wikipedia.org/wiki/Law_of_Demeter.

that return internal calls to the caller that then demand that the caller execute further calls in order to reach its goal violate the Law of Demeter (see Section 10.5).

The goal of all these principles is to create public interfaces that support chunking. If they are adhered to, public interfaces can be processed faster as knowledge units. If we also observe the basic principles of coupling, we have gained a lot of knowledge that helps us to chunk when learning to understand a program.

5.1.2.3 Coupling

In order to understand and change a building block within an architecture, developers must obtain an overview of the building block that is to be altered and its neighbors. All the building blocks that the first building block cooperates with are important in this context. To make a modification, the developer must understand these additional blocks, at least to a certain degree (see [Noak 2007]). The more dependencies there are between building blocks, the more difficult it becomes to analyze the individual participants using limited short-term memory and to form suitable knowledge units.

Loose coupling is the computer science principle that comes into play at this point[8]. Coupling refers to the degree of dependency between the building blocks of a software system. The more dependencies there are in a system, the stronger the coupling.

Loose coupling

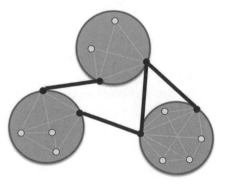

Figure 5-5

Interconnected units with public interfaces and loose coupling

---

8   see [Booch 2004], [Gamma et al. 1994], [Riel 1996] and [Züllighoven 2005].

Unit and public interface
→ loose coupling

If the building blocks of a system have been formed into units and the public interfaces developed according to the principles detailed in the previous two sections, the system should automatically consist of loosely coupled building blocks (see fig. 5-5). A building block that performs a contiguous task will need less additional building blocks than a building block that performs many different tasks. If the public interface is delegating according to the Law of Demeter, then the caller only needs this public interface. It doesn't have to skip from public interface to public interface in order to complete its task, performing a lot of additional coupling along the way.

5.2   Pattern Consistency

In the early 1990s, Erich Gamma radically changed computer science with his doctoral thesis on design patterns. Suddenly we had a name for what we had already been doing for many years. And that is exactly the point—we simply can't work without patterns and/or schemata.

5.2.1 Establishing Schemata

The most far-reaching means used by humans to structure complex relationships are *schemata*—i.e., units of knowledge that combine abstract and concrete knowledge. At the abstract level, schemata contain typical properties of the relationships they schematically depict and define value ranges for these properties. On the concrete level, a schema contains a number of examples that represent prototypical characteristics of the schema[9].

The teacher schema

For example, if we are informed that a person is a teacher, then on the abstract level our schema contains different assumptions and ideas about the associated activity: teachers are employed at a school, they do not have an 8-hour working day, and they have to correct class tests. Specifically, we will remember our own teachers, who we have stored as prototypes of the teacher schema. From our knowledge of prototypes we also draw conclusions about the other person.

---

9   see [Norman 1982].

The opposite effect can be seen in the following example. If someone tells you their father was a hemmer, your brain attempts to find a suitable schema. In a matter of seconds, most of us realize that we don't know this profession and a question mark pops up in our minds. What is a hemmer? At the end of the 18th century, hemmers used donkeys to transport goods along the mountain slopes of the Alps (the hems) from Germany to Italy and back. Today, there are other transport routes available, but back then this was the job description that people had to rely on.

The hemmer schema

The design patterns applied during software development use the power of the human brain to work with schemata. The description schema developed for design patterns contains an abstract representation of the pattern along with different implementation variants, which can be understood as prototypes. If developers have already worked with a design pattern and formed a schema based on it, they are able to more quickly recognize and understand the program texts and structures that use this design pattern.

Design pattern = schema

Discussions on design patterns repeatedly point out that design patterns are not invented, but rather discovered and created from experience. The same observation was made in cognitive psychology: schemata can only be developed by experience, and strengthened and refined by new, similar experiences. Changing individual defining characteristics is usually quite difficult because it questions the entire schema. For example, shortly after mobile phones hit the market I was surprised to see a stranger passing me on the street holding a monologue. Usually, if someone walking behind me is talking, I would expect two or more people to walk past. I had to relive this experience several times until I adequately adapted my schema to include a single person talking on a mobile phone.

Discovered, not invented

Schemata and chunking are two mechanisms that humans often use in combination. A situation is grasped using a schema and then processed into a knowledge unit (i.e., a chunk). Let's look at an example. In an experiment, chess masters and beginners were shown positions on a chessboard for about five seconds. If the pieces were arranged in a meaningful way, the chess masters were able to remember the positions of more than twenty pieces. They saw patterns of known positions and stored corresponding chunks in their short-term memory. The less experienced players could only

Chess, schemata, and chunking

map out the positions of four or five pieces because they had to remember the positions of the chess pieces individually. In a similar experiment with the chess pieces arranged randomly, the chess masters were no longer at an advantage. There were no existing schemata that they could use to condense the meaningless distribution of the pieces into larger units of knowledge.

Deductive understanding   With the help of a group of schemata relating to a specific issue, an expert in the field can find their way around faster than a newcomer who does not possess corresponding schemata. This speed gain is due to the expert's ability to directly retrieve memories using schemata to recognize patterns in the environment. This ability distinguishes the expert from a layperson, who is forced to construct knowledge units and develop new schemata from the ground up using a deductive approach. Deductive understanding of connections leads to serial processing in the brain, which, according to cognitive psychologists, the human brain is less suited to. The human brain is better suited to parallel processing, during which information spreads and patterns are recognized. Accordingly, the development of expertise in a specific field goes hand in hand with a transition from deductive solution strategies to solution strategies such as pattern recognition, to which the human brain is better adapted.

The construction of schemata provides decisive speed advantages when it comes to the understanding complex structures. This is also why patterns found their way into software development at a very early stage.

5.2.2 Transfer to Design Principles

The *establishment of schemata* is reflected in pattern-based software development. Patterns can be found on a small scale in design patterns and on a larger scale in architectural styles. Patterns have the advantage that they limit the solution space available to the development team, thus making it easier to understand existing solutions.

Incorrect patterns slow   Anyone who writes software is familiar with the opposite effect:
us down   a system uses a class that contains the name of a well-known pattern but does not match this pattern. Imagine, for example, a class

called XYFactory (see fig. 5-6). Anyone who is familiar with this pattern has certain expectations regarding the public interface and the behavior of the class. It creates objects based on an abstract type and/or configuration.

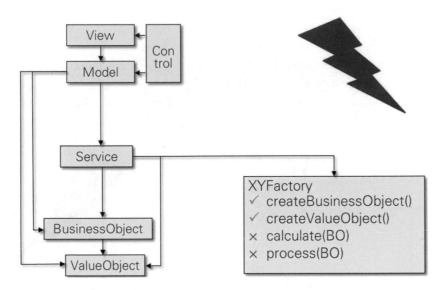

Figure 5-6

Mismatched pattern

The XYFactory class not only creates objects, it also offers methods that perform calculations on the generated objects. The result is that the process of understanding is slowed down! We then ask ourselves why the programmer developed this solution. There must have been a good reason, so how do we find out what his intentions were? Do we have any clues as to who developed the class? Is the developer still with the company? Perhaps he simply misunderstood the factory pattern. Or did he not know what to do with the calculation methods and simply integrated them into the XYFactory class? Or perhaps he didn't do any of the above and just happened to name his class this way? Do we have to refactor here? These are some of the questions you will need to ask in cases like this. And you can't take advantage of a schema and understand the program from the top down. Such erroneous or unwise use of patterns in software systems is a big problem. They nullify the speed we gain from using patterns during the understanding and modification process, just like the meaningful and random setups of chess pieces described in the previous section.

Missing and unknown

patterns   If patterns are missing in a software system, the developers will
not be able to establish a schema. This can become a painful experience if you are programming systems that are only partly based
on patterns. Let's imagine that we have to fix a bug in the selection
of business objects in the user interface. To find the bug, we go
through different patterns in the source code and end up at the
service that is responsible for this type of business object. We also
find the actual business object class (see fig. 5-7). During our investigation of the selection algorithm in the service, we suddenly come
across a class that does not match any of the patterns already used
in the system.

Figure 5-7

Unknown pattern

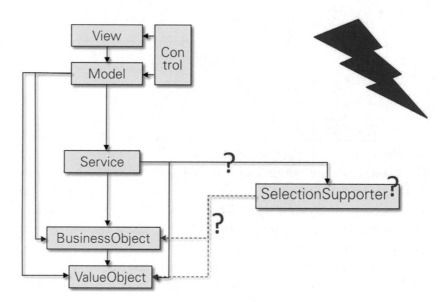

Such a class could be called `SelectionSupporter`, for example. Our
system so far contains no Supporter pattern. Of course, the name
tells us that the class will have something to do with the problem,
and probably supports a different class with its work. But the role
of `SelectionSupporter` in relation to the surrounding classes remains
unclear. Can `SelectionSupporter` work on the business objects? Can
it use the service to improve selection? We can only understand the
solution implemented here by looking at the cooperation between
these classes in detail, and this takes time! If the developer of `Selec-
tionSupporter` had chosen one of our existing patterns or added the

Supporter pattern to the existing pattern repertoire, we would have made much faster progress during our bug fix.

Design patterns should give developers clues about the tasks of each class and how they are meant to work together. This usually strengthens the focus on clear tasks (i.e., modularity). If a pattern is used incorrectly, or differently, or in not all the appropriate places, it hinders the establishment of schemata.

However, it is not only the use of design patterns at the class level that is important in the context of these considerations. The way the development team implemented the planned (target) patterns in the program code is just as interesting. Can the planned patterns be found within the code?

Target architecture as a model

Nowadays, most programming languages and development environments offer two means for mapping the target architecture to the source code. These are:

- The packet structure governing classes in the programming language in question
- The project structure and the associated division into build artifacts in the development environment in question

If the packet structure and/or the build artifact structure correspond to the architectural specifications, the developers can navigate the program much more easily. Figure 5-8 shows the package tree of a Java system in which the actual architecture contains a total of 28 packages. The package tree starts on the left-hand side with the top-level package de. de contains the package unihamburg and continues down the line to the system name jcommsy. The package tree then splits into four. These four packages display the four layers of the system as planned by the architect. The package nodes shown in figure 5-8 are color-coded according to their corresponding layers.

Patterns in the actual architecture

In this example, the architects did their job very well and the planned subsystems can be found in the actual architecture. The pattern that the target architecture delivered to the developers is clearly recognizable through the names and the level structure.

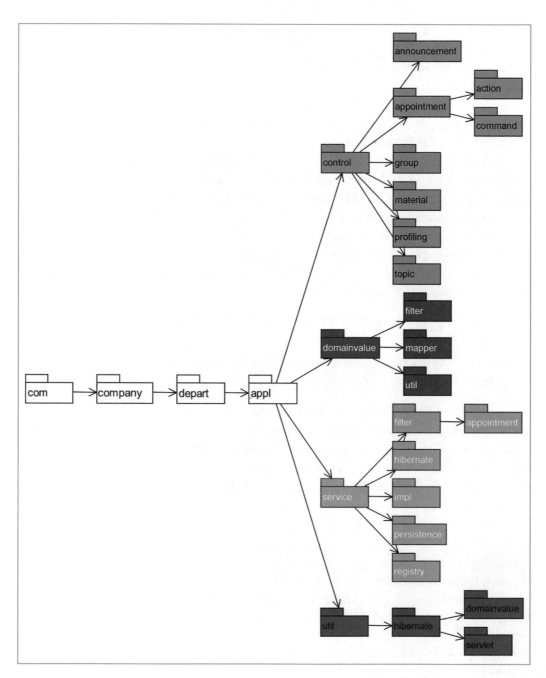

Figure 5-8

Subsystems within the

package structure

Rules for pattern consistency in architecture
The building blocks of a pattern-consistent architecture must: 1) Correspond to the specifications for building blocks in the target architecture 2) Be of a consistent design in accordance with uniform models

Pattern consistency in architecture

In the next chapter we will get to know which architectural styles and patterns most efficiently support the construction of schemata. The use of patterns and architectural styles in practice is explained in Chapters 7 and 8.

5.3 Hierarchy

As early as the 1960s, Dijkstra pointed out that ordered structures are useful in the development of software systems [Dijkstra 1968]. Let's look at what cognitive psychology has to offer in the context of Dijkstra's layered system concept.

5.3.1 Formation of Hierarchies

Studies in various areas of cognitive psychology show that hierarchies play an important role in the perception, understanding, and memorizing of complex structures. In such experiments, trees (mono-hierarchical) or directional acyclic (polyhierarchical) graphs are regarded as hierarchical structures (see fig. 5-9). Different relations are used to order the elements, including categorical subordination (normal for the superordinate and subordinate terms in inheritance hierarchies), part-whole relationships (as used to transform smaller units into larger ones during aggregation relation), and also mind maps, in which terms are related to one another (usage relations). The authors all conclude that people can absorb knowledge well, reproduce it, and navigate around it if it is presented within hierarchical structures[10].

Hierarchical structures

---

10 see [Norman 1982].

Figure 5-9

Hierarchical structure of
parent and child nodes

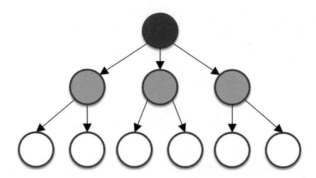

Ability of memory   The authors cite sample studies on learning-related word categories, the organization of learning materials, text comprehension, text analysis, and text reproduction. When reproducing long lists the memory performance of the test subjects was significantly better if they were offered decision trees with categorical suborders. Test subjects who used hierarchical chapter structures or mind maps grasped educational content much faster. Where there was no existing hierarchical structure, the test subjects tried to arrange the text hierarchically anyway. A hierarchy is obviously the model preferred by all the test subjects.

Asked to reproduce text, the test subjects produced a further interesting effect. They were better able to remember text located at higher levels within the structure, such as the main terms or summaries. The more detailed parts located lower down in the structure were much more easily forgotten. However, text comprehension depended heavily on whether the text itself helped the test subjects to recognize the hierarchical structures within it.

These cognitive psychological studies come to the conclusion that hierarchically ordered content is easier for people to learn and process. Content can be retrieved much more efficiently from a hierarchical structure.

Hierarchies and chunking   Over and above these findings, human beings also tend to combine hierarchies with chunking (see Section 5.1.1). Knowledge units (i.e., chunks) are mapped in memory with the help of hierarchical structures. For example, a house can be memorized as a high-level knowledge unit that contains smaller knowledge units representing the individual rooms.

Using hierarchies to   The advantages of hierarchies can also be seen in studies of
understand programs   top-down program understanding. If developers are familiar with

the hierarchies within a software system, they can carry out maintenance work more efficiently than developers who don't know the hierarchies. The latter have to analyze the unknown software system from the bottom up. They have to develop their own hierarchies and chunks, which takes a lot of time. Note that developers use hierarchies to view software systems on different levels, hiding parts of the system and its structure in order to reduce complexity[11].

5.3.2 Transfer to Design Principles

In programming languages, the *formation of hierarchies* is supported by the aggregation relationship. Methods are encapsulated in classes, classes are encapsulated in packets, and so on. However, this doesn't apply to all other types of relationships. We can link any class and interface in a source code base with a use relationship and/or an inheritance relationship to create interwoven structures that are not hierarchical in any way. For example, if class A inherits from class B and class B also uses class A, a non-hierarchical structure is created.

Aggregation, inheritance, use

The possibility of using inheritance and use relationships to implement hierarchical structures remains. In software architecture, the goal is to create a "cycle-free" system. An architecture is cycle-free if a building block doesn't lead back to itself via the relationships it and its related building blocks contains. Such a structure is referred to as a directed acyclic graph.

Figure 5-10 shows two directed graphs. The blue nodes form a cyclic structure, while the white nodes belong to the graph but not to the cyclic structure.

Cycles and cycle groups

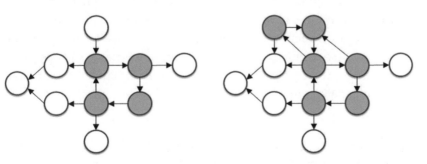

Figure 5-10

Cycles in a directed graph

11 see [Storey et al. 1999], [Wallnau et al. 1996] and [Mayrhauser & Vans 1997].

The structure on the left in figure 5-10 contains a cycle involving four nodes, while the one on the right shows a cycle group consisting of three individual cycles. For the sake of simplicity, the following sections use the terms cycle and cycle group synonymously.

Today, various arguments can be found in the relevant textbooks as to why ordered structures are preferable to cycles. These generally technical arguments partly pick up and extend the arguments against cyclical structures gained from cognitive psychology[12]:

- *Extensibility:* Cyclic structures are difficult to expand because they are difficult to understand. Developing modules in parallel can be inhibited by cycles, because changes made to one module can cause modifications in the modules linked to it.

- *Testability:* To minimize errors in software systems, corresponding test classes have to be written. Cyclically linked blocks cannot be tested in isolation, so all blocks involved in the cycle have to be tested. Working with mocks is a solution for this problem.

- *Evolution:* Compared to the rest of the software system, cyclical building blocks change more frequently and are more prone to errors. Furthermore, cyclical structures spread because new classes are added to the existing cycles when a system is extended.

- *Partitioning:* If a software system is to be divided into individual components that are delivered or deployed separately, the components must not contain any cyclic dependencies.

- *Comprehensibility:* Components contained in a cycle can only be considered as a unit. If you want to understand and change a block, you have to gain an overview of all the blocks linked that are to it. Building blocks involved in cycles often play several roles within the architecture. Different responsibilities arise from these roles, which in turn make it more difficult to grasp the big picture. In addition, building blocks within cycles are proportionally larger than other building blocks, making them more difficult to manage and understand.

---

12 [Binder 1999], [Bischofberger et al. 2004], [Feathers 2004], [Fowler 2001], [Lakos 1996], [Martin 2013], [Neumann 2005] and [Zimmermann & Nagappan 2006].

> **Rules for a cycle-free architecture**
>
> The relationships between the building blocks in a cycle-free architecture have to be free of return relationships on all levels

Cycle-free architecture

Although cycle-free architecture is a relatively old concept, it is still a rare exception today. In Chapter 9 we will take a closer look at some contemporary systems.

5.4 Cycles = Failed modularity + Pattern

The *Comprehensibility* entry in the list in the previous section contains a very important message about modularity and pattern consistency, namely: classes within a cycle are often larger than other classes and have multiple roles that include specific tasks. The desire to create cycle-free software is therefore not a means to an end! It is less about satisfying the technical/structural idea that cycles must be avoided and is more about creating a comprehensible design.

Freedom from cycles is not an end in itself

If the individual building blocks are modular and have only one task, the design should be cycle-free. A module that provides basic functionality should never require functionality from the module it is based on. If the tasks involved are clearly distributed, it will be obvious which module has to use which others in order to fulfill its task. A reverse (and therefore cyclical) relationship shouldn't arise at all.

The same argument also applies to pattern consistency. If you make sure that the individual building blocks match the selected patterns and adhere to the corresponding rules during the design phase, the result is a cycle-free architecture. The example used in Section 8.6 and at the beginning of Chapter 9 clearly demonstrates how cycles, modularity, and patterns influence each other.

5.5 Consequences for Architectural Analysis

Today's software systems (and therefore the ones examined here) are often very large. This makes it impossible for developers and architects to be experts in all areas of a system. Additionally, the maintenance of software systems is often carried infrequently. If you edit a piece of source code rarely and the pauses between maintenance phases are long, it is impossible to become (or remain) an expert on all levels. Even the best developers won't have suitable hierarchies, schemata, and chunks on hand for all parts of the source code.

Understanding programs iteratively   Depending on the task at hand, developers instead have to identify the components and source code that need to be altered. Studies have shown that developers combine top-down and bottom-up approaches in order to comprehend the source code and identify the parts that need to be modified (see [Wallnau et al. 1996]). At the beginning of a search, the developer typically uses hierarchies and schemata to explore the system as far as possible from the top down. If the schemata and hierarchies are no longer useful, the developer will switch to the bottom-up technique to gain further understanding of the code. This also leads to an increase in chunking. During this (usually) iterative process, the developers gain an understanding of the parts of the program that have to be changed and the ways they interact. Furthermore, they will localize the side effects that may be triggered by modifications.

Summary   For this process of understanding and changing the program to run as quickly and error-free as possible, software systems must:

◼ Consist of modules that are meaningfully connected on different levels of abstraction in order to facilitate *chunking* (modularity)

◼ Be constructed without cycles in order to support the formation of hierarchies (cycle-free structure)

◼ Offer recurring patterns at different levels of abstraction from which patterns can be formed (pattern consistency)

A software system with an architecture that supports these processes will be easier for developers and architects to understand and modify.

It is therefore essential to investigate these aspects of the architectural in order to successfully analyze and improve it (s. fig. 5-11). These areas offer room for improvement, as you will see in the detailed examples in Chapters 8, 9, and 10.

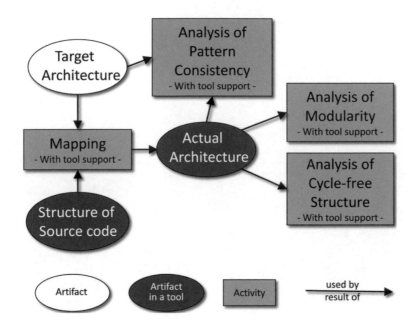

Figure 5-11

The architectural analysis

and improvement process

6 Architectural Styles that Reduce Technical Debt

During the past 30 years, developers and architects have discovered various architectural styles in the course of their work. Architectural styles are a proven means of establishing guardrails for the design space of the entire architecture. Architects and developers form schemata based on these guardrails and, with the help of these schemata, learn to navigate around the source code and quickly carry out maintenance or add extensions. Furthermore, most architectural styles provide specifications for modularity and promote cycle-free structures.

The following sections take a look at which guardrails common architectural styles offer, and which architectural styles are best at supporting our three basic principles.

6.1 Rules of Architectural Styles

Architectural styles specify the structure of a software system, and thus also the elements it contains and the relationships between them[1]:

Elements and rules

■ What types of elements does the architectural style have?

■ Which architectural rules exist for this architectural style?

   • *Element rules* only affect one element type. Element rules define the public interface of an element type or specify the modules from which it is constructed.

---

1 see [Bass et al. 2012], [Fielding 2000], [Garlan 2000], [Hofmeister et al. 2000] and [Knodel & Popescu 2007].

- *Permissions* define the relationships between specific element types.
- *Prohibition rules* prohibit relationships between specific element types

Pipes and Filters Due to these restrictions, only some of the possible combinations between elements and relationships are permitted. For example, the "pipe-and-filter" architectural style contains two types of elements. Filters are executing elements that transform data while pipes act as connection streams that pass data between the filters. An important rule for this style is that pipes can only be linked to filters but not to one another.

Compared to other architectural styles, the pipes-and-filter architectural style is extremely limited due to having only two element types. This structure can only be used to make rough specifications for the design space. In the following sections, we will get to know other architectural styles that offer more element types and thus provide more detailed specifications for the design space.

6.2   Separation of Business and Technical Building Blocks

A simple but essential architectural style used in high-quality architecture involves the separation of the domain and technical building blocks, according to the tenets of Quasar (**Q**uality-**D**riven **S**oftware **A**rchitecture[2]). Business building blocks are those that contain source code for the application domain, such as business rules, calculations, validations, and so on. Technical building blocks solve purely technical problems, such as database connections, user interfaces, and so on. The basic principle of this architectural style is that each building block contained in an architecture may only be responsible for either of these two aspects. This separation is postulated by Quasar because the domain and technical aspects of software systems usually have very different change cycles. If this separation can be maintained, the result will be a well modularized system.

---

2   see [Voss et al. 2006]

This Quasar-based idea became manageable with the introduction of "blood types" for software components. I think this model has not really become established because the blood-type analogy for software is pretty far-fetched. Nevertheless, this style provides some very important hints that should be obvious to every software architect:

Software "blood types"

- *Blood group A* includes all software components that implement domain functionality. They represent the actual aim of the project (e.g., customer, account, invoice, order, and so on).

- *Blood group T* is assigned to all technical software modules that can be defined by having at least one technical API (e.g., a database connection, user interface technology, communication with remote applications).

- All software modules that represent a mixture of A- and T-type modules have the *blood type AT*. This type of software should be avoided and, if necessary, separated from the rest of the system (e.g., functional classes that are implemented as EJBs or inherit from technical classes for other reasons).

- *Blood group R* is reserved for all software modules that perform the transformation between A and T modules. R building blocks are a necessary mild form of AT building blocks. They are usually small, do not contain too much logic, and are used as transitions between A and T building blocks (e.g., database mapper classes, FormBeans in Struts).

A sample class of the unwanted blood type AT could look like this:

Blood group AT

```
public class UserGroup extends ArrayList<User> {…}
```

Here, a domain class that is used to represent groups of users inherits from a technical class. Such a solution is forbidden by Quasar due to its blood types. Even the most experienced developers and architects would call such a solution a code smell. A reasonable implementation of such a class would involve giving the class UserGroup a copy variable of the ArrayList<User> type.

From a style point of view, the four blood types are Quasar's architectural elements. Each has:

■ Element rules for each individual blood type. For example: "R building blocks are small and contain little logic".

■ Prohibition rules for cooperation between blood types. For example: "A-Software and T-Software must not know each other".

Quasar coarse structure   If this separation is maintained consistently within a system, a rough structure is created for the entire system (see fig. 6-1).

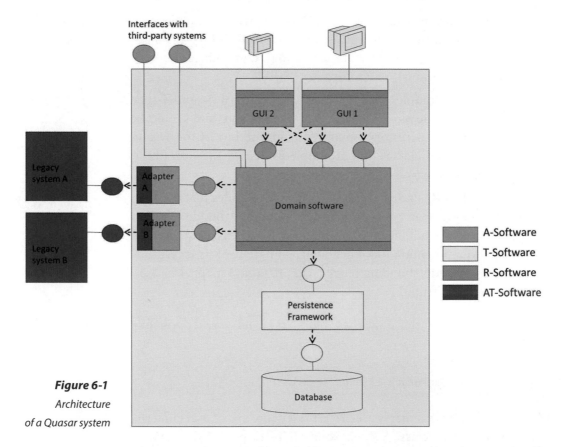

Interfaces with
third-party systems

GUI 2   GUI 1

Legacy
system A

Adapter
A

Domain software

Legacy
system B

Adapter
B

A-Software
T-Software
R-Software
AT-Software

Persistence
Framework

Database

Figure 6-1

Architecture

of a Quasar system

Pattern, modularity,   These specifications from the Quasar architectural style provide all
and freedom from cycles   building blocks with a rough location within the overall system, resulting in a pattern that can be followed by developers and architects. At the same time, the blood types make statements about the division of tasks and cooperation within the system. This separation

between blood types also leads to better modularity, and the rules for cooperation between the blood types mean that the source code has a rough hierarchical structure.

6.3 Layered Architecture

Layered architecture is one of the architectural styles most frequently described in literature and most often used by corporations[3]. The layer is the only type of architectural element that a layered architecture defines. Layers combine a software system's building blocks into larger units, making the layer itself a kind of building block too. Layers are sorted hierarchically, and architecture rules are defined that prevent deeper layers from accessing the layers above them.

The first layered software system was Dijkstra's THE system. This system was built on a strict layering pattern that permitted each layer to access only the one lying directly beneath it. The transition from one layer to the next was thereby considered to be an abstraction to a higher level of language. Operating systems are usually developed according to this strict layering model, as shown by the ISO/OSI layer model.

Strict layering

Application software, frameworks, and libraries generally do not use layering that restricts the access of each layer to the layer below. As a rule, the building blocks in the higher layers may access several layers, and sometimes even all the layers below. The reason for this weaker layering is that the goal is not to create a higher language level (as is the case with operating systems) but rather to avoid any upward relationships between layers.

Layering in applications

Today's layered architectures commonly use only two-layer dimensions, namely: technical and domain layering.

6.3.1 Technical Layering

In order to achieve a technical layer model, the building blocks in a software system are classified and hierarchized according to their technical tasks. Hence, layers are created that reflect the technical

---

3 see [Bass et al. 2012], [Fowler 2003], [Hofmeister et al. 2000], [Jacobson 1992] and [Züllighoven 2005].

structure of the system. The technical layering model proposed by Eric Evans divides layers into presentation, application, domain, and infrastructure layers. The individual layers usually have public interfaces that restrict the access of other layers to their content[4].

Figure 6-2

Technical layering

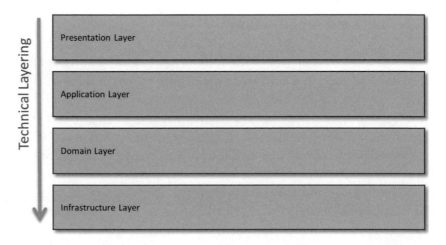

Semantics of layers In his article *On a "Buzzword": Hierarchical Structure* [Parnas 1974] David Parnas criticized the way many authors speak of a hierarchical structure in their system without clearly stating how the system is layered or which kinds of relationships exist between the layers. Any building blocks of a software system can be combined into a layer without rhyme or reason. The technical layering shown in figure 6-2 attempts to overcome this dilemma. Certain tasks are defined for each layer, thus producing a semantic enrichment of the layers according to technical aspects.

Modularity in layers This discussion clearly shows that freedom from cycles (i.e., relationships that contravene the layer model) cannot be the only reason to use layers. On the contrary, the question remains regarding how modular division of a system in the technical dimension can work. If you find cycles between the layers, then the division of the layers (i.e. their modularity) has not been successfully implemented (see also Section 5.4).

---

4   see [Evans 2004] and [iSAQB 2019].

6.3.2 Domain Layering

Traditional technical layering is generally not enough for large software systems, as the resulting large technical layers cannot provide sufficient orientation to make chunking possible. Creating more subdivisions and hierarchies based on the domain is the obvious approach to take for systems that exceed a certain size.

Large software systems often support different departments in an organization (for example, credit, investment, or stocks) as well as functions that overlap departments, such as customer management and customer relationship management (CRM). This is why architects and developers of larger software systems often add domain-oriented layering in addition to the technical layers.

Organizational divisions

With the domain partitioning as a foundation, architects also need to define rules for the relationships between the domain-based building blocks. For example, a central module (such as customer relations) can be used by other modules (such as the credit or investment units). However, the building blocks used by customer relations aren't usually used by the other, higher-level building blocks.

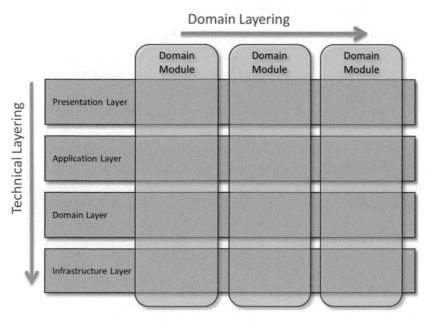

Figure 6-3

Domain layering

Domain modules   Domain-oriented layering divides the system into vertical modules[5] that traverse the technical layers (see fig. 6-3). Each module represents a business unit or a business area, and each domain module contains the parts of the technical layers (presentation, application, domain, infrastructure) that belong to the corresponding domain. The individual domain modules are also layered, which further limits the relationships between them. For example, the basic Customer Administration module can be used by all modules it is based on (i.e., credit, stocks, and investment). However, these "add-on" modules may not use each other, whether they match the domain or not.

Domain-based   The professional modules are the architectural elements of pro-
relationships   fessional layering. These architectural elements are also subject to the rules of their relationships. The permitted relationships between business areas are defined as architectural rules. As with technical layers, relationships between domain modules are only allowed in one direction, thus creating a hierarchy of domain modules.

In Section 6.5 we will see how the new microservices trend is related to dividing a system into domain-oriented modules.

6.3.3 The Infrastructure Layer

Locating the infrastructure layer at the bottom (see fig. 6-3) causes difficulties, as some of the layers above the infrastructure layer can access certain building blocks within the infrastructure layer while others shouldn't be able to.

Infrastructure ≠ lowest   Figure 6-4 shows some exemplary relationships between the
layer   higher layers and the infrastructure layer. All layers can use the logging framework, while the widget library should only be used by the presentation layer. Other libraries (such as the print library and the OR mapper) have similar difficulties too. If the infrastructure layer is the lowest layer of the architecture, such layer violations are not obvious. The pattern "Higher layers may call all underlying layers" does not work for this layer. This makes the pattern more complicated because it involves an exception.

---

5   see [Larman 2004] and [Züllighoven 2005].

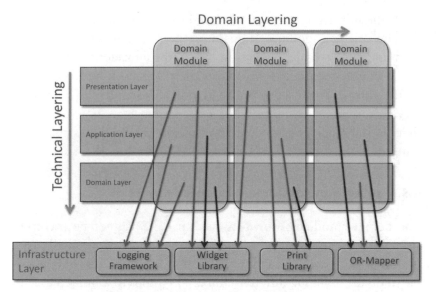

Figure 6-4

Infrastructure layer issues

In order to solve this predicament, the infrastructure layer must be classified as the lowest module in the technical layering model. Figure 6-5 shows this new placement.

Infrastructure layer = bottommost module

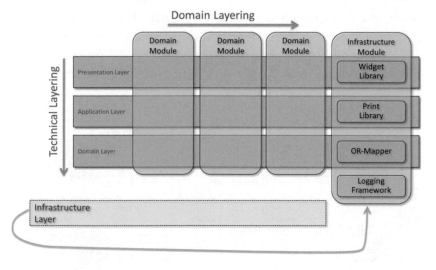

Figure 6-5

Judicious positioning of the infrastructure layer

This new arrangement leads to clearly definable rules for the relationships between the modules and layers. The basic pattern then becomes mandatory throughout the architectural style. In other words, higher layers—both in the technical and domain dimensions—may use the lower layers. This is a clear and consistent pattern.

Domain first   If the infrastructure layer is placed as a foundation beneath the domain-oriented modules, domain-oriented layering should be the predominant layering dimension. With the hexagonal and onion architectures, Section 6.4 introduces the reversal of the relationship to the infrastructure layer through port & adapters. The microservices discussed in Section 6.5 introduce an architectural style that declares domain-oriented layering to be the first structuring criterion.

6.3.4 Integration of Domain-oriented Layers

The domain modules shown in Section 6.3.2 cannot be traversed from the presentation layer to the business domain layer in all cases. If a software system has an integrated user interface, it is only possible to divide it among different domain modules to a limited extent. All parts of the user interface must have access to each domain in order to properly display the complex presentation. A similar question can also arise in a business process engine. The individual processing steps can be implemented as independent domain modules, or using a clear domain-oriented layer model. However, the business process engine must then integrate these individual processing steps.

Broad integration layer   Here, a similar solution is required as for the integrated user interface shown below. Figure 6-6 shows an extreme form of this type of interface-based integration.

Figure 6-6

Broad Integration of the domain modules via the user interface

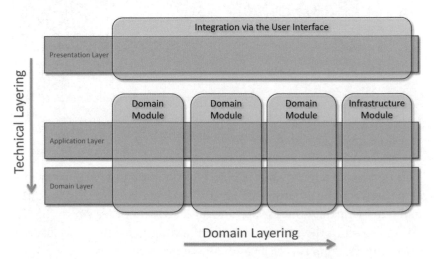

A somewhat softer approach could be to divide the user interface into individual domain parts that are then assigned back to the domain modules. What remains is the thinnest possible integration layer (see fig. 6-7).

Thin integration layer

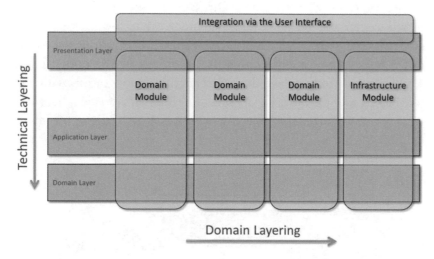

Figure 6-7

Narrow integration of domain modules

This narrow integration of domain modules forms a typical solution for web applications developed according to the principles of microservices.

6.4   Hexagonal, Onion, and Clean Architecture

In recent years, more architectural styles have evolved that incorporate and enhance aspects of layered architecture (see Section 6.3) and Quasar (see Section 6.2). These include:

- Hexagonal Architecture (also known as Ports & Adapters architecture) introduced by Alistair Cockburn in 2005[6]
- Onion Architecture introduced by Jeffrey Palermo in 2008[7]
- Clean Architecture introduced by Robert C. Martin in 2012[8]

---

6   *http://wiki.c2.com/?PortsAndAdaptersArchitecture*
7   *https://jeffreypalermo.com/2008/07/the-onion-architecture-part-1/*
8   *https://blog.cleancoder.com/uncle-bob/2012/08/13/the-clean-architecture.html*

Although these styles differ somewhat in their details, they all pursue the same modularity goal addressed in this book. They all achieve this goal by emphasizing the separation of the business and technical building blocks and layering of the domain modules.

Figure 6-8 summarizes these different architectural approaches. In the center the business building blocks that form a three layered "onion" with outside-in-relationships. The onion is broken down into domain modules that are indicated by the dotted lines. The hexagon surrounding the onion enables cooperation with the technical building blocks via ports and adapters or also via gateways or transformation. See the websites listed below for more details[9].

Figure 6-8

Hexagonal, onion, and clean architecture

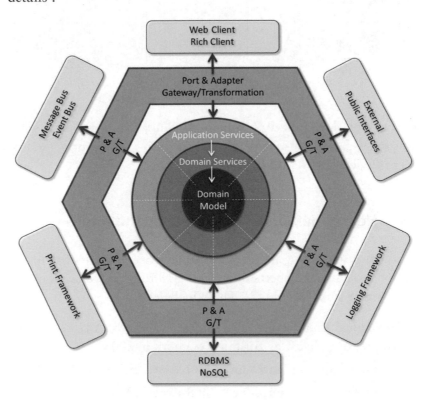

9   *https://herbertograca.com/2017/11/16/explicit-architecture-01-ddd-hexagonal-onion-clean-cqrs-how-i-put-it-all-together/*
https://www.thinktocode.com/2018/07/19/ports-and-adapters-architecture/
https://blog.cleancoder.com/uncle-bob/2012/08/13/the-clean-architecture.html

This architectural style makes the business building blocks independent of the technical ones. The domain modules can be tested without involving the user interface, database, web server or other external interfaces. Additionally, because the domain modules know nothing about the rest of the world, the user interface, database and public interfaces can be altered or exchanged without affecting the rest of the system. This is a clear improvement over the infrastructure layer found in the layered architecture. Like layered architectures and pattern languages, theses "onion-layered" architectural styles, can be analyzed using Sotograph. I have already carried out two corresponding analyses with two separated teams.

Once the onion has been divided into domain modules and if independent deployable units are part of the plan, the next step involves using microservices and Domain-Driven Design.

6.5   Microservices and Domain-Driven Design

In recent years, microservices have emerged as a new architectural style. Many developers and architects originally thought that this architectural style was simply about dividing software systems into services that could be deployed independently of each other while accelerating development using a synchronous team structure. If this were the case, microservices wouldn't belong to the scope of this book.

Independent services

By combining microservices with Eric Evans'[10] principles of strategic Domain-Driven Design, the focus is placed on the domain while splitting a software system into microservices. This is a clear and, in my opinion, very important development toward domain-oriented structures in software systems (see also Section 6.3.2). Evans' style of strategic design provides development teams and business analysts with guidance on how to break down the domain of their software system into sub-areas known as "bounded contexts". A microservice is developed for each bounded context and the rough domain structure is mapped directly onto the structure of the software system.

Bounded context
→ microservice

---

10 [Evans 2004], [Vernon 2017]

Ubiquitous language
in a microservice

Within a bounded context, all business language concepts—or, as Eric Evans says, the "ubiquitous language"—are clearly and unambiguously defined. On the one hand, there are concepts in every domain that can be uniquely assigned to a bounded context, while on the other hand, the same concept can exist with a slightly different definition in two separate bounded contexts. This can happen simply because two departments in a company think differently about the same concept. This semantic shift of concepts between contexts is adopted during the implementation of the business language in the various microservices. Hence a class that represents a business concept from a bounded context in *Microservice A* can be expected to exist under the same name in *Microservice B*. The only difference should be the implementation. For example, the Account class in the *account management* microservice is implemented differently to the Account class used in the *credit* microservice. Both classes certainly have similar parts (such as the account number or the deposit or withdrawal amount). However, other functionalities, such as the overdraft limit for current accounts or the installment payment for credits, will only be available in one or other of the two implementations.

Microservices and
modularity

If development teams divide their microservices using the bounded contexts within their domain, the result is an architecture with a strong focus on modularity (see fig. 6-9) that grows out of the business requirements. Developers and architects try to design microservices that can serve as domain-based units for chunking. Great importance is attached to a minimal public interface and loose coupling. Fowler writes in his article on microservices: "The aim of the microservice style is to be as decoupled and cohesive as possible" (see [Fowler & Lewis 2014]). This architectural style is therefore a real boon to modularity and domain-oriented decomposition.

Communication

As already indicated by the double-headed arrows in figure 6-9, the microservice-based design not only involves domain-oriented separation, but also clarifies how the communication between the individual microservices is implemented. Fowler & Lewis say that communication between services should be as lean as possible and that the public interfaces between microservices must be explicitly described. The logic shouldn't be implemented in the connection between the microservices, but rather in the microservices themselves (see [Fowler & Lewis 2014]).

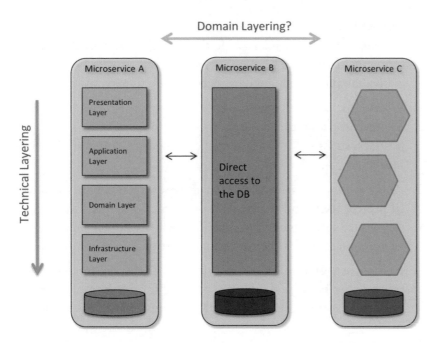

Figure 6-9
Microservices with different implementations

For cases where this rule is not observed, Fowler & Lewis make the following observation: "You quickly think that everything is fine if you look at the inside of a component, but you don't see the chaotic connections between the services."

Public interfaces and context mapping

In order to conceptualize the chaos of the connections between the services (i.e., the public interfaces), the DDD (Domain-Driven Design) strategy proposes seven different options. Eric Evans calls the collaboration between bounded contexts and the public interfaces between microservices "context mapping". The tighter the collaboration, the more the teams responsible for the microservices or bounded contexts have to coordinate. The types of context mapping described by Evans are ordered below from those with the closest collaboration to those with no collaboration at all:

- *Shared Kernel:* Multiple microservices share a part of their model—i.e., there are some classes that are the same in both microservices and can only be modified in unison. The teams responsible for these bounded contexts have a lot to discuss.

- *Customer/Supplier:* The supplier microservice provides certain services to the customer microservice. These services are agreed upon by the customer team and the supplier team.

■ *Published Language:* A published language is a well-documented information exchange language that enables easy use and translation of any number of microservices. All those who develop and evolve the published language need to talk to each other.

■ *Open Host Service:* A microservice offers its services as an public interface that can be used by other microservices. An open host service often offers a published language at its public interface.

■ *Anticorruption Layer:* A microservice uses an additional layer to protect itself and its model from legacy systems. Changes to the service's own model are possible, while changes made to the legacy system only affect the anticorruption layer.

■ *Conformist:* One microservice precisely maps the model of another, either because there is no funding for a new model or it is obvious that the other microservice already embodies the perfect model.

■ *Separate Ways:* Microservices are not connected at all. Each has its own model and no data is exchanged between them.

Freedom from cycles and microservices   These types of context mapping do not create a cycle-free order. Even the *DomainEvents* introduced in more recent versions of DDD do not solve this problem. *DomainEvents* certainly decouple more than REST or RPC calls, but don't automatically lead to orderly communication. Every organization that develops microservices in teams must therefore think carefully about how communication between its microservices should be organized.

First experiences   Section 7.5 deals with the experience I have had in the last couple of years converting applications to microservices.

6.6   Pattern Languages

Pattern languages take layered architecture, microservices, and the Quasar architecture a step further. The specifications of the layered and Quasar architectures relate to a relatively unrefined level of an architecture. As an example, imagine the architecture of a system with 250,000 lines of code. The architecture probably consists of three to four technical layers and just as many domain modules. These modules and layers contain many classes. Layer architecture and Quasar do not provide any guidelines on how to order the structure of these classes. Architectural styles that remedy this are called *pattern languages*[11].

Pattern languages are architectural styles that extend the use of design patterns to the entire code base. A pattern language defines a set of pattern elements at the class level and specifies rules for the individual pattern elements. These rules determine which responsibilities the individual pattern elements have (element rules). They also specify how the pattern elements may interact with one another (permission and prohibition rules) [12].

Matching design patterns

Examples of such pattern elements are "business object" and "service". Three rules for these two pattern elements could be:

- Services are stateless classes (element rules)
- Services work on business objects and change their state (permission rule)
- Business objects are not allowed to use services (prohibition rule)

Because they operate at the class level, these pattern elements and rules are much more precise than layer definitions. Pattern languages semantically enrich the elements at the class level so that a class is no longer just a simple class, but rather a particular type of class. Developers need to know the pattern elements and rules in order to understand the interaction of classes. This will help them make modifications that do not violate the rules. The elements and rules of a pattern language create an extended level of communication and understanding with which developers can build new patterns and schemata.

Semantic enrichment

Mature pattern languages are used consistently in all areas of a software system, generally without exceptions. Thus, pattern languages provide consistent patterns for the entire architecture—something that is very valuable from a pattern consistency viewpoint.

Pattern consistency and pattern languages

---

11 The "pattern language" concept goes back to the architect Christopher Alexander, who developed a language of patterns for real architecture (see [Alexander 1982], [Buschmann et al 2007] and [Züllighoven 2005]).

12 see [Evans 2004], [Fowler 2003], [Voss et al. 2006] and [Züllighoven 2005].

Modularity and pattern languages   Pattern languages are not just a clever way to enable developers to easily set up and use schemata, they also affect modularity and freedom from cycles. A pattern language uses element rules to define the task of a class—for example, a business object tasked with managing its own data. The object's tasks do not include displaying stuff on the user interface or the transport of packets on the network. This example shows how pattern languages significantly improve modularity.

Freedom from cycles and pattern languages   When it comes to creating cycle-free software, pattern languages are—surprisingly—hierarchical. This means that there are no cycles between the various pattern elements, but rather a clear usage direction. However, pattern languages do not prevent cycles between classes of the same pattern element. This direction of use is generated by the language's prohibition and permission rules. We have already seen two examples of this: services work on business objects and change their state (permission rule), while business objects are not allowed to use services (prohibition rule).

We will now take a closer look at the Tool & Material and Domain-Driven Design (DDD) pattern languages. We will then look at patterns that are typically introduced into software systems via frameworks.

Project-specific pattern languages   Many development teams have developed their own exclusive pattern languages[13]. Frequently, these project-specific pattern languages rely on the patterns provided by the frameworks used by the project. Based on their own experience, development teams add their own elements to these framework patterns.

All of these pattern languages, whether developed in projects or taken from existing literature, have similarities and can be used in architectural analysis, as we will see in Chapter 8.

6.6.1 The Tool & Material Pattern Language

The Tool & Material (T&M) approach represents a general approach to software development. It is focused on domain-orientation as well as high usability and software quality. It also provides guidance on how to perform iterative software projects with prototyping and workflow analysis, as well as mission statements,

---

13 see [Kim & Garlan 2006].

workplace types, and design metaphors that help developers during the design phase[14].

The T&M approach defines a pattern language for software design, and offers the following pattern elements (see fig. 6-10):

Elements of the T&M pattern language

■ **Domain Values** model user-defined values from their corresponding domain. They have a defined value range and are implemented internally using standard data types. They have no identity and cannot be changed. For example: IBAN, container number, telephone number, and so on, are modeled as domain values and implemented accordingly.

Domain-specific values are transferred

■ **Materials** represent objects or concepts that become part of the result of an assignment. Materials must be suitable for processing and can be derived directly from the objects in the domain's concepts. They embody a domain-specific concept by identity and ensure its domain consistency. Typical materials that can be transferred to software systems are accounts, medical records, containers, ships, contracts, offers, payments, e-mails (as an image of a letter), and so on.

Domain objects and concepts are displayed

■ **Domain services** combine the business knowledge of a domain that cannot be mapped into individual materials. They bundle related domain objects or processes and offer a consistent service for tools and machines. They are stateless and independent of the front-end. Services often match Materials—for example, an account management service or a contract service. Higher-value specialist tasks, which process several materials, could be: BookingService (payment, account, offsetting account), PolicyService (request, contract).

Domain services bundle materials and domain values

■ **Tools** embody domain-specific activities and working steps in order to complete tasks interactively. Tools are used to examine and change Materials. They must be redesigned as software because their tangible counterparts in the domain are not directly transferable to software (for example: pen, hammer). They must be suitable for the job and easy to handle. New tools created for the computer could, for example, be a *PortMonitor* to monitor the port, a *ContractEditor* to edit contracts, a remitter to enter remittances, and so on.

Tools need to be redesigned

---

14 see [Züllighoven 2005] and [Riehle & Züllighoven 1995].

Routine activities are automated

- ▪ **Automatons** perform recurring routine tasks. They automate sequences of work. They also have a defined result and, following initial setup, run without further external intervention. Typical automatons are ATMs or continuous transfer machines that usually run at nighttime.

External services are connected

- ▪ **Technical services** encapsulate external services. They obtain the materials and domain values required by the application from a database or via external services.

Figure 6-10

The Tool & Material (T&M) pattern language

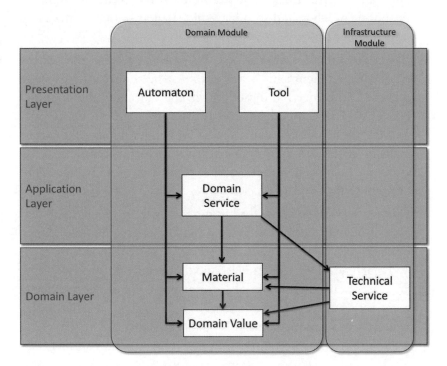

The arrows in figure 6-10 represent the use relationships that are permitted between pattern elements within the T&M architecture. Inheritance relationships are prohibited between T&M pattern elements and can only exist for general superclasses or classes provided by a framework. These restrictions can be mapped using permission and prohibition rules. The public interfaces of the individual pattern elements are determined by element rules[15].

---

15 see [Knodel & Popescu 2007].

6.6.2 The DDD Pattern Language

In his book *Domain-Driven Design* (see [Evans 2004]), Eric Evans presents the strategic design that demonstrates how bounded contexts can be used to dissect microservices and get them to collaborate (see Section 6.5). He also uses this tactical design approach to develop a pattern language that specifies how the inner structures of bounded contexts or microservices can be constructed. The layer architecture used in Domain Driven Design (DDD) corresponds to the four technical layers presented in Section 6.3.1.

The DDD pattern language provides patterns for application, domain, and infrastructure layers (see fig. 6-11):

Elements of the DDD pattern language

- **Value Objects** do not have their own identity. They describe the state of other objects and can consist of other Value Objects (but never of entities). This pattern corresponds to the domain value pattern in the T&M approach.

- **Entities** are the core objects of a domain with an unchangeable identity and a clearly defined lifecycle. Entities map their state to value objects and are practically always persistent. Here we see similarities to the materials in the T&M approach.

- **Aggregates** encapsulate connected entities and their value objects, usually have a single entity as entry point (root), and are considered a unit with regard to modifications. Aggregates use the root entity to ensure domain consistency and the integrity of the entities they contain. Aggregates are equivalent to complex materials in the T&M approach.

- **Domain Services** represent domain sequences or processes that cannot be executed by entities. Services are stateless, and the parameters and results of their operations are aggregates, entities, and value objects. In the T&M approach, this pattern element has the same name.

- **Application Services** form the capsule for their domain module, and provide a public interface for calling the domain functionality implemented in domain services, entities, and aggregates. Application services do not contain any domain-oriented functionality. This pattern has no T&M equivalent.

■ **Factories** encapsulate the creation of aggregates, entities, and value objects. Factories work exclusively within the domain and have no access to the technical building blocks. This is one of the GoF (Gang of Four) patterns and has no T&M equivalent.

■ **Repositories** encapsulate the technical details ("T") of the (technical) infrastructure layer with respect to the domain layer. Repositories provide object references to entities that need to be read from databases. The T&M equivalent is the technical service.

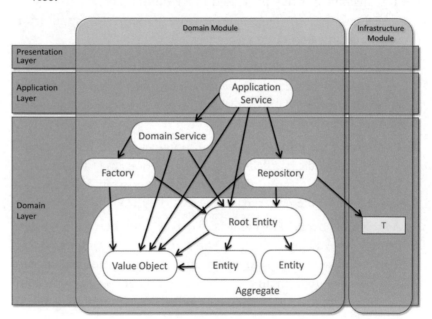

The arrows in figure 6-11 represent the permitted use relationships between the pattern elements within the DDD architecture. The aggregate is an envelope for one or more entities. The aggregate is not found as a separate class within the source code, and the root entity maintains domain consistency. The architecture elements and the rules for their relationships must be used in every domain module of an architecture in order to restrict the design space. This ensures a consistent structure for all the domain modules.

6.6.3   Typical Framework Patterns

Java, C#, and C++ projects use frameworks, which usually provide their own patterns. In the course of my analysis, I have encountered framework patterns from the following categories (although many other pattern groups exist too):

■ *UI pattern:* The Model View Controller (MVC) pattern is the one generally used for user interfaces. It is available in a variety of variants (MVVM, MVP, PAC) in all common frameworks and programming languages[16].

MVC

■ *Data Patterns:* Common data storage and transfer patterns are Data Access Object (DAO), Data Transfer Object (DTO), Persistent Entity (in Hibernate), and Repository (in Spring). (See [Fowler 2002].)

DAO and DTO

■ *Rich client platform patterns:* Entire platforms such as Eclipse and NetBeans are designed for the development of rich client applications. They define the patterns for public interfaces, different types of dialogs, data storage, and integration.

RCP

■ *General patterns:* Since the first books on patterns were published in the mid-1990s, the term "Gang of Four" (GoF) patterns is a recurring theme. The GoF [Gamma et al. 1994] patterns I most often come across are Adapter, Command, Builder, and Factory (although Dependency Injection is now making this one redundant). Other non-GoF patterns that also occur frequently are Handler, Provider, Converter, Listener, Action, Extension, and Item.

GoF

Prior to each analysis, you can guess which patterns are likely to occur based on the frameworks in use. These often appear in combination with self-developed pattern languages or pattern languages taken from existing literature. The exciting thing here is identifying how the pattern language is linked to the framework patterns.

---

16 An overview of all MVC variants can be found at *mvc.givan.se.*

6.7   Sustainability and Architectural Styles

If applied correctly, the architectural styles presented in this chapter all have a positive effect on the sustainability of a software system. The separation into business and technical building blocks, layer architecture, microservices, and pattern languages support modularity, hierarchy, and pattern consistency to different degrees and in different ways (see table 6-1).

Table 6-1

Effects of architectural styles

Architectural Style	Modularity	Hierarchy	Pattern Consistency
Separation of business and technical building blocks (6.2)	Business and technical tasks of the various "blood types"	Relationship rules for "blood types"	Definition of technical and business building blocks
Technical layering (6.3.1)	Layer names/tasks Public interfaces of layers	Layering in two dimensions	Large structure Mapping to the structure of the source code
Hexagonal, onion, clean architecture (6.4)	Business and technical tasks	Layering and relationship rules for ports & adapters	Definition of technical and business building blocks
Microservices (6.5)	Separation into domain modules with corresponding domain names Pubic interfaces, loose coupling	Technical layering can be expected within microservices	Integration of functionality and own database
Pattern language (6.6)	Names/tasks and public interfaces of the pattern elements	Relationship rules for pattern elements	Semantics through clearly defined pattern elements

The following chapters will show how these architectural styles interact with real software systems in real-world settings.

7 Pattern in Software Architecture

Many architectural variants and ideas can be found in the wild. In this chapter we look into how the architectural styles described in the previous chapter present themselves in a source code base. We will also look into some of the specific characteristics you will encounter out there.

7.1 Mapping the Target to the Actual Architecture

The architects and developers of smaller systems (less than 250,000 LOC) usually answer my first question on the architecture of their systems with quotes like, "Our system has GUI, business logic, and database mapping layers." This answer is not a surprise, as this kind of rough technical layering is typical for systems of this size. But I would still prefer to hear a different answer! What I would like to see is domain-oriented layering, as you will see below. For larger systems, the question of structuring is more urgent, and answers like, "Our system is divided into XY components and has layers" are common. In these cases, the division of the domain supplements technical layering.

Unfortunately, technical only

Statements like this, made by architects and developers, make it clear that there is a pattern for the system's architecture. If such a pattern is used well, it can help all those involved to navigate their way successfully around the system.

Architecture as a pattern

Architects and developers usually use the language's packet concept (above the class level) to map the target architecture using technical layers. If additional build artifacts exist above the packet level, these will also be used to map the architecture. This can work well or badly, depending on the situation at hand.

Architecture within the source code

An example of an attempt that still needs improvement is shown in figure 7-1. This Java package tree has four sub-packages below

Bad mapping

the second root node, and the arrows lead from the parent package to its children. Additionally, the blue and green sub-packages have their own sub-packages. The first step in modeling this architecture was to clarify which packages within the tree belong to each other. These relationships are shown by the different colors in figure 7-1, which reveal that the package tree only partially matches the architecture. Specifically, the purple and orange components have packages located at different levels within the tree and are also partially located below package nodes that form the root nodes of the blue and green components. In figure 7-1 these two components are identified by the red and black dotted lines.

Figure 7-1

Target architecture

in a Java package tree

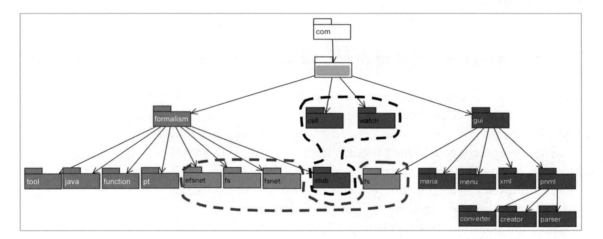

In this example, the architecture pattern is difficult to trace in the package tree, and the developers have to keep this anomaly in mind when navigating the package tree. In many cases, such a mismatch between the target architecture and the package tree results in the developers' understanding of the architecture becoming increasingly vague over time. This package tree requires urgent refinement.

The bigger the better

It is interesting to note that all systems with more than 1.5 million LOC have good packaging, whereas smaller systems are usually more chaotic. As a result, modeling the architecture of smaller systems is more complex—the layers and components are composed of different sub-trees, some of which are located on different levels of the package tree. Or there are package nodes that, according to the architects, contain classes of different components.

Somewhere along the way past the one million LOC mark, the architects of large systems manage to bring order to their packaging. There is obviously a point at which the build artifacts or the package/directory tree have to be cleaned up to keep the system manageable. Additionally, the architects clearly gave their teams strict rules on how the tree should be designed. These rules also determine where the classes should be put. The architects of the large systems obviously attach significant importance to the task of checking these rules constantly and—preferably—automatically.

Large systems need order

If it becomes obvious during architectural analysis that the packaging doesn't correspond to the planned structure, you have to consider what it is that prevents the development team from adapting the packaging to changes in the target architecture.

The following arguments are typical:

Reasons for chaos

- *Lack of budget:* The fundamental restructuring of a system takes time. A modification that doesn't extend the functionality of the software system and "only" improves its structure is often neglected when it comes to allocating time and/or money (see Section 1.3.4).

No time or money

- *Test effort:* For many Java/C#/C++ architects, restructuring the system appears to be a major refactoring effort, especially if classes or packet trees have to be moved between build artifacts, or if completely new build artifacts have to be created. These restructuring processes need to be validated by a series of component, integration, and user tests, which is why architects often shy away from this effort.

Major refactoring = high testing costs

    This argument doesn't exist in the ABAP world. Since all elements are listed in the system-wide dictionary, package assignment has no effect on the runtime system.

- *Stubborn technology:* Teams that use restrictive and (fortunately!) outdated source code management systems such as CVS have little motivation to move classes. Such management systems delete the classes when they are moved from their original location and add them as new classes at the destination. By deleting and recreating a class, the history of the moved class and all its modifications is lost. Case studies show that this is a common reason

Outdated technology

why architects are reluctant to move classes within the packet structure. One architect even claimed that once it has been created, the packet tree should never be changed. Fortunately, most teams nowadays use more advanced source code management systems.

Source code structure =
target architecture

> **Target architecture in the source code**
>
> Strengthen the architectural patterns for your developers and guide them through the source code by regularly aligning the structure of packets or projects with the target architecture. Use the same names and hierarchies.

So how does an ideal system structure look in an ideal scenario in which we have money, a great development team, and appropriate technical support?

7.2   The Ideal Structure: Domain-Oriented or Technical?

Statics and deployment   Every development team has its own way of mapping an architecture. All architects use the existing structuring mechanisms of their programming language and development environment (i.e., the packet structures and build artifacts surrounding them). Using these two tools, developers and architects want on the one hand to express static architecture (i.e., the existing building blocks and how they should relate to each other), while on the other hand, they also prepare deployment of individual artifacts to different clients and servers by dividing them into build artifacts. First, let's look at the static architecture to clarify whether technology or the domain should have priority. Once we have done this, we can then address the question of deployment for different types of architecture (rich client, web application, and so on).

The first criterion   If the architects want to express technical layering and a domain-oriented division using modules, we basically have two options: we either use the technical layering as our initial structuring level and form the domain-specific structures beneath, or vice versa. Figure 7-2 illustrates these variants using a Java package tree.

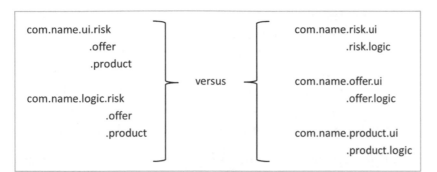

Figure 7-2

Package trees for a layered architecture

The use of build artifacts in this structure is also a valid choice. In this case, we could either have two technical build artifacts (UI and Logic) or three domain-oriented build artifacts (Risk, Offer, and Product).

In most small projects that implement limited functionality, we find that technical layering was chosen as the main structuring method. The larger a system becomes, the more the architects switch to domain-oriented divisions for their structuring.

Small = technical

Due to their technical education, most developers tend to think in terms of technical layers. Domain-orientation makes life more difficult for them because they have to understand the application level too. However, our goal is to create a good model of the domain. Without good domain-specific design, not even the first draft of our system will meet the prescribed user requirements. Further extensions and troubleshooting in a poorly modeled system will be equally problematic. If you have divided your system into technical build artifacts with individual projects for the user interface, business logic, and so on, the transparency of the content will suffer. In the context of this kind of division, domain-specific relationships can only be identified in smaller systems that use very good naming conventions.

Domain first

To strengthen the domain-oriented modularization of a system, you need to apply the following concept:

Domain over technology

Choose the domain-oriented division of a system as the most important criterion for the packet or artifact structure within your system.

Deployment structure   If you use deployment of the software to various processes or devices as an architectural criterion, you may need an additional level above the functional structure. This level splits the source code into several build artifacts that can be deployed to different processes or computers. For example, you could separate the client code from the server code or the various microservice deployments. The detailed structure of your system could then look like this:

- A *rich client application* or *native app* with a *server component*: The top level consists of a basic client, server, and common/shared structure used to map the deployment (see fig. 7-3). Shared parts that are to be used by the client and the server are usually combined in a shared area called *Common* or *Shared*. Domain-oriented build artifacts then exist beneath these three areas. The domain-oriented build artifacts on the client are often more roughly structured than those on the server. This is because the client integrates various server components (see Section 6.3.4).

- For a *web application*: The high-level structure consists of an integration layer (see Section 6.3.4) and domain-oriented build artifacts.

- For a pure *server application*: The domain-oriented build artifacts form the initial structure.

Structuring in domain-oriented build artifacts   Below the first level of domain-oriented build artifacts, all architecture variants are structured the same way. The domain-oriented build artifacts are further subdivided until you arrive at features that cannot be broken down any further into domain-oriented artifacts. These packets, with their individual functional features, then contain the corresponding classes of all technical layers required by the implementation. If a pattern language is used, a set of pattern elements can be found here (see Section 6.6).

Figure 7-3 shows the division of a client-server application into client, server, and common areas. The build artifacts are then located beneath these three deployment areas. The other, lower levels below are not shown in figure 7-3.

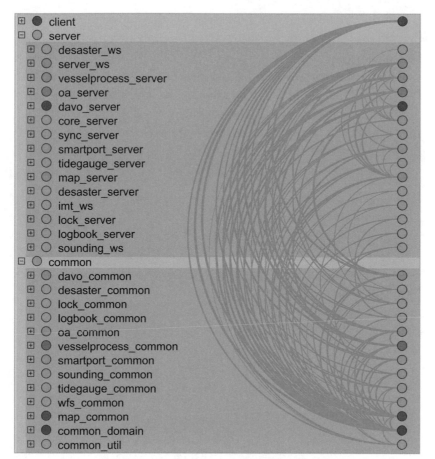

Figure 7-3

The deployment and domain-oriented build artifacts of a rich client application

Systems become difficult to manage when the switch from technical layering to a domain-oriented division is partially implemented, or where technical and domain-oriented structures coexist side by side. In such systems you will find domain-oriented and technical packet nodes on a single level. The (older) developers of these systems do not have a well-structured architectural concept, but tend instead to navigate the source code using a series of parallel schemata. Younger developers have difficulties navigating such structures.

    The architectural analysis of such systems requires a lot of modeling effort, and mapping the source code to the target architecture requires a lot of knowledge of the various architectural patterns. Architects and developers usually claim that budget limitations and recalcitrant technology are the reasons for this "construction site"

Mixture in transition

Investigating a construction site

condition (see Section 7.1). Either that or they simply have no idea that there is an architecture that could be expressed using the structure of the system.

Figure 7-4 shows such an inconsistent system. This is a Java system with 700,000 LOC. The system was developed in four interdependent Eclipse projects. The packages are distributed across all four projects and, in some cases, the same package exists in multiple projects. For more information on the "split packages" code smell see Section 3.1.

Figure 7-4

Mixed domain and technical package nodes

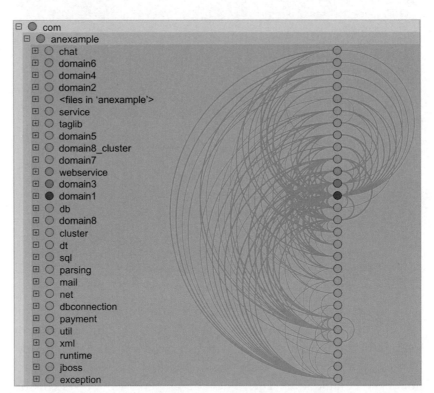

Chaos in components   Also problematic are software systems in which a consistent domain-based structure was chosen at the highest level but where completely different structures exist beneath the top level. The result is that each component in the system has to be explained individually. Architects often cite the following arguments when explaining inconsistent structures:

- *No collective code ownership:* Packaging inconsistency is caused by the fact that individual developers are each responsible for "their" part of the software system. Each developer has her own personal ideas about the structure of her part of the system. Consistency is not intended and therefore doesn't arise. Microservices go one step further with their idea of independent technology decisions for each microservice. Different microservices are implemented in different programming languages and technologies as the developers see fit.

My code, your code

- *Artist at work:* An architect told me that he could not enforce a unified structure. His developers insisted on living out their talents as software "artists" and added new structures and patterns to the system every year. He told me that this results in a system with annual growth rings of patterns.

Self-fulfillment

As you can tell from my remarks in the previous sections, I generally speak out for consistency over self-fulfillment. However, I can still be convinced by good arguments that certain technologies and programming languages are better suited than others to solving certain problems, resulting in a heterogeneous architecture. In spite of this, the structures of the different system parts can still be built in a consistent manner.

Consistency before self-fulfillment

> **Consistent Patterns**
>
> Use consistent patterns to structure your architecture (both domain-oriented and technical) that can always be found in the packet tree or the build artifacts

Once you have agreed on the basic division of the system into technical and domain-oriented units, the next question to ask will concern your choice of public interfaces.

7.3   Public Interfaces for Building Block

The first Java systems I analyzed gave me the impression that public interfaces are not really an important Java concept.

Do we need public interfaces in a system?
This was particularly obvious in a Java system that had been built by a team that had previously programmed in PL/1. This group of developers attached great importance to their internal public interfaces, just as they were used to doing in the past. They defined public interfaces for the building blocks right from the start. This was of course accompanied by code ownership, with each developer responsible for a building block that she designed and implemented. The interaction between building blocks was communicated via the public interface, so nothing worked without public interfaces.

Documented public interfaces
Public interfaces were the decisive means used by this team to keep the system architecture stable, and the architects were particularly keen on keeping the public interfaces of their building blocks maintained. Teams that work this way usually provide comprehensive documentation of all their public interfaces. The documentation forms the core of the architecture description and is always adapted when changes are made to the system. Modules may only be used via the classes and methods that are described in the documentation. During analysis, the architects of systems like this remain convinced that their software only remains expandable and maintainable because they subjected themselves to these restrictions at the development stage.

Public interfaces come later
In contrast, most developers who grew up using object-oriented languages do not design public interfaces for their system's building blocks at the beginning of a project. Public interfaces are obviously very important to architects, but they nevertheless do not consider the definition of public interfaces to be necessary or useful at the beginning of a project. The general attitude among architects at this stage is that the building blocks are still too small and that the entire content resides in the public interface.

Public interfaces usually begin to show up in the building blocks when a system reaches a size of 400,000 LOC or more. The first public interfaces can often be found in client and server source code. This is a natural process caused by the desire to decouple the client from the server. Such a public interface consists of the server classes and interfaces that are used in the client's source code.

Just as they do when layering (see Section 7.1), architects and developers begin implementing a public interface on the technical layers rather than between domain-oriented modules. As during layering, it makes sense to design the public interfaces between domain-oriented modules early on.

Domain-specific public interfaces

Public interfaces between domain-oriented modules

Start designing the domain-oriented public interfaces as soon as the first division into domain-oriented modules becomes apparent

---

If you don't pay attention to this aspect, you might run into a situation similar to that of an architect for whom I ran an architectural analysis some time ago. His fairly large Java system had around 850,000 LOC, but public interfaces for building blocks had not yet been made available within the architecture. When he realized that it was possible to check the public interfaces using Sotograph, he asked us if we could also check the inverse set. He requested that we run a query to determines which classes had not yet been used externally in the individual building blocks, followed by a daily check to ensure that nobody starts using these classes.

Public interfaces came too late

The question to answer here is: Where can the system's public interfaces be found? Development teams organize their public interfaces in various ways:

Patterns for public interfaces

1. *Distributed public interface:* The public interface is formed by all interface files that can be found in any packets within the packet structure of the building block.

2. *Root packet public interface:* The elements of the public interface are located in the root node of the module (i.e., the topmost packet).

3. *Public interface packet:* Each module contains a special packet for the public interface, which is placed directly below the root node of the module.

4. *Public interface project:* The public interface is outsourced to a separate project.

Distributed public interfaces

Distributed public interfaces are often found in smaller, younger systems where all the developers are familiar with the entire source code. Figure 7-5 shows part of a system in which two namespaces (Consultant and BranchManager) exist on the service layer. Both namespaces contain the interface and implementation files of the corresponding services. However, only the interfaces should be used outside of the service layer, not the implementations.

Figure 7-5

Distributed public interfaces

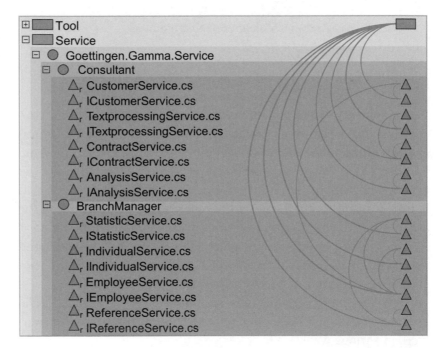

Distributed public interfaces cloud the view

Distributing public interfaces over the entire packet structure is not a good solution. If a user of this module wants to look at the public interface, he has to navigate through the entire structure of the packet to gain an insight. The architects of such solutions often argue that if you have questions regarding the implementation, you can find the interface file directly next to the specific class, thus enabling you to navigate more quickly to the class in question. However, since most development environments can evaluate the inheritance or implementation relationships and display the corresponding subclasses to the developer, this argument doesn't convince me. In addition, the public interface often includes exception classes for which there is no interface file.

The *root packet public interface* variant is a step in the right direction. All classes and interface files belonging to the public interface are kept in one place (see fig. 7-6). They can be examined together, and the spatial proximity makes chunking possible. Of course, this doesn't necessarily mean that there is a connection between the files within the public interface.

Root packet public interface

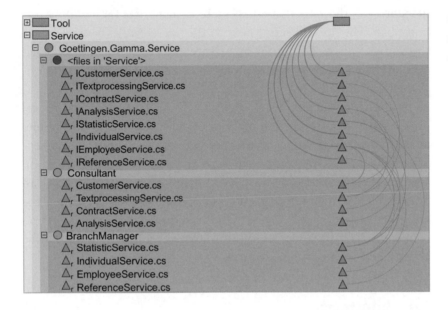

Figure 7-6

Root packet public interface

The problem with this option is that not only the classes and interface files are often placed in the root packet. Development teams often look for a location for utility classes that are used throughout the module. Since there is no obvious location for these, they are often placed in the root packet. This creates a mixture of public interface and utility classes within the root packet, in turn muddying the user view of the public interface.

Root node for public interfaces and utility classes

This ambiguity is resolved by variant #3, *public interface packet* (see fig. 7-7)—i.e., using a named packet for the public interface. Some teams (such as the Eclipse team) call this packet api, while others call it interface or public. If a packet named impl exists and contains the entire implementation, the developer is well supported. He is guided by a consistent pattern for all building blocks and finds the public interface in one place.

Public interface packet

Figure 7-7

Public interface packet

in Java

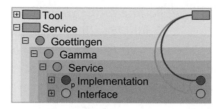

In figure 7-7 the two namespaces are called interface and imple-mentation. The "p" subscript next to the implementation namespace shows that this node should be private. The arc from the applica-tion layer that leads to implementation is red because these relation-ships are prohibited by the architecture.

Public interface project

If the development team divides its source code into several projects, the idea of creating individual public interfaces and imple-mentation projects often arises (i.e., variant #4 above). This sep-arates the public interface even further from the implementation and has the advantage that a project based on another project can be compiled with the public interface project on its own (i.e., the implementation project is not actually required). The next section details the risks that such a solution involves and why it should be approached with extreme caution.

7.4   Interfaces:
The Architectural Miracle Cure?

There are a number of established principles in software develop-ment related to interfaces and public interface projects. Ways to make software more flexible and modifiable are:

- Encapsulation and loose coupling
- Dependency on abstractions
- Programming against abstractions

Issues facing public

interface projects

Interfaces and public interface projects become hazardous when they are used to resolve cycles. There is no doubt you can resolve cycles using interfaces, and many books recommend precisely this procedure. However, I simply don't like this approach. Interfaces were invented to offer and facilitate different implementations for an abstract description. Interfaces are not there to resolve cycles.

Figure 7-8

A dual cycle at class level

Let's take a closer look. Imagine you have programmed two classes, A and B (see fig. 7-8), and that these two classes require each other. This creates a class-level cycle.

We have a cycle

There are two ways to resolve this cycle:

1. Revise the design of the classes so that the cycle is no longer required
2. Use interfaces

7.4.1   Basic Therapy

Of course, I favor strategy #1 (i.e., use a better design). Applying strategy #2 involves creating a structure consisting of two classes and an interface (see fig. 7-9).

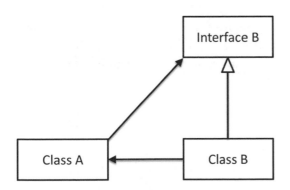

Figure 7-9

Resolving a two-class cycle using an interface

Class B implements interface B, so the relationship is transferred from class B to interface B and you don't have a cycle from class B anymore.

If the main focus of a project manager or quality manager is to look good in the metrics, the introduction of interfaces is the obvious solution for cyclically coupled classes. All quality measurement tools used in the project will ignore cycles and the result will be awesome!

Interfaces camouflage cycles

But is the design improved by dividing a domain concept—which hopefully represents class B—into two parts? Certainly not! The previously static cyclic dependency between classes A and B has now been moved into the runtime environment.

Building block cycles

The problem becomes even more obvious if we imagine that class A and class B play important roles as services in two different building blocks. This means we have a cycle not only at class level, but also at the module level (see fig. 7-10).

Figure 7-10

Two-element cycle at building block level

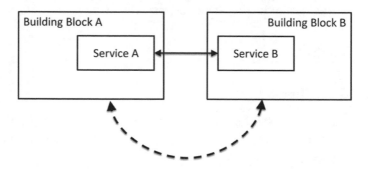

If we now apply our magic interface, it won't improve the situation.

Building block cycles using interfaces

Interface B is put into building block B together with class B. The cycle between the two building blocks is still there, and decomposing service B to form an interface and an implementation doesn't help (see fig. 7-11).

Figure 7-11

Interface within a two-element cycle

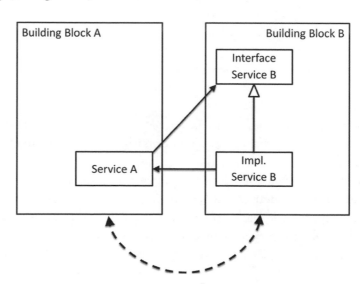

Ways I have found in the field to get rid of cycles between building blocks are either assigning the interface of service B to building block A (see fig. 7-12) or storing the interface of service B is in a separate building block (see fig. 7-13).

7.4.2 Side Effects

The option shown in figure 7-12 proves very successful in plug-in architectures. Here, module A defines an interface for a plug-in that must be supplied by other modules for module A to function. This solution not only provides an implementation for interface service B from module B, it also provides a number of other modules that will have their own implementations. All these implementations inherit from the interface of service B. In this variant, the concept "interface" is used exactly as intended by the inventor. Remember: interfaces are abstract descriptions that can be offered to and used by various implementations.

Interfaces in plug-in architectures

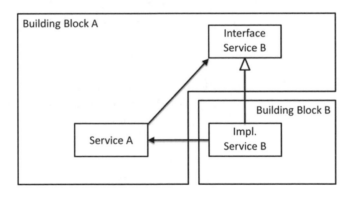

Figure 7-12

Breaking down building blocks to make cycles invisible

In order for the plug-in solution to work, component A obviously needs the appropriate implementation for its interface at runtime, which is supplied either by component B or by some other component that offers an implementation of the plug-in interface. Nowadays, there are various dependency injection frameworks available that can perform this task. Alternatively, a factory located outside of building block A can be used. Otherwise, the cycle between blocks A and B will be re-implemented into the system.

Dependency Injection

It will quickly become apparent whether the plug-in solution works (i.e., whether it is a good idea to assign service B's interface

No plug-in architecture, though!

to module A). This will occur if other modules apart from module A want to use the service B interface. If this is the case, the interface of service B can no longer be a plug-in interface for module A. In this case, the interface of service B is (unfortunately) only the interface of the implementation of service B. Service B's interface has nothing to do with module A and we are still stuck with our cycle between module A and module B (see fig. 7-11 or fig. 7-12).

Figure 7-13

Breaking down building blocks to make cycles invisible

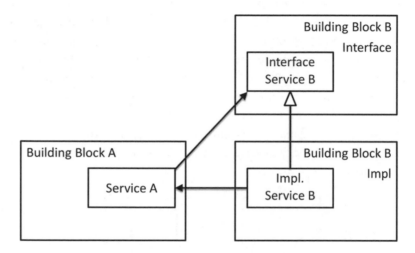

Public interface project?   In order to avoid this problem, the variant shown in figure 7-13 is often chosen. In this example, the interface is moved into its own building block. All interface files of building block B are usually assembled in the public interface project of building block B. For the sake of clarity, the problem is simplified by using building blocks that only have a single class and interface.

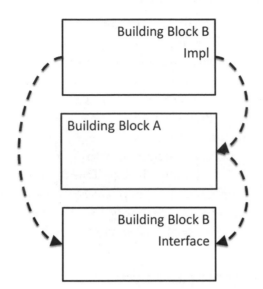

Figure 7-14
Interface building block

Splitting building block B into two parts creates the structure shown in figure 7-14. Building block A and building block B Impl require the building block B Interface. The mutual relationship no longer exists. In order to arrange these relationships hierarchically, the components of building block B must be distributed around building block A. The domain-oriented building block B is broken down into two building blocks that are no longer close to each other within the system.

Separate building blocks that belong together

If we continue to play with the interfaces in order to avoid cycles, a public interface project will eventually become necessary for building block A (see fig. 7-15).

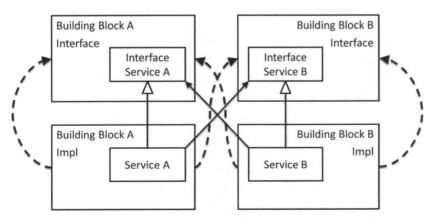

Figure 7-15
Each domain-oriented building block has two technical parts

Public interface projects
as patterns

Assuming building blocks A and B already have a separate public interface project, this pattern will eventually become the template for the rest of the development. Each project must have a pubic interface project to access its services. Alternatively, you could create one large public interface project in which all interfaces for the entire system are collected (see fig. 7-16). Both approaches sound like great architecture patterns, don't they?

Public interface projects
conceal architectural
problems

In reality, however, division into projects only obscures the dependencies between building blocks. True modularity (e.g., in the sense of domain-oriented modules or microservices) is not achieved this way (see fig. 7-16). A better way to achieve technical freedom from cycles is to disassemble domain-oriented units that belong together.

Figure 7-16
One public interface
project for all

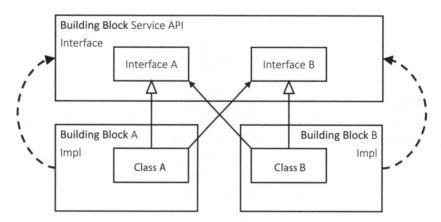

7.4.3 Field Studies on "Living Patients"

One public interface and
one implementation
project cover everything

The following sections detail two examples to help you visualize this issue as it occurs in real-world systems. The first system has 715,000 LOC with 7,400 C# classes, and is divided into 590 projects. Visual Studio doesn't allow cycles between projects and DLLs, so projects that cause potential cycles have to be split into separate interface and implementation projects. In this particular system, 552 projects have interface and implementation projects. The only other option would have been to create a few very large projects.

The image on the left in figure 7-17 shows this wonderfully layered system consisting of 590 projects. On the right you can see what happens when we merge the interface and implementation

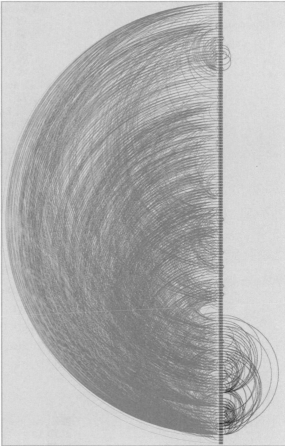

projects. A series of red arcs appear, representing relationships that contravene the direction of the layers.

There is a clear bunching of interconnected projects in the lower part of the system where the basic functionality is located. The domain-specific discussion of violations during the analysis helped the architects solve a lot of issues while refining the design.

The second system is one in which the architects and developers placed all the interfaces in a common project. As a result, all other projects have only one entry point for accessing the functionality of the other projects.

Figure 7-17

Single system with and without separation of interface and implementation projects

One project for all interfaces

Figure 7-18

All projects use ServiceAPI to call each other

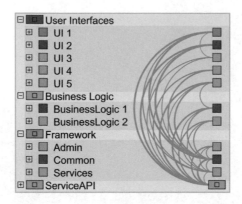

ServiceAPI

This system has 190,000 LOC and 2,000 Java classes divided into 42 projects. In figure 7-18 you can see that all the projects have relationships to ServiceAPI. This is because ServiceAPI contains all the interface files, so all the resulting relationships lead there from the individual projects. The individual projects hardly call each other at all. The places where direct relationships existed between the individual projects (i.e., UI 1 → UI 3, UI 5 → Business Logic 1, access to Common and Services) were regarded as violations by the developers and architects and were further examined during our analysis.

Figure 7-19

Interfaces assigned to implementations

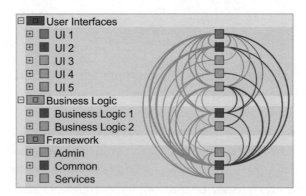

Interwoven domain

If interfaces are integrated into the corresponding domain-specific projects, a completely different picture emerges (see fig. 7-19). The various projects are strongly linked to each other. The Common project in particular is used heavily, especially by the projects located above it in the structure.

7.4.4 Fighting the Monolith

Many development teams and architects take this path and decon-struct their building blocks into interface and implementation proj-ects. This is mostly because the teams want to modularize their increasingly large systems along domain-related lines. This enables them to work on smaller projects without having to gain an over-view of the entire project. Teams using a development environment such as Visual Studio or a build system such as Maven have to ask themselves whether the system has a hierarchical domain-oriented structure.

Domain-oriented hierarchies in monoliths?

Why? Because projects developed in Visual Studio or built using Maven should not be linked by cycles. The easiest way to deal with this limitation is to create interface projects. Figure 7-20 summa-rizes the most commonly used divisions.

No technical workarounds please!

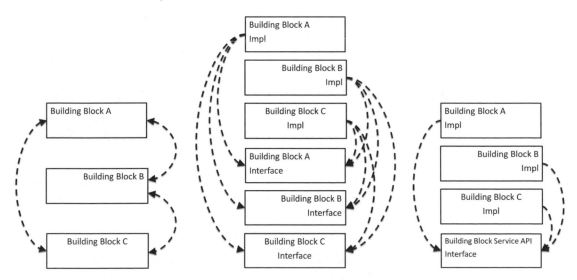

This type of division is a workaround that you should not use if you want to create a sustainable architecture!

Figure 7-20

Three cyclic building blocks and two ways to hide the cycles

Figure 7-21

A system with many cycles

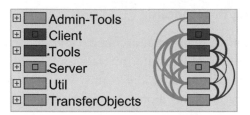

Breaking up the monolith

If you want to divide a monolithic system like the one shown in figure 7-21, into several projects, I suggest the following procedure:

Client-server separation

■ First, split your system into two projects, preferably at the point where a cycle-free break should automatically occur—i.e., between the client and server sections of the code. If this seems too tricky, the system probably has a weak structure (or no structure at all) and you will have a lot of refactoring work to do (see Section 11.1).

Separation of interface and business logic

■ In a web architecture, you take the best place in the source code where the user interface logic and the business logic can be split.

Server-to-client interface project

■ If you want to compile the client code independently from the server code, place the server code interfaces in a separate project.

■ The server interface project should only be used by the client(s). Other server projects should continue to work directly with the server classes.

Domain-specific modules on the server

■ Now start examining the server project source code. If you used a modularity-focused, pattern-based, cycle-free approach, it should be possible to create domain-oriented slices in the server project with only one direction of use between them.

■ You should then provide public interfaces for the individual domain-oriented server projects. These public interfaces should be located in the corresponding server project and may be called by the higher-level slices.

Domain-specific layering and microservices

■ This is how to create draft domain-oriented layering in your system (see fig. 7-22). If your goal is to create microservices, you have to consider the communication between the domain-oriented modules. Later on, you can run them in different processes.

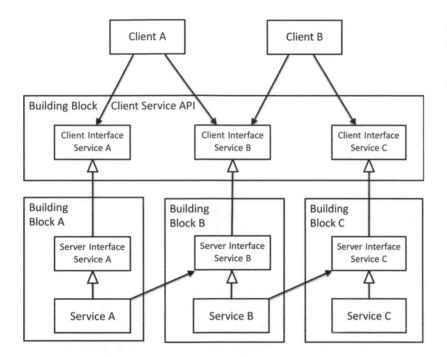

Figure 7-22

*Splitting the building
blocks in a sustainable
architecture*

Place interfaces in modules

Place the interfaces for a functionality implemented in a module in the same
project as the classes that implement the functionality

7.5   The Need for Microservices

Several companies have approached me over the past couple of
years with requests to examine their systems and see how they can
be broken down into microservices. Such requests are very exciting because many companies have only a vague idea of what it
means to split a system into microservices. A corresponding analysis
should begin by clarifying what microservices really are and how
the company might benefit by introducing them.

You need microservices

The stated aims are often better scalability or simply some kind
of vague idea about improving the architecture using microservices because that's what everybody is doing right now. If you add
DevOps and an automated deployment pipeline to the equation,
you are riding the complete wave of current hype. There is no doubt

The current major hypes

these are all useful and important topics, but the kind of analysis I do is about the comprehensibility of an architecture, which is why I always begin by looking at the source code and its structure.

A microservices–based architectural style leads to a domain-oriented system split (see Section 6.5) based on the "domain first, technology second" theory outlined in Section 7.2. This is a highly legitimate wish. In all microservice-based analysis that we have looked at so far, none provided the necessary prerequisites for a simple domain-specific division. With a few exceptions, these systems mostly have good technical layering. In the domain-related dimension, however, I was often confronted with the famous "big ball of mud".

Figure 7-23 shows the domain-related split of a goods ordering system. The software is written in C# and, following about nine months of development, has about 100,000 LOC. The system is still relatively small but will soon grow to include additional product categories with specific Orders processes. To ensure that the system can cope with a large bunch of requests while retaining a high level of performance, it would make sense to divide it into microservices.

Figure 7-23
A first domain-oriented
split

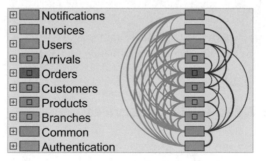

The domain-oriented structure shown in figure 7-23 was not present in the system's namespaces and directories. The first order in the system was technical layering—a common phenomenon in systems of this size (see Section 7.2). While analyzing this system, we spent most of the time doing architectural work and developing a meaningful domain-oriented structure. The result shown in figure 7-23 represents a first step that results in 25,804 relationships on the left (in green) and 587 relationships on the right (in red).

One potential division could involve combining Orders and all the elements above it into an "Ordering" microservice, with

Customers, Products, and Branches combined to provide a second domain-based microservice called "Core Data" (see fig. 7-24).

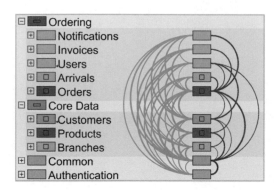

Figure 7-24

Splitting the system into two microservices

However, before these two microservices can be labeled as such and deployed separately, the team would have to devote itself to the following tasks:

The necessary steps

- Define a public interface between the Orders and Core Data microservices (see Section 6.5 for more on types of context mapping).

- Streamline the public interface between Orders and Core Data so that communication across process boundaries can take place while retaining high levels of performance.

- Clarify how the two components Common and Authentication can be taken apart and added to Orders or Core Data. One option would be to use a shared kernel model (see Section 6.5) with both copied into both microservices.

All these tasks would result in a lot of time-consuming refactoring work. Even in such a young, relatively small system, it would have been better to think about the rough technical layout beforehand.

Time-consuming refactoring

> **Planning microservices in advance**
>
> Once you can foresee that your system will need to be split into microservices, you should begin by creating a domain-based structure and defining the public interfaces for each microservice. The later you start the harder it will become to introduce appropriate structures.

8 Pattern Languages: A True Architectural Treasure!

At the University of Hamburg where I studied, pattern languages were an integral part of software engineering education. We built software according to the Tool & Material approach using the T&M pattern (see Section 6.6.1). Whenever I analyze software systems, I automatically look for pattern languages. Pattern languages are an architectural treasure that should be cared for and cultivated!

8.1 The Treasure Hunt

About one in ten of my analysis reveal right from the start that the system was developed using a pattern language. In such cases, the development team refers to a published pattern language such as Domain-Driven Design. In five per cent of cases, the teams developed their own custom, company-internal pattern. In these cases, the developers and architects answer question about layering by saying something like, "We have our own thing", and then they talk about their patterns. Some companies even have training materials for their pattern language, and new employees are taught the different types of classes, interfaces, tasks, and relationships in a "master class" course that lasts several days.

The treasure's already there

However, 90% of the time the following happens: When analyzing the architectural violations on the technical layers and the domain structure, developers and architects end up talking repeatedly about certain class types. The participants say things like: "But a business object is not allowed to do that" or "Why does this view use that service? That has to be done via the controller!"

First signs

In cases like this, it is worth uncovering the pattern language. There are several ways to do this: you can model it directly using an analysis tool, or start with a blackboard sketch to get an idea of how the various patterns fit together (see fig. 8-1).

Figure 8-1

A first look at a pattern language

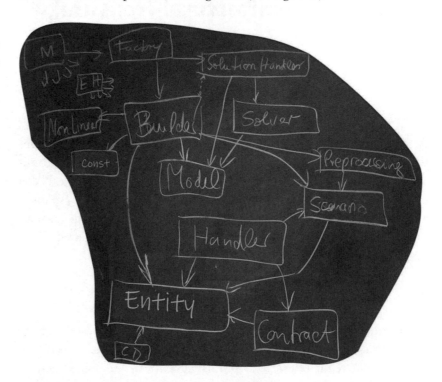

The treasure map

Figure 8-1 shows an (anonymized) pattern language for an 800,000 LOC C++ system. The names of the individual pattern elements—such as model, builder, handler, entity, contract, and so on—specify the tasks of the corresponding classes for this team. The task of a class also determines which methods can typically be found in the public interface. Figure 8-1 also specifies how the pattern language's classes are allowed to work together. The development team always has the pattern language in mind while it works, and uses it to decide where and how which adaptation or extension should be implemented. The Beta case study (see Section 11.3) explains exactly how we modeled this pattern language during our analysis.

To find out if there is a pattern language in use, ask your team the following questions:

Searching for clues

> ### Are we using a pattern language?
>
> The following questions will help you determine whether your project uses a pattern language:
>
> - Do the developers and architects talk about the system's design in terms of patterns, or do they just discuss classes?
> - In addition to pattern elements, are there rules that restrict the relationships between the different pattern elements and lead to a hierarchical structure?
> - Are the pattern elements and rules binding for the entire development team or are they only used in some parts of the system?

8.2 Software Archaeology

Once you have defined the target pattern language with the team, the fun of modeling and checking the pattern language in the source code begins. During the analysis there are three ways to make the pattern element of a class visible in the program text:

Pattern languages in source code

- *Naming Conventions:* When a team uses naming conventions, class names have extensions that indicate which pattern they belong to—for example, "BO" for BusinessObject, "DV" for DomainValue, "UC" for UseCase and "I" for Interfaces. Additional extensions such as "Service", "Factory", "Handler", "Exception", and so on, can of course be added too.
- *Structure conventions:* All classes of a pattern element are stored in a single packet. For example, all exceptions are stored in the exception packet.
- *Typing:* In this case, the teams use interfaces and superclasses to indicate that a class belongs to a certain pattern. By introducing superclasses and interfaces, the development team ensures that classes are uniquely assigned to a pattern. A marker interface is often sufficient. Alternatively, you can make the standard functionality of the pattern element available to all subclasses.

■ *Annotation:* In Java and C#, you can define your own annotations. Some frameworks, such as Spring, now offer annotations for common pattern languages such as DDD. If each pattern element has its own annotation, these can be used to uniquely assign classes.

Naming conventions are the most common

Systems in which the team uses *naming conventions* are the most common. Classes are given names from which the pattern element can be derived. Sometimes, when patterns don't have a meaningful name extension, teams also combine *naming* and *structure conventions*. This usually occurs when the development team is modeling the domain and chooses class names that directly match the names of objects or concepts within the domain. The container is then represented by a class called `Container`. An extension such as "BO" reduces the degree of direct mapping to the domain. *Typing* is a rare technique that is only used by teams that have written their own framework for their pattern language.

Structural conventions only

I have met two teams that made their patterns visible using only package names—in other words, using *structural conventions*. Both teams explained that they had decided not to "pollute" their class names with extensions. This decision was based on a rejection of the Hungarian notation by these teams. Hungarian notation is a system that was introduced in the 1980s to clarify the task and type (of a variable or method) using its name. There are several arguments against Hungarian notation—for example, the names are complicated to read and can confuse developers, or simply because a typed language doesn't require a variable or method's type to be part of its name.

Although these arguments make sense for variables and methods, they are not valid for pattern languages. Adding extensions to the class names in a pattern language can lead to the creation of a new level of language understanding that is not part of the programming language or its type checks.

Disadvantages of structural conventions

In addition, the use of structural conventions means that the classes belonging to a single use case are distributed over a number of packets, depending on the pattern to which they belong. If you want to make changes to or extend a use case, you won't find the corresponding classes in one place. The following recommendation therefore applies:

> **Make your pattern language visible in your class names**
>
> Make the pattern elements of your pattern language obvious using exten-
> sions to the names of your classes. If you want to avoid doing this for classes
> in your domain, use annotations, or introduce marker interfaces or super-
> classes for the corresponding pattern elements.

8.3   From the Treasure Chest

Almost every system contains hints of a pattern language. Sometimes the developers and architects are aware of the patterns, while
at other times, patterns and the connections between them were
something completely new to the team.

The example shown in figure 8-2 is a Java system with 320,000
LOC. The team responsible added name extensions to almost all its
classes: XYService, XYProcess, XYImporter, and so on, and only the
business objects don't have name extensions. However, the business objects are identifiable because they are contained in their own
package within the various projects. This use of naming and structuring conventions made it easier to model the pattern language

Modeling a pattern language

In order to bundle all the classes of a pattern into a layer or
subsystem, you can use regular expressions in Sotograph. All the
classes for the Services layer were collected using the expression
Service. (i.e., using the name suffix Service). For the BusinessObjects layer we used the expression: **/businessobjects/**
that collected all the classes that were in the Businessobjects package. At *www.sustainable-software-architecture.com* you will find
a video which shows the structuring of a system according to a
pattern language in detail with Sotograph.

Regular expressions

Figure 8-2

*The pattern language
of a Java server*

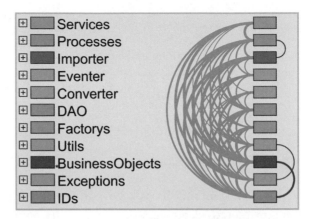

*Bringing the pattern
to light*

Modeling a system this way creates a whole new, pattern-based view of the architecture that can't usually be found in the packet or build-artifact structures. This is how you uncover an architectural treasure that is hidden within the system. If developers and architects do use a pattern language to structure their system, it makes them very happy to see that they have done a good job.

A good example

In teams with pattern experience, about 80-90 per cent of the source code can usually be assigned to patterns. A nice example is shown in figure 8-2. The system depicted provides web services (i.e., it doesn't have its own user interface), which is why figure 8-2 doesn't show any user interface patterns. During our analysis we were able to assign 93 per cent of the source code to these patterns—a truly remarkable value. Almost all the patterns in this system form a sequence of layers built up on top of one another. There are only a few violations (0.2 per cent), caused by just eight relationships between 12 classes. We found solutions for these violations very quickly during our analysis. This project team deserves high praise for its great design work.

Another good example

The system shown in figure 8-3 has almost as good a structure as the one in the previous example. This system was programmed in C# and has 210,000 LOC. Again, 90 per cent of the source code is clearly assigned to patterns. A total of 18 relationships that don't follow the pattern specifications are represented by the eight red arcs. In this case, the violations of the pattern language account for just one per cent of the relationships. The team behind this system also did a very good job.

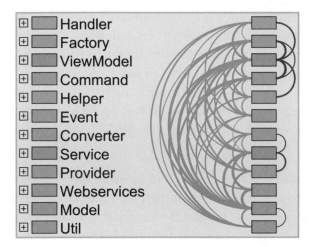

Figure 8-3

*The pattern language
of a C# system*

The system shown in figure 8-3 reveals typical challenges posed by pattern languages:

Typical challenges presented by pattern languages

- *Fuzzy definition:* During the discussion with the team that created the pattern language shown in figure 8-3, we quickly noticed that the pattern elements "Service", "Provider" and "Converter" have similar tasks. It wasn't immediately clear to the developers why one class became more of a "service" while others became more of a "provider" or a "converter". Such mutually overlapping pattern elements dilute a pattern language and need to be either very well defined or removed.

  Fuzzy definitions

- *Framework connection:* The classes `Handler`, `Command` and `ViewModel` represent the connection to the GUI framework in this system. Either the GUI framework has unclear structural specifications, which creates cycles, or the development teams interpret the GUI framework and its pattern elements differently, and thus construct their own cyclic structures.

  Framework pattern

- *Universal patterns:* Most systems have patterns (Such as `Factory` or `Builder`) that have relationships with various patterns within the language and thus evoke cycles. For example, a `Factory` can create a command and be used by another command to create a `ViewModel`. These universal patterns must be examined separately when looking into the pattern language.

  Universal patterns

Utils and Helper

■ *Utility classes:* Static helper methods for which it is unclear which pattern elements they should be assigned to usually end up as static methods in classes called things like "Utils" or "Helper". This typically results in large classes with cyclic relationships. In figure 8-3 this issue is still in its infancy. Methods and classes like these require discussion to find out which class should have the task and whether "Utils" or "Helper" classes are necessary (see Section 8.6).

A degenerate pattern language

The following example is a Java system with 800,000 LOC. In response to my question about patterns, the developers of this system immediately told me about several pattern categories. The result of our modeling is shown in figure 8-4. Due to the large number of patterns, we created groups for some of them. In total we were able to assign 86 per cent of the source code to patterns, which is a great result for a first look at a pattern-based system. Here, the development team obviously programmed using patterns.

Figure 8-4

Pattern language in a Java system

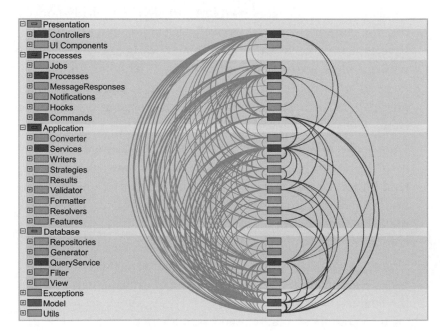

Nevertheless, figure 8-4 shows more violations than the two previous examples, with 4.5 per cent of the relationships violating the layout dictated by the patterns. More than 200 classes are involved in these violations, and the high number of pattern violations reflects the general state of the system very well. Overall, this team had collected quite a lot of technical debt:

Technical debt in pattern languages

- Because neither technical nor a domain-based decomposition is possible, the whole system can only be assembled as a build artifact.

- Fifteen per cent of all classes are involved in cycles. A large cycle involving 270 classes coupled the entire system into a monolith that is virtually impossible to decompose.

- The unit test coverage is less than 10 per cent, which is not surprising given such strong coupling.

- Some patterns are not clearly defined, and their relationships to other patterns are not obvious. Based on figure 8-4, the Utils patterns can do just about anything, although utils should normally only be allowed to be used.

Following our analysis, this team had a lot of work to do to make the system maintainable and extensible. The pattern analysis was particularly important because the patterns were intrinsically very important to the development team and because they make a good starting point for restructuring the architecture. The team successively resolved the violations between the patterns and found a way to dismantle the monolith.

Patterns as starting points for refactoring

8.4 How Much Gold Is There?

The discussion of the examples in the previous section reveals some obvious criteria that we can use to assess pattern languages. In order to evaluate the quality of a pattern language, you have to ask the following questions:

Evaluation of pattern languages

- Are there patterns and rules regarding how the relationship between the patterns should look?

- Are the relationships between the patterns hierarchical?

- How much of the system can we assign to the pattern language and/or which percentage of the source code is not part of the pattern language?
- How many violations are there between the pattern elements?
- How many pattern elements are there in the entire system?
- Are there groups of pattern elements?

Entering the pattern language via cycles

Perhaps you already think that I am investigating pattern languages with the goal of uncovering cycles, but that isn't the whole story. I analyze pattern languages to check the consistency and standardization of the patterns involved, and also to determine whether the development teams comply with the design rules set by the patterns. Fortunately, these design rules often result in the individual pattern elements working together without cycles (see Section 6.6), and are easy to verify.

The much larger part of the design rules, which describe the tasks of a pattern element and the design of its public interface, can only be examined indirectly using analysis tools. In order to analyze these design rules, you have to step into the source code with the developers and architects, and cycles or layer violations are a good indication of where to start.

> **Use pattern languages to improve quality**
>
> Train your developers and architects to use pattern languages. Ensure that they know the pattern languages that exist for this kind of application area. Initiate regular discussions about the patterns used so that the pattern language remains in good condition.

8.5   Annual Growth Rings

Software systems accumulate "growth rings" over time. This usually happens when new developers join the project. They don't know the system and bring their own development philosophy and patterns with them, eventually resulting in areas within the system that look different from the rest. Other patterns and, sometimes, different naming conventions get used, or perhaps changes are suddenly implemented in a different way than the team is used to.

It is not generally a bad thing when new developers or architects introduce new stimuli into a development team. New ideas, new architectural concepts, and new patterns are a boon, but often give rise to questions such as: "Why did you do it this way? Wouldn't it be much better that way?" This is the moment when the development team needs to make time for discussions, otherwise uncontrolled growth (i.e., "growth rings") will result.

Growth rings from different generations of pattern languages accumulate technical debt in a system. Patterns that do similar things but need to be explained by different developers are a good indicator for this kind of proliferation. Or statements like: "X and Y know that bit. The other part is only known by Z." The problem with growth rings is that for each enhancement or maintenance step you make, you have to retrace and understand the patterns that led to the growth ring you are adjusting.

Avoid annual growth rings in patterns

Be very careful when extending your pattern language. Ensure that the patterns are standardized and used consistently.

New patterns may only be included in the pattern language following detailed discussion with the development team.

8.6   Unclear Patterns Provoke Cycles

If a team does not bother to take care of its patterns, or is not aware that patterns are good for the structure of the system, the patterns will break over time and accidental patterns will be introduced. Figure 8-5 shows 22 classes connected by a single class cycle, which means none of the classes can be removed from the cycle without refactoring.

Patterns can be hard work

The left-hand side of figure 8-5 shows a "star cycle" structure that is typical of older Java systems. In this case, several `command` classes are grouped around the `PluginManager`. They all know the `PluginManager` and the `PluginManager` knows them in return, resulting in a direct bidirectional relationship. This part of the cycle wouldn't be an issue if it occurred locally and in isolation, but other classes are attached to it, thus creating a much larger, even less

Star cycles

comprehensible structure than a star cycle. For starters, let's have a look at when star cycles usually occur. We will then discuss the real-world issue illustrated in figure 8-5.

Figure 8-5

Broken patterns

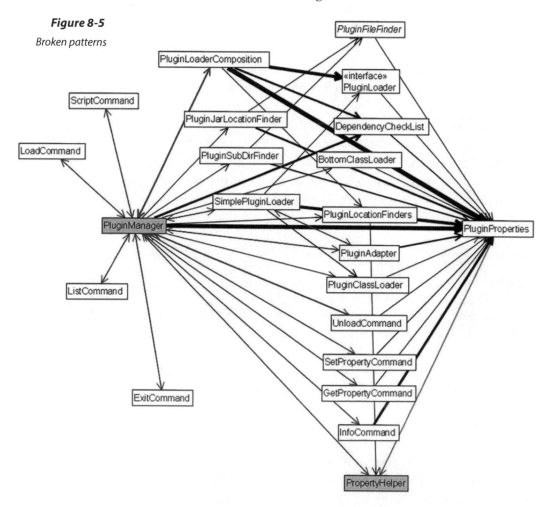

Star cycles, like the one surrounding the PluginManager in figure 8-5 usually follow two common patterns:

Star cycle around
Factories

■ All leaf classes in the star cycle are created either by a central class, a factory, or a manager, and are then made available to other classes. At the same time, the leaf classes use the factory or manager to gain access to their sibling classes. It would be better at this point if the factory or the manager were to provide the leaf classes (at creation) with the other required classes via dependency injection. This way, the leaf classes would not need to know the factory or the manager and could be created differently.

■ All leaf classes in the star cycle have a central superclass that knows about their subclasses. In this case, in addition to the role of providing common functionality for all classes, the superclass was also assigned the task of a factory for the objects of the subclasses. Here, it would be better if the two tasks were distributed amongst two classes—otherwise, each time a new subclass is added, the superclass has to be adjusted, and all other subclasses must be recompiled.

Star cycle around super classes

The issue in the class cycle shown in figure 8-5 is not the star cycle surrounding `PluginManager`, but rather the relationships that arise around the `PluginProperties` class. A class called `PluginProperties` should only provide properties—i.e., it is used by other classes to query properties. However, this class should be at the end of the call chain, and shouldn't call any other classes by itself. Unfortunately, the `PluginProperties` class cycle has a relationship to the `PropertyHelper` class (indicated by the red arrow).

Properties are simple

Helper classes can be found in increasing numbers of systems and are a highly problematic development. The problem here is that the "Helper" pattern is extremely generic. The name makes it obvious that it is a helper class, but doesn't restrict the cooperation of the helper class with any other classes. A helper class can be used from anywhere and can use any other class. Sometimes I get the impression that helper classes are the new utilities. Word has kind of got around that Util classes are not a good idea, and "Helper" sounds somehow better. Unfortunately, Helper classes are no better in practice than utility classes.

Help is available anytime, anywhere

Avoid fuzzy patterns

Avoid helper and utility classes whenever possible. Instead, look for an appropriate domain-oriented class in which the helper or utility functionality can and should be integrated.

9 Chaos Within Layers: The Daily Pain

If you and the development team descend slowly from the technical layering through the domain-oriented modules to the class level, you will find the real pain points in a system. Classes are stuck in strongly coupled cycles that are difficult to understand, adjustments are time-consuming, and the testing effort is high. Cycles in software systems have different characteristics that allow us to reach certain conclusions about the quality of the system at hand.

Pain points

Over the past few years, I have come across a number of systems whose development teams created layered architectures without too many violations. Nevertheless, the teams' development speed steadily decreased the longer they worked on the software. I call this phenomenon "all show but no substance". The issues in systems like these do not lie in the coarse structures of the architecture, but are instead found on the class level, where the developers need to do the most work. Developers don't program layers or modules, but are instead busy programming classes.

All show but no substance

The following example details a system with about 120,000 LOC. The architect, who joined the project at a later stage, requested an analysis because his team had extreme difficulties extending and tweaking the system. After modeling the technical layers in the source code, the following picture emerged:

It's getting more and more expensive!

Figure 9-1

Technical layering

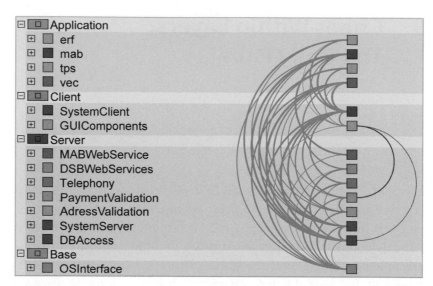

Good technical layering

In figure 9-1 we see four technical layers (Application, Client, Server, and Base) with their respective building blocks. Figure 9-1 shows that the technical layering has worked well. There are only two red relationships between DBAccess and GUIComponents, and our analysis showed that these two violations could be refactored. Our initial conclusion was that the system has good technical layering.

Inner Chaos

This result surprised me, so I had another conversation with the architect. He told me that in the previous three months he had invested all his energy in fixing the layers, but he had still not been able to reduce the problem load for his developers. The development effort and testing times were still far too high for a small system like this. I had to get to the bottom of this predicament, so I went ahead and investigated the class level. That is where I found what I was looking for:

- 30 per cent of all classes were tangled up in class cycles

- Two classes (Campaign and MainFrameEx) knew 20 per cent of all the other classes.

Figure 9-2 shows these two classes and all the relationships between them in one of the larger class cycles in this system.

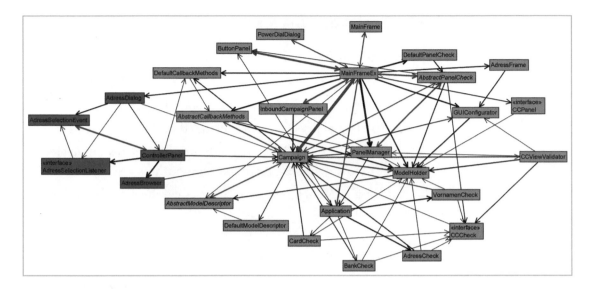

A cycle of 29 classes is not very large, and you will get to see much greater chaos in the course of this chapter. The reason this cycle is particularly painful during development and troubleshooting is the large number of direct cycles between pairs of classes that it contains (indicated by the blue arrows in figure 9-2). These are evidence of a missing planned relationship order for the classes concerned. This structure has no indication of where top and bottom should be, and is exacerbated by the fact that the tasks of the classes (and their modularity) are not obvious (see Section 5.4). The real technical debt in this system can be found on the class level in the individual subsystems and layers. Technical debt is actually quite low at higher levels of the architecture.

Figure 9-2

A cycle of 29 classes

Bidirectional relationships

> **Modularity leads to loose and orderly coupling without cycles**
>
> Build your classes and larger building blocks so that they perform clearly describable tasks. If you do this, you will automatically get orderly, loose coupling in your system.

9.1   Evaluating the Mess

You can use metrics that cover different aspects of cycles to assess how much damage they cause in a system:

- *Scale:* What is the percentage of classes in cycles?
- *Scope:* How many classes are included in the large cycles?
- *Interconnectedness:* How strongly are the classes connected by cycles? How many bidirectional relationships are there?
- *Hiddenness:* Which relations in cycles cannot be seen in the class public interfaces?
- *Range:* Are the cycles located in a building block or do they extend beyond building block boundaries?

In addition to metrics, you also need common sense to judge cycles. Numbers alone can only ever be indicators of potential problems—they do not contain proof or a solution.

9.1.1   The Extent of the Chaos

I consider the percentage of classes in cycles to be a good initial indicator of the extent of a system's disarray at the class level. You can also use this number to deduce how many classes will probably not have test classes. In most systems, classes that are involved in cycles don't have direct unit test classes.

Correcting scale   Before we can draw conclusions from this percentage, we have to check several aspects of the calculation:

1. Are the inner classes counted as classes when assessing cycles? If so, we have to remove them from the equation.

2. Did the developers transfer the relational model for the business objects directly from the database into the class model? If the developers chose this path, the business objects will be in a single cycle because each relationship is bidirectional. I don't like this kind of structure any more than I like cycles in other areas of the source code. The problem is that a modification at this point would affect the basis of the application. If this business object class cycle is well defined, the business classes can be ignored in the calculation.

Decomposing such a system into microservices (see Section 7.5), unfortunately, is almost impossible.

3. Does the system contain a lot of two-class cycles that always follow the same pattern? If so, we should examine the pattern separately and not take it into account when calculating the scale of a cycle.

If we adjust the results as suggested above, we can make some initial assumptions based on the result. In a system where less than 10 per cent of the classes are involved in cycles, the chaos on the class level isn't too great, and you are looking at a system with a hierarchical design at the class level. With a result between 10 and 20 per cent, you will have a lot of work to do unraveling cycles. When a system has more than 30 per cent of its classes in cycles, then the system is already heavily eroded or never had a meaningful design at the class level at all. If a system has less than seven per cent classes in cycles, my expectation of finding a well developed pattern language increases (see Chapter 8). Of course, these are only initial assumptions based on a percentage. For these assumptions to become reliable statements, the scope, interconnectednessas, and range of the cycles (see Sections 9.1.2 and 9.1.3) have to be considered too.

10% < 20% < 30%

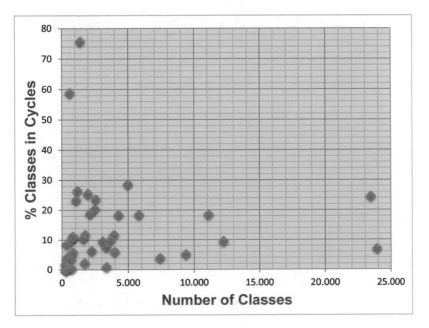

Figure 9-3

Percentage of classes

in cycles

The evaluation shown in figure 9-3 illustrates the percentage of classes in cycles for 40 different-sized Java/C# and C++ systems. A lot of these systems have less than 10 per cent classes in cycles, while some fall into worse categories with more than 20 per cent classes in cycles. There are even systems in existence where virtually every class is caught up in one cycle or another.

If you plot the percentage of classes in cycles against the number of lines of code (LOC) you get a similar picture. The size of the system doesn't influence the proportion of classes in cycles.

9.1.1.1 Architectural Styles and Cycles

Pattern languages reduce cycles

If you look at the architectural styles used in systems represented in figure 9-3, you will quickly notice a relationship between pattern languages and a reduction in the number of cycles. Figure 9-4 shows the percentage of classes in cycles relative to the type of architectural style used. For this evaluation, the two systems with very high values (76 and 58 per cent in figure 9-3) were omitted because their architects did not define a pattern language or even a layered architecture in order to avoid cycles. The architect of the system with 76 per cent classes in cycles told me, "Cycles were not one of our criteria".

Figure 9-4

Percentage of classes in cycles in relation to architectural styles

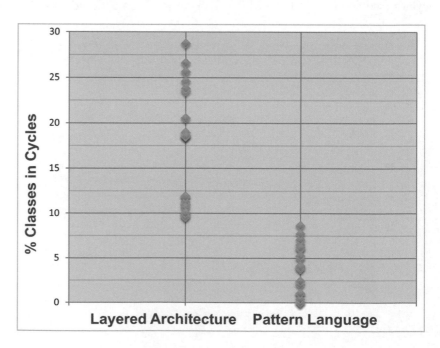

Figure 9-4 suggests that pattern languages usually lead to a lower proportion of classes in cycles than layer architecture.

One of the systems from figure 9-4 that I classified as having a *Degenerated pattern* pattern language has quite a few (8.7 per cent) classes in cycles (#5 *language* in table 9-1). This high value can be explained by the history of its development. During our analysis of the system's architecture, the maintenance developer told me that the system had originally been developed using a pattern language. It was then taken over by a maintenance team that had no experience of the pattern language used by the previous team.

An additional difficulty was that the original development had *Lost knowledge* been carried out by external staff who were no longer available after the task was handed over to the new maintenance team. After two years of maintenance by a different group of developers, the system was incomprehensible and difficult to master for the maintaining developers. To remedy the situation, the maintenance developer was assigned to one of the original developers, who discovered that the extensions made during the previous two years had ignored various specifications from the pattern language. As a result, the structure of the system had degenerated. The team was able to improve on the situation by doing some refactoring work.

Documentation and transfer of pattern languages

Document the pattern languages you use comprehensively so that subsequent generations of developers understand the design rules you used to structure your system.

9.1.1.2 Lines of Code in Cycles

Cycles have obvious structures, and studies have also revealed that classes involved in cycles are potentially larger than classes that aren't. This effect can also be found in the data I collected.

In the systems examined here, the proportion of program lines *Classes in cycles are larger* of all classes in cycles was 1.5 to 3 times greater than the proportion of classes in cycles (see table 9-1). The data in table 9-1 is sorted according to the percentage of classes in cycles. The corresponding architectural style is denoted by the fill color (pattern languages = white, layer architecture = light gray, no style = dark gray).

Table 9-1

Executable lines of code in class cycles

#	RLOC	% Classes in cycles	% RLOC in cycles
1	10,679	0.0	0.0
4	21,591	0.0	0.0
9	43,969	0.4	2.0
3	16,314	1.0	3.5
2	13,219	2.0	2.8
10	49,428	3.8	9.9
12	70,266	4.1	5.2
7	33,651	5.0	20.7
21	629,674	5.2	9.6
17	133,095	6.5	17.2
22	1,296,455	7.1	15.3
5	22,957	8.7	16.9
6	23,478	10.1	23.4
11	65,284	11.0	23.8
13	84,480	11.3	26.1
18	143,101	11.9	17.2
16	120,964	19.0	40.7
23	1,384,260	24.6	59.2
15	112,675	25.6	35.9
14	93,593	26.6	40.3
8	36,671	59.0	66.4
20	344,911	75.9	90.4

Classes that store are even larger The value for system #7 (20.72 per cent RLOC in cycles) represents a noticeable deviation from the other pattern languages. Here, you can see a tendency that we observed for all the systems we examined. Classes that are responsible for accessing the database or importing and exporting external files are two to three times larger than other classes. Classes that save, import, or export data often implement the complete process procedurally, or a main class is developed that controls the entire process and provides basic functionality. This results in large classes which, when integrated into cycles, lead to extreme values. In system #7, nine of the 31 classes involved in cycles are responsible for storing objects in the database or importing external files, and are therefore very large.

9.1.1.3 Dependency Injection and Cycles

In addition to ugly structures and larger classes in cycles, there is another measurable phenomenon that makes cycles tricky to deal with. In 2006, Hayden Melton and Ewan Tempero examined the scale and scope of the class cycles in 85 Java systems [Melton & Tempero 2006].

Melton and Tempero also evaluated whether cycles can be iden-   *Hidden calls create cycles*
tified in the public interfaces of classes, checking along the way whether the cyclic calls to other classes could only be found within method implementations. In such cases, the class method was addressed directly by the method implementation, or an object was created using the keyword "new" to make the actual call. Melton and Tempero's results show that these hidden calls are the main cause of large cycles. They posit that this phenomenon results from the effort to keep internal implementation details outside of the public interface.

Fortunately, around 2006, the new idea of dependency injection   *Dependency injection*
found its way into software development. Dependency injection   *as an improvement*
means all objects used by a class must be injected into the class via its public interface, so the relations classes have to each other and their cyclic relations become visible via the public interface, making them easy to spot for developers. A look at the import statements will also help you spot cycles. If you look at a class instead, you are more likely to focus on the available methods rather than on the imports.

> **Making dependencies visible**
>
> Specify in your team that all objects a class needs must be submitted via its public interface. This makes cycles visible early on and easier to avoid.

9.1.2   Scope and Interconnectedness

If two similarly sized software systems have a similar number of   *Big or small?*
classes in cycles, the resulting chaos can still look very different. In extreme cases, one system may contain many smaller cycles involving three or four architectural elements, while another may contain just one huge interconnected cycle. For developers, many small

cycles present a less complex problem due to the small size of the problematic structure. If large cycles exist, issues concerning comprehensibility, extensibility, testability, evolution, and partitioning are intensified[1].

In addition, the classes in a cycle can be linked to each other to with varying degrees of interconnectedness, so the effort required to dissolve the cycle varies greatly. The cycle shown figure 9-5 consists of sixteen classes that become a cycle because of a single relationship between two classes. This relationship is caused by two constants that are not otherwise used in the entire software system. By shifting these constants into the class that actually uses them, this cycle can be easily resolved[2].

Figure 9-5
Loosely interconnected
cycle

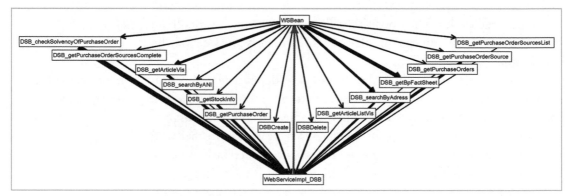

In contrast, figure 9-6 shows a strongly interconnected cycle. Even though it is less than half the size of the cycle shown in figure 9-5, with only with seven classes, it has many more direct cycles. While working with cycles, it quickly becomes obvious that ones like this can only be resolved through a fundamental redesign of a number of the classes involved.

The most striking features of the cycle shown in figure 9-6 are the four direct cycles/bidirectional relationships marked in red. To resolve these bidirectional relations, the tasks of the classes involved must be discussed and the overall functionality required by these

---

1   see [Binder 1999] and [Lakos 1996].
2   see [Melton & Tempero 2006].

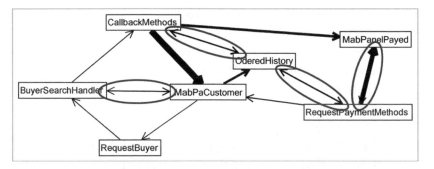

Figure 9-6

Strongly interconnected cycle

classes has to be redesigned. In some cases, it might even be easier to re-implement the entire functionality.

When it comes to studying interconnectedness, a comparison of different architectural styles is also worthwhile. Figure 9-7 clearly shows that pattern languages have relatively few bidirectional relationships within their cycles. The pattern-based system with the highest percentage (9.6 per cent) is system #5, as already shown in Section 9.1.1. This system was developed using a pattern language that eroded in the following two years due to a lack of knowledge on the part of the developers maintaining the software.

Unraveling pattern languages

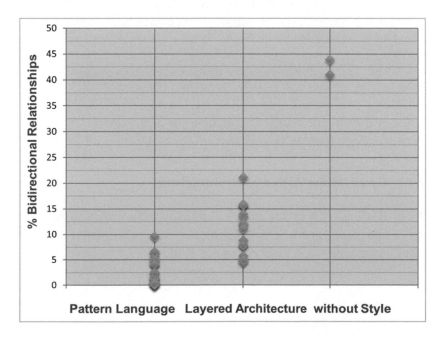

Figure 9-7

Number of bidirectional relationships in cycles

Classes that don't fit   Within the systems that used pattern languages, it was also surprising to find that cycles were usually caused by the classes that couldn't be linked to any element of the pattern language. Strictly speaking, these classes shouldn't even exist in a system modeled using a pattern language! Typical examples are classes that launch parts of the software system, ones that handle exceptions, and ones that manage user login data and/or database access. For such classes, the developers lack the guidance provided by the rules of the pattern language, which determine which role the class plays within the system. Without rules like these, cycles occur more often near the boundaries of a pattern language.

Small cycles   The cycles we saw in the previous sections were still relatively small, containing just seven, 16, and 29 classes. Cycles of this size can be quickly identified, and relatively simply fixed or redesigned by arranging the individual classes hierarchically and analyzing the erroneous relationships.

> **Unraveling small cycles**
>
> Sort your classes into hierarchies while disregarding the existing relationships between them. Of course, some of these classes can exist on a single level. Discuss the tasks of the different classes and their desired interaction with the other classes in the cycle with your team. Then examine the relationships that do not match your new design because they create cycles.

You can do this for cycles that involve up to 30 classes. For larger cycles you will have to use other methods (see Section 9.2).

9.1.3 Cycle Range Within an Architecture

When dealing with cycles, you will quickly realize that some class cycles take place within a building block while others cross building block boundaries (see fig. 9-8 and fig. 9-9).

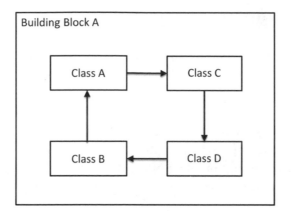

Figure 9-8
Local class cycle

The class cycle shown in figure 9-8 is not relevant at the build-   *What belongs together?*
ing block level because all the classes involved belong to building
block A. Figure 9-9, however, shows a class cycle that goes beyond
the boundaries of building blocks A and B. Both cycles, whether
local or boundary-crossing, are a problem for developers. However,
the location of the four classes in the single building block illustrated in figure 9-8 shows that these four classes belong together.

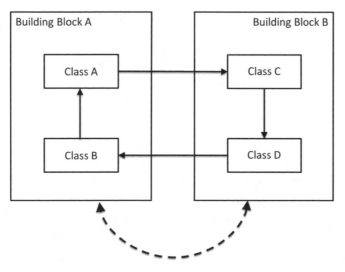

Figure 9-9
Class cycle across building
block boundaries

In contrast, the distribution of the classes into two building blocks
(as shown in fig. 9-9) gives the impression that classes A and B
belong together, and that classes C and D belong together. Divisions
like this obscure the fact that the four classes are actually tidily
coupled.

Placement for classes in cycles

Assign classes that are involved in cycles to a single building block. This makes the strong coupling of these classes visible.

Building block cycles without class cycles

In addition to class cycles that cross building block boundaries, cycles also exist at the building block level that do not consist of class cycles (see fig. 9-10). In this case, there is a cycle between building block A and building block B, which is caused by the relationships between class A and class C, and between class D and class B.

Figure 9-10

Building block cycle without a class cycle

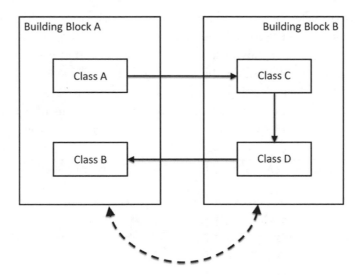

Resolving building block cycles using relocation

Pure building block cycles usually indicate that the classes they contain have not been assigned to the correct building blocks. Such cycles can often be resolved by restructuring. For example, the building block cycle shown in figure 9-10 could be resolved by shifting class A or class B to building block B. However, You have to make sure this kind of shift doesn't make the situation worse. For example, if you move class A to building block B but class A is used by other classes in building block A, you haven't gained anything. Building block A continues to use building block B and the only difference is that it now uses other classes.

Correct restructuring

The open source project *Infoglue*, which we introduced in Section 2.3, contains a good example of proper restructuring. Basically, *Infoglue* is divided into four layers, each containing additional building blocks (see fig. 9-11). In Section 2.3 we resolved two layer violations, while the violations between Util and Service could not be resolved by rearranging the classes, and instead require an extensive redesign. In the situation shown in figure 9-11 these violations still exist. They are shown in yellow to distinguish them from those not yet investigated.

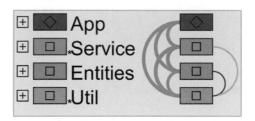

Figure 9-11

The Infoglue *architecture*

The cycle between the Util and Entities layers serves as an example for the resolution of a building block cycle. In order to examine this cycle, a filter is applied to the classes that cause the layer violation (indicated by the red arc in fig. 9-12). Here, `DefaultInterception-PointComparator` uses `InterceptionPointVO`.

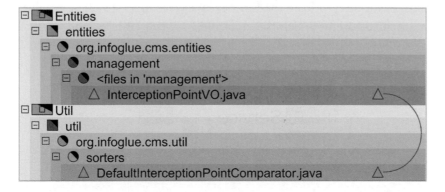

Figure 9-12

Layer violation between

Util and Entities

Looking at figure 9-12 it isn't immediately obvious how this violation can be resolved. That's why we have to extend the filter to reveal all the relations between the `InterceptionPointVO` and `Default-InterceptionPointComparator` classes. Figure 9-13 shows the result: the `InterceptionPointVO` class uses the two Util classes `StringValidator` and `ValidatorFactory`.

Deeper inspection

Figure 9-13

Resolving a building

block cycle

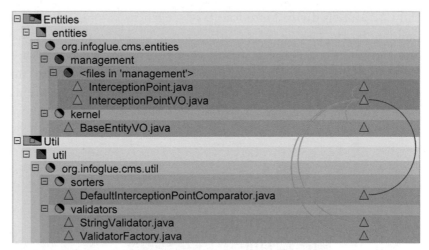

Elegant resolution
This building block cycle can be very elegantly resolved by moving the class `DefaultInterceptionPointComparator` to the Entities layer. `DefaultInterceptionPointComparator` does not use any other class except `InterceptionPointVO`, so its natural location is in the same package as the `InterceptionPointVO` class anyway. `Interception-PointVO`, on the other hand, should not be moved. Doing so would cause a new layer violation because `InterceptionPointVO` uses the class `BaseEntityVO` from the Entities layer (see fig. 9-13). The result is an architecture in which the violation between Utilities and Entities is resolved (see fig. 9-14).

Figure 9-14

Restructured architecture

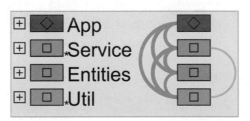

In contrast, a class cycle usually requires a more complex redesign of several classes and their interactions, as we will see in the next section.

9.2   The Big Ball of Mud

Large cycles are impressive structures. Figure 9-15 shows a partic- *A monster cycle*
ularly large specimen. This colorful and structurally beautiful form
consists of 480 classes, all of which need each other. Here, you
can get back to every starting point from each class simply by taking different paths through the cycle. The different colors stand for
the different packages that contain the classes. The classes that are
interconnected the most within the cycle are in the center, while the *Figure 9-15*
outer classes have fewer relationships to the other classes. The fol- *Class cycle involving*
lowing sections explain how to deal with monsters like this.   *480 classes*

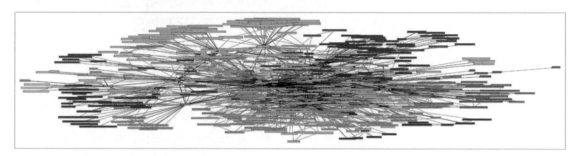

Large class clusters are usually found in systems that have no (or
virtually no) automated unit tests. If the developers write a unit
test for each class while programming the productive classes, they
would automatically avoid cycles, because they want either to produce as little context as possible for a class during unit testing and
like to avoid mock objects.

Unfortunately, the test coverage in this system was zero. There *Serious chaos*
was little source code on the server because most of the functionality was kept on the client, and the system's business object classes
were also used on the client only. When the customer requested a
new functionality, the architects realized that they would also need
the business objects on the server in order to comply. Unfortunately,
the business objects on the client were woven into large cycles of
460 and 220 classes, so it wouldn't have been possible to migrate
the business objects to the server without a major rebuild and a lot
more testing. This particular issue was solved by transferring all
the client classes, including the GUI interface and controller, to the
server as a library so that the business objects could be used on the

server. A little more attention to unit testing, freedom from cycles, and modularization would certainly have led to a simpler transformation in this case.

Automated tests produce small, controllable cycles

For new developments you should specify that there must be a test class for each class in which the essential functionality of the class is checked via positive and negative tests. Implement Test-Driven Design (TDD) so that the tests are written before the functionality.

Assuming you already have a large codebase, specify that any developer must first write a unit test for each modification or extension. The test is intended to safeguard the modification before it is implemented. This step-by-step process will help you develop a larger test suite.

9.2.1 The Black Hole Effect

By creating automatic tests, the design of the class will instantly improve. Additionally, either no class cycles will creep in at all, or the ones that do will be small and manageable. If you don't have any rules in place or unit tests that encourage freedom from cycles, cycles that start off small will become larger and larger as the project progresses.

The initial situation   Some time ago I was hired by a client to work as an architect. My tasks were to discuss public interfaces with the providers of the various externally developed systems and to monitor their quality. One of these systems underwent a sad development in the course of the project. My initial analysis of the system (700,000 LOC, C++) revealed various cyclic structures (see fig. 9-16).

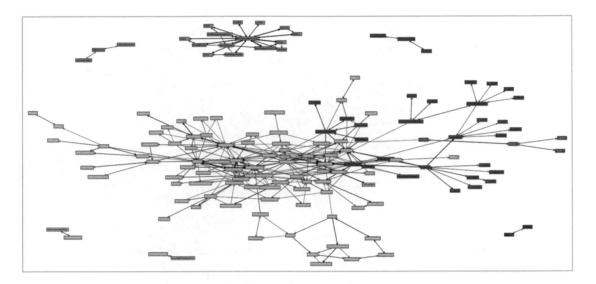

Figure 9-16 shows 147 classes that are color-coded according to the building blocks they belong to. In the center there is an obvious large class cycle that contains 119 classes from the green, pink, dark blue, and light blue building blocks. Six smaller cycles involving two, three, and 15 classes are arranged around this larger cycle. Unfortunately, my client hadn't defined any technical quality criteria during the contract negotiations. The service provider accepted our findings but insisted on charging extra to tackle the ensuing quality problems. Of course, this also delayed delivery.

One year later I analyzed the system again. The service provider's estimates for change requests had risen significantly in the intervening months, and simple enhancements that used to cost two days now cost five days. The estimates for larger extensions or conversions had shot up exponentially. What was going on?

The system had grown by 200,000 LOC during the intervening year and I was shocked to find out that the developers had significantly worsened the class cycle situation. The cycles in figure 9-16 had meanwhile become a contiguous structure encompassing 410 classes (see fig. 9-17).

Figure 9-16

Cyclic structures revealed by initial analysis

Some cycles already exist

Increasing effort when making changes

Things had got worse!

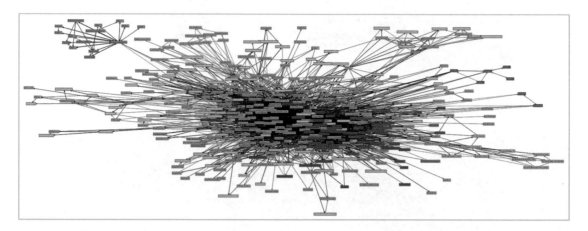

Figure 9-17

*Cyclic structure revealed
by the second analysis*

Comparing the two images reveals the following:

- All 410 classes are now connected. There are no longer any separate cycles as there were in figure 9-16. Furthermore, the beige cycle with 15 classes shown in figure 9-16 is now connected to the main cycle.

Degradation

- The green and purple blocks are much closer together.

- The number of classes in the green and the light-blue blocks has risen significantly.

*A huge cycle sucks
in classes*

This development is typical and inevitable for large class cycles. The coupling within a large class cycle becomes stronger and stronger the more it grows. Large class cycles are like **black holes**. They suck in classes and, over time, pull them ever closer toward the center of the main cycle.

Take a look at the light blue classes in figure 9-17 and imagine adding a new variant to these classes. How would you go about it? You would probably copy an existing light blue class, change the necessary lines, and add the new class to the mechanism that links the other light-blue classes to the overall system. And there you have it—you have already added another class to the cycle. The more connections there are, the tighter they get, and the closer the light blue classes move toward the center of the cycle.

> **Avoid large cycles**
>
> Do not allow large, strongly-coupled cycles to develop in your system. Enhancements and change requests in structures like these are expensive and error-prone.

9.2.2 Breaking Free

Today's analysis tools offer some support in breaking cycles. The thinnest relationships within the cycle are usually identified because the tool developers assume that resolving these relationships requires the least effort. Alternatively, the tools compute groups of relationships that would have to be cut to break up the cycle into smaller cycles or cycle-free structures.

I have never gotten far using graph theory views of cycles. In my opinion, solving cycles is only possible on the basis of criteria that grow out of the system's architecture and its domain. If a system has cycles, it is because the tasks of the classes involved are not clearly defined. The classes don't have good modularity and developers will have difficulties processing them as a chunk. You have to ask yourself which task should be assigned to whom and which relationships have to be broken down, regardless of the strength of these relationships and the smaller cycles that may result. *Graph theory solutions aren't real solutions*

I even consider the idea of looking for the thinnest relationships in cycles to be dangerous. Time and again, I come across systems in which cycle relationships exist due to copy-and-paste programming. The first programmer of a new functionality accidentally built in a relationship that leads to a cycle, and subsequent programmers copy this solution, unwittingly strengthening the unwanted relationship. If, instead of the unwanted relationship, you dissolve a different one that coincidentally consists of fewer calls, you will further dilute the system's architecture.

It is better to dissolve class cycles by dividing the classes in the cycle into rougher units. These units reduce the number of elements and make it easier to examine the cycle. All systems usually permit a rougher structure based on patterns (see Chapter 8). The only question is how well the roughly divided units help to unravel the larger cycles. I regularly use the following four rough *Create rougher units* structures in my analysis. They are sorted according to their effectiveness:

1. *Technical layers:* If the class cycle involves multiple technical layers, it can be broken down into smaller cycles by dissolving the layer violations. Once the cycle involves only a single layer, it is necessary to avoid the structures it contains (see points 2-4).

2. *Pattern language:* Pattern languages usually define a clear hierarchy for the pattern's classes. If the cycle's classes are sorted into layers according to the patterns, the relationships that need to be dissolved become visible as violations.

3. *Domain-oriented building blocks:* In some systems, the domain-oriented building blocks have a hierarchizing effect similar to that of technical layering. In this case, the domain-oriented building blocks play a useful role in breaking down cycles.

4. *Packages/Namespaces/Directories:* The weakest structuring tool is the lowest level of the system's building blocks. Unfortunately, developers don't often use this level for hierarchization.

> **Breaking down large cycles**
>
> Search for a structuring tool at a higher level than the classes. Look first at class cycles that extend beyond the boundaries of the technical layers. If you are lucky and the system is based on a pattern language, continue working with the layer's patterns. If your system is separated into domain-oriented building blocks, then use this structure instead. The last, often weaker option is to follow the system's package structure.

We will now look at two examples of how large cycles can be broken down using technical layering and pattern languages.

9.2.3 "Weaponizing" Technical Layering

Some time ago I analyzed a 710,000-LOC Java system that contained, among other things, a class cycle involving 134 classes. This cycle spanned seven of the system's nine technical layers (see fig. 9-18).

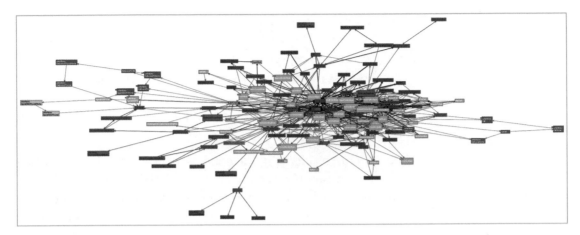

All the other class cycles in this system were much smaller and were contained within the layers. In order to reduce coupling between the layers and resolve the cycle, we approached the large cycle at the layer level (see fig. 9-19).

In figure 9-19 the filter is set to show the classes involved in the cycle, which is why the corresponding layers are shown as black triangles. The black triangles indicate that not all classes assigned to these layers are part of the selection. For example, all the Service layer's classes (and their relationships) that are not involved in the large class cycle were ignored. We can only see the relationships that cause the class cycle.

Figure 9-18

Cycle involving 134 classes

Concentration on technical layers

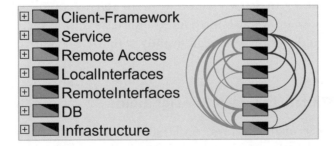

Figure 9-19

Class cycle at layer level

Due to the layering shown in figure 9-19, the 134 classes are automatically arranged hierarchically as the development team intended. Instead of a 134-class issue, we thus reduced our problem to a seven-layer issue, with the violations indicated by the red arcs. At a first glance, there seem to be a lot of violations—however, the strength of

20 violations remain

the arcs in relation to each other is logarithmic, not linear, and there are only 20 relationships between classes that cause violations. In contrast, the green arcs represent a total of 598 inter-class relationships.

Remarkably, most violations are caused by relationships between the Service layer and the other layers. An analysis of these relationships revealed that two relatively typical mistakes were made during the implementation:

1. *Location of constants:* In the course of development, teams often introduce constants or enums that they integrate into the class in which they are first used. Increasing numbers of classes need these constants and use the class in which the constants are declared. If you separate the constants from the class, this part of the cycle dissolves easily.

2. *Missing Dependency Injection:* The public interfaces of the classes in the five layers below the Service layer were not designed so that they can be handed objects or data as parameters, as required by their methods. Instead, the classes access the service's class objects in their method implementation and fetch the required objects or data there. Correcting these violations is more time-consuming than correcting violations caused by constants. You have to include parameters in the methods' public interfaces so that the data and objects can be injected. The same adjustments also have to be made for the method's calls.

By refactoring these two issues, we were able to completely resolve this class cycle. We also introduced unit tests during the rebuilding process and were able to significantly stabilize this part of the system.

9.2.4 Pattern Language as a Lighthouse

Things can always
get worse!

In another analysis (Java, 650,000 LOC) I came across a very large class cycle involving 463 classes in 50 packages. At the class level, this cycle is highly interwoven (see fig. 9-20). Compared with figure 9-16 and figure 9-17, you can see that this cycle has fewer satellites surrounding the main cycle. In addition, classes from the same packages (identifiable by their color codes) are distributed throughout the cycle.

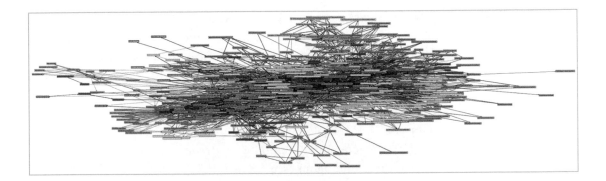

Fortunately, the developers of this system used a pattern language. In figure 9-21 you can see the nine layers that the result from sorting the 463 classes in this cycle using the supplied patterns.

We marked one relationship that was not permitted due to layering constraints as permitted (indicated by the yellow arc). Each controller/view pair was built so that they know each other bi-directionally.

Figure 9-20

Class cycle with

463 participants

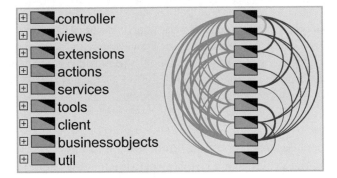

Figure 9-21

Class cycle in a pattern

language

At first glance, this class cycle looks just as interwoven at the pattern language level (fig. 9-21) as it does at the class level (fig. 9-20). Looking at the metrics, it is encouraging to see that only two per cent of the relationships shown in figure 9-21 are prohibited and therefore shown in red. So many correct relationships and so few bad ones lead us to assume that the pattern language, if used correctly, has a good hierarchizing effect. In the following sections, we will look at how this effect can be used to resolve the cycle.

A closer look at figure 9-21 shows that a large proportion of the violations in this cycle emanate from the classes that belong to the

A lot of good, a little bad

Business objects =

relational model

businessobject pattern. The entire class cycle contains 203 business objects. In this system, the relational model was mapped directly from the database into the business objects. This means that each class represents a table and that the relationships between the classes are bidirectional. The classes therefore always know each other if there is a relationship between the two corresponding tables in the database.

I have encountered mapping of a relational model into business objects time and again (see Section 9.1.1). this solution because it turns the business model into a completely interwoven cluster, you should only revise it very carefully at this point. The business model of a system is fundamental to all the system functionality based on it. Reconstructing such a system would be akin to redeveloping it from the ground up.

Business objects ≠ relational model

If you could develop a system from scratch, then my recommendation would be:

> **Business model and relational model**
>
> Build the business model of your application without cycles. This gives you stronger guidance for modularizing the individual classes according to their tasks. The hierarchy of the business model also provides a functional layer for the functionality based on the business model. You will benefit from this while dividing it into domain-oriented modules.

Forget cycles between business objects

The large class cycle shown in figure 9-20 and figure 9-21 makes it clear that the cycles that exist between business object classes cannot be changed. However, the relationships that originate from the business object classes contradict the pattern language. The developers didn't work cleanly here. In total, 97 of the 203 business object classes involved in the cycle have relationships to higher layers. A large number of these violations (emanating from 87 classes) connect to just a few classes in tools and client.

Mixing factory and utility

These classes in tools and client are typical classes with two tasks: on the one hand they work like a factory and create certain class structures out of business objects and tools, while on the other hand, the developers have integrated utility functionality into them. The tool and client patterns have significantly fewer design rules than the other patterns, so it is not surprising that the developers misused these classes for double tasks.

Once these relationships have been dissolved, only 10 business object classes remain, and these need to be investigated more closely. If these business objects are removed from the cycle too, there is still a cycle involving 184 classes and several small cycles involving a total of 76 classes left (see fig. 9-22).

The remaining cycle without the business objects

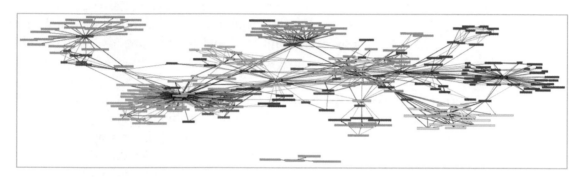

If we view the residual cycle on the pattern language level, it becomes much easier to manage (see fig. 9-23).

Figure 9-22

Class cycle without business objects

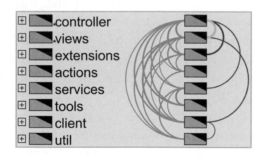

Figure 9-23

Class cycle without business objects at pattern level

If you dissolve the remaining red relationships shown in figure 9-23, the 184-class cycle disintegrates into its individual parts. Only local cycles remain, and these are usually grouped around a central class to form star cycles (see Section 8.6).

Star cycle

In figure 9-22, star cycles can be found at top left and top center (green/purple), at bottom left (light blue), at bottom right (yellow), and at the perimeter (purple).

By using the refactoring approach described above (remove business objects, remove pattern violations, break the star cycle) we were able to significantly scale down this very large class cycle.

Of course, we also introduced unit tests to safeguard such a large refactoring effort.

9.3   Uneven Modules

The compulsion to create cycle-free systems: a blessing or a curse?

Based on the previous sections and their coverage of cycles, you may be thinking that every team should ensure that cycles are prohibited during the development/build process. Various technologies (Maven, Netweaver, Build in Visual Studio) already exist that do this job perfectly. However, from my point of view caution is still advised!

The pseudo-solution

Faced with a monolith that you want to restructure, you should refrain from using technologies that prohibit cycles. You will either end up in the interface trap (see Section 7.4) or you will inevitably choose the pseudo-solution that goes under the name "Uneven Modules". This particular solution consists of several modules that work together without cycles, but which are very different in size.

Cycle-free component model

Our example here is a Java system with about 420,000 LOC, developed initially without Maven and split later into Maven artifacts. Maven does not allow cycles between Maven artifacts. At the beginning of the analysis, the team told me that their system consisted of nine Maven artifacts arranged in three layers. However, the team's explicit request to me was, "Can't we model the architecture properly after all? We actually have 17 sub-systems!"

Options and preferences for architecture

Figure 9-24 illustrates the result. The tabbed, colored rectangles represent the building blocks defined during our analysis. They are arranged into five layers from top to bottom. The BaseUtil building block on the lowest layer is used by all higher-level building blocks, and, to improve readability, I have omitted the relationships to it.

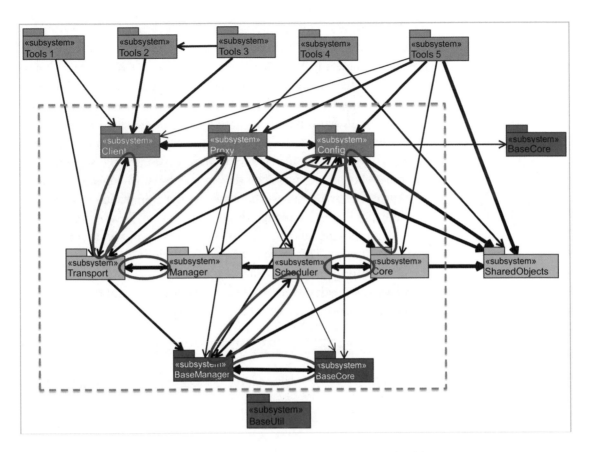

Figure 9-24 shows a series of relationships between the nine building blocks in the middle. These either contravene the layering or are
direct cycles (shown in red). These relationships are the reason why
the ostensibly cycle-free architecture of this system consists of only
nine Maven artifacts on three layers. One of these nine artifacts is
very large. This large building block is displayed in figure 9-24 as a
green dotted box. The corresponding Maven artifact contains about
80per cent of the total code and all cyclically connected building
blocks are hidden inside it.

The separation into nine building blocks is really a joke and it
would have been OK to leave them as they were. We were faced
with a monolith orbited by eight small satellites. This is NOT genuine modularization! The only thing the team really did well was to
form a cycle-free BaseUtil component outside of the large central
building block.

Figure 9-24

Uneven Modules

Officially cycle-free

80 per cent of the code in one component

At a dead end   The developers of this system would have liked to tidy up their architecture and break down the cycles. Unfortunately, they were not given the budget to carry out the necessary restructuring and refactoring (see Section 1.3.4). In effect, they were forced to live with the disguised monolith and simply make occasional minor improvements. Due to Maven's forced freedom from cycles, the developers had little opportunity to visualize the 17 subsystems and five layers in their minds visible in the actual architecture, which is aligned to the nine Maven artifacts. The developers have to repeatedly translate form one structure to the other in the minds. In order to follow the development team's discussions, every new employee has to understand the planned architecture (as opposed to the code's actual structure). This is a very tricky situation!

We can only hope that management wants the monolith to be dismantled someday—otherwise the level of technical debt will simply become too painful with each new extension.

Balanced breakdown of cycle-free components

Dismantle your system into similarly-sized, cycle-free modules and check the proportions of your system before using technology that forces freedom from cycles.

The compulsion to create   These technologies make sense if you have already structured your
cycle-free build artifacts   source code using a good design. They enable you to break down domain-oriented building blocks without cyclic relationships and can be used to prevent the erosion of architecture. However, you have to ensure that the architects and developers who are building the system regularly exchange information about the architecture.

10 Refining Modularity

Throughout the discussion of layer architecture, public interfaces, pattern languages, and cycles detailed in the previous chapters, the questions we repeatedly ask are: What are the tasks of the building blocks involved? Are the responsibilities assigned in a meaningful way? The question of modularity is therefore a constant part of our thinking, even when we are investigating other aspects of a system.

In order to assess how well a development team paid attention to modularity, the analysis should review the basic rules for building a modular architecture (see Section 5.1). Building block modularity cannot be measured directly using a single metric, but you can still assess it using metrics such as the size of the building blocks, the number of incoming and outgoing relationships, the complexity of methods, code duplicates, and—for example—by examining naming conventions.

Verifying modularity

Like the metrics for cycles, these metrics are only indicators for building blocks with low modularity. Whether the public interface of a module really is a capsule and whether the methods of the public interface represent a coherent task can only be determined indirectly. A real judgment can only be made in the course of discussions with a system's developers and architects.

Metrics as indicators

At the beginning of each analysis I ask the development team if they use a metric tool and, if they do, which one they use. I also try to find out how the team integrates the metric tool's findings into their development process. The answer to these questions gives me an idea of how the team deals with the source code and architecture quality. Their answers can also help me to estimate the degree of metrics detail I have to go into myself.

Use of metric tools

Using metric tools

Use one of the common metric tools to evaluate your software projects. Regularly examine the classes, methods, packages, and building blocks that exceed the limits you define.

Metric OK,
comprehensibility zero

However, you should avoid the approach that I was introduced to one day at a customer site. During salary discussions, bonus payments were linked to achieving certain metric values. The individual developers used their time to alter the source code in order to meet the requirements of these metrics. Unfortunately, a lot of the modifications they made were meaningless—for example, domain-oriented classes which exceeded the metric "lines per class" were simply split down the middle, and a range of similar tricks were applied in order to fulfill the new requirements. As a result, the software metrics looked quite good, but the comprehensibility of the code had been trashed.

10.1 Building Block Cohesion

Good Name = Cohesion

A simple way to study the cohesion of building blocks is to look at their names. If the building blocks have appropriate names that describe a system's task you can assume that modularity played a role in the system's design.

Figure 10-1

Class with high cohesion

```
public class Account {
    void deposit (Amount b)...
    void withdraw (Amount b)...
    bool isAmountCovered (Amount b)...
    Amount getBalance()...
    AccNr getAccountNumber()...
```

Figure 10-1 shows a domain class that bears the name of the corresponding domain concept (Account). The method names and parameter types are also closely linked to the terms of the application's domain. In contrast, the ProgramManager class shown in figure 10-2 contains a collection of services that—among other things—manage an event queue, a printer queue, and the system's service registry. Each of these three tasks rally deserves a class of its own. Due to the varied services included in the ProgramManager class, this class will probably be quite large and will likely be linked to many other classes.

```
public class ProgramManager {
    void initializeEventQueue()…
    void sendEvent(Event event)…
    void registerForEvent(Event event)...
    void shutdownEventQueue()…
    void initializeServiceRegistry()…
    void registerService(Service service)…
    Service getService(String name)...
    void shutdownServiceRegistry()...
    void initializePrinterQueue()…
    void printDocument(Document document)…
```

Figure 10-2

Class with low cohesion

Bad names that I come across time and again are:

Bad names

- *Manager:* When you no longer know what to call a class, you call it a manager. The task of such a class is not really restricted by the choice of an imprecise name and, in principle, a manager can be anything you like. This is why these classes are typical repositories for a lot of functionality.

- *Handler:* Where a class takes care of something but isn't a manager because it has to be a bit smaller, then it's usually called a handler.

- *Util or Helper:* These classes mostly contain collections of static methods that are not really connected. Util building blocks usually consist of classes that couldn't be linked to any domain or technical area.

It goes without saying that, in addition to the domain classes, you will need a whole series of technical classes that include Util classes. It is important to give these classes or building blocks a meaningful description of their tasks and how they cooperate with other classes. A catch-all for everything that can't be accommodated elsewhere is not the right solution.

Util needs cohesion too

> **Select suitable names**
>
> Be sure to increase the cohesion in your designs by choosing appropriate names. Difficulties in defining names are a clear signal that you need to revise your design.

Measuring cohesion

In addition to names, many authors propose measurement of cohesion via coupling. Building blocks are examined to check whether the elements contained within them are coupled more strongly to one another than to the ones located outside. For example, the coupling between a package's classes determines the cohesion of the package as a whole. If the classes have more relationships to each other than to the classes in other packages, the package has high cohesion. Cohesion at class level is determined by whether (and to what extent) the methods of a class are linked to each other and to the attributes of the class.

Cohesion of packages and classes

Measuring high cohesion within packages and larger building blocks based on coupling is a sensible option, whereas measuring cohesion based on coupling between attributes and methods in classes appears more difficult. Let's take another look at the classes `Account` and `ProgramManager` from this point of view. We expect the class `Account` to have the attributes `AccountNumber` and `balance`. The class `ProgramManager` has an `EventQueue`, a `PrinterQueue` and a `ServiceRegistry` as its attributes. In `ProgramManager`, the relevant method groups will work with the matching attributes without overlapping. A corresponding metric would fit our impression that this class has little cohesion and should be decomposed. There are also two groups of methods for the `Account` class, namely: all methods that work on the balance, and a method that can be used to query the `AccountNumber`. If you follow the recommendation to divide methods without common attributes into separate classes, you would clearly be working against the business concept of the domain.

> **Strengthening cohesion in packages, modules, and layers**
>
> Make sure that classes within a package, module, or layer interact more with each other than with classes outside of the building block that encloses them.

Copied code fragments are another indication of poor cohesion. When a code snippet can be found in several places in a system in a very similar form we talk about "code duplication". Code duplicates are problematic from the modularity viewpoint because two or more units perform the same task. This could be because the responsibility for the task is not clearly assigned. Furthermore, code duplicates can cause quality issues, as they generate redundancies and inconsistencies:

Code duplicates = poor cohesion

- Duplicates increase the size of the codebase. Large codebases are harder to maintain than small ones.

- Duplicates increase the required testing effort because every version has to be tested in its own setting.

- Duplicates are likely to be overlooked during maintenance when they actually need to be dealt with consistently and uniformly.

Most analysis tools provide comprehensive support for finding duplicated code (see fig. 10-3).

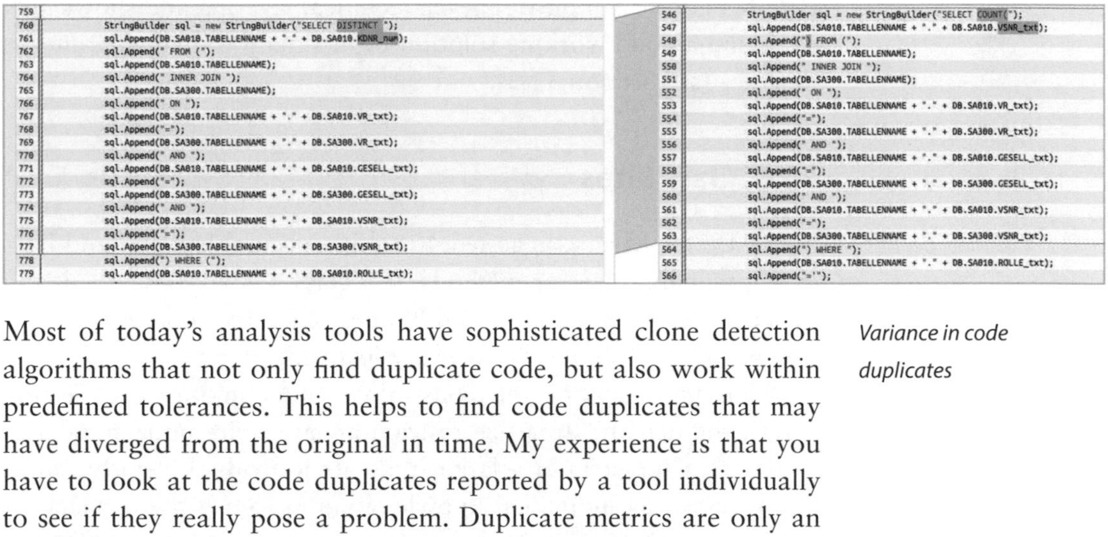

Figure 10-3

Code duplicate (light blue) with the deviating digits highlighted in purple (shown in TeamScale)

Most of today's analysis tools have sophisticated clone detection algorithms that not only find duplicate code, but also work within predefined tolerances. This helps to find code duplicates that may have diverged from the original in time. My experience is that you have to look at the code duplicates reported by a tool individually to see if they really pose a problem. Duplicate metrics are only an indicator.

Variance in code duplicates

Avoid code duplicates

Scan your source code regularly for code duplicates. After an initial examination of all duplicates, pay special attention to recent duplicates.

10.2 Building Block Sizes

5-40 classes per package

Bertrand Meyer—the inventor of the Eiffel programming language and the Design by Contract model—established that packages should contain between five and 40 classes. They should be developed by one to four people and should be capable of being understood by any individual. The existence of large packages and building blocks can, liked classes and methods, be measured using metric tools (see Sections 10.3 and 10.4). Again, you should look here at the larger units.

During analysis, special attention needs to be paid to the relative sizes of the technical layers, as well as those of the domain modules and the building blocks they contain. If the development teams understand that large units are not a good idea, you can expect the size of the units to be balanced at this level too. If not, you probably have a case of "uneven modules" (see Section 9.3). The other option lies in the development team viewing the building blocks not as modular units but rather as locations. Our case study C++ system *Beta* is a good example of uneven technical layering and shows how we found a good working solution for a situation involving uneven modules (see Section 11.3).

10.3 Class Sizes

1,000 lines per class

In the 1970s, Myers suggested 40 to 50 executable command lines as a reasonable size for methods. If a class has 20 methods, it can thus contain a maximum of 1,000 lines of source code. Any exception to this rule should be carefully justified.

Large units and chunks

Thinking back to the constraints of chunking (see Section 5.1.1), the demands for size restrictions are quite understandable. In order to understand a larger unit, its individual elements must be processed as individual knowledge units. Since the capacity of short-term memory is limited, a large unit shouldn't contain too many elements.

Object orientation favors small units

Nowadays, most object-oriented systems show that their development teams are trying to implement these requirements. The following diagrams illustrate a system that successfully implemented an object-oriented class level design (see fig. 10-4 and fig. 10-5).

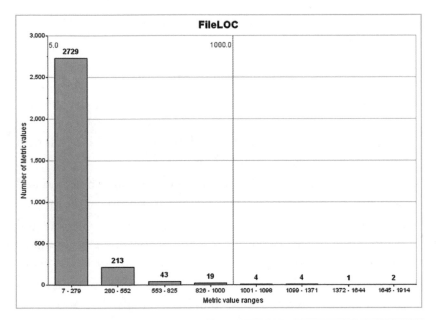

Figure 10-4

Number of lines per file

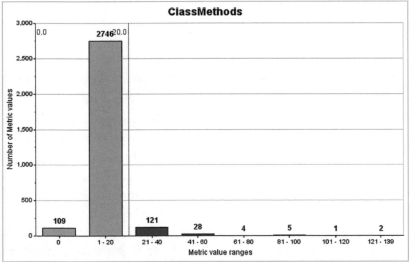

Figure 10-5

*Number of methods
per class*

Ninety-nine point four per cent of the files in this system have less than 1,000 lines, while 94.7 per cent of the classes have fewer than 20 methods.

The classes that cross these boundaries are the most interesting. Depending on how many large units appear during the evaluation, you should investigate the worst offenders at the extreme ends of the scale. We try to identify entire groups of large building blocks

Typical large units

by means of patterns. Typically, systems contain large classes that belong to the following categories:

- *Generated code:* Classes that were generated by an external or a self-developed framework or library can be ignored when evaluating their size or modularity. An evaluation of whether the generator generates modular source code of no interest here. Only pre-generated template classes which the developers later fill with source code are worth a closer look.

- *DB/file interface classes:* Classes that import and export files and database public interfaces are often developed procedurally.

- *Disposable classes:* These classes are developed for one-time migration of data sets to a new database, or for initial data import. Despite their temporary nature they are often nevertheless kept.

- *Central framework superclasses:* When assessing a framework, central superclasses are often found to be huge. The developers equip these classes with ever-increasing functionality over time and splitting them into multiple smaller classes is not easy because a number of specific classes inherit from the central superclass. In addition, many classes within the framework use the central superclass type—another factor that makes a rebuild expensive.

- *Central business objects and services:* In most cases, the central business object and service classes tend to grow increasingly large over time. Because the system's users are always coming up with exciting new ideas, new functionality and data are constantly being added to them. If you miss the right moment to divide these classes, it will be just as difficult to accomplish later as it was with the central framework superclass. The entire application is based on these few central classes and a rebuild requires large numbers of adjustments. This situation can be avoided by applying strategic design of Domain-Driven Design (see Section 6.5 and 6.6.2).

- *Utility classes:* Many systems use utility classes that contain all the methods that don't fit in anywhere else.

Nip it in the bud! For all these cases I can only advise you to nip the effect in the bud. Remember that large units are difficult to comprehend, usually perform too many simultaneous tasks, and are often involved in cycles. They are a code smell that you won't normally want to have in your codebase.

As well as analyzing the number of lines, you can also examine the publicly visible interfaces a developer is confronted with when using a class (see fig. 10-6 and fig. 10-7).

Public interface

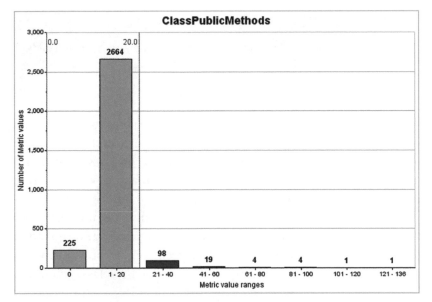

Figure 10-6

Number of public methods

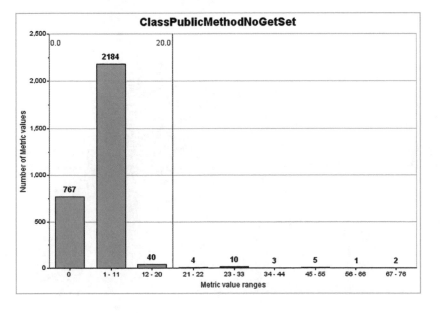

Figure 10-7

Number of public methods per class without set/get

The public interfaces of the classes in this system are well structured, with 96 per cent of the classes containing fewer than 20 methods (or 99 percent if you exclude all set/get methods). The number of classes with more than 20 methods is therefore manageable and they can be examined without too much effort.

> ### Limit class and method sizes
>
> Assess the sizes of the classes and methods in your source code regularly, and pay special attention to the cohesion of the classes and methods that continually increase in size.

Some tools can analyze the relative sizes of classes and supply an indicator for how urgent an alteration might be. For example, Seerene analyzes the relationships between large classes, how frequently the classes were modified, and how many developers were involved in the code modification (see fig. 10-8 and fig. 10-9).

Software as a city

Figure 10-8 shows a software system divided into modules (large rectangles separated by thick grey lines), packages (separated by light grey elevations), and classes (green, yellow or red towers). The height of a tower represents the size of the class, while the

Figure 10-8

The relationship between class size and the number of developers depicted using Seerene (© http://www.seerene.com/)

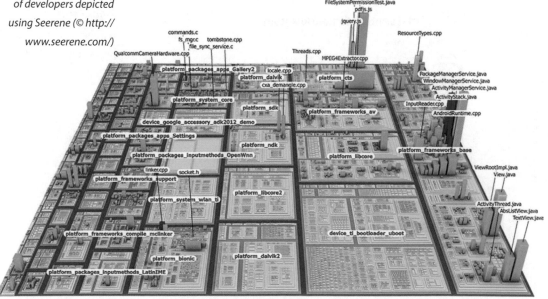

colors show how many developers are working on a class. Red means that only one developer worked on a class over a pre-selected period, yellow represents two or three developers, while green class towers represent classes programmed by many different developers that are therefore "safe".

Figure 10-9 shows a similar evaluation, but this time with red representing the classes that have been altered most frequently. Yellow classes are modified fairly often, while green classes are rarely touched.

If you have an evaluation like this at your disposal (see fig. 10-9) along with one that shows the number of changes made for each large class, then you should have a pretty good idea where to start. Figure 10-8 and figure 10-9 look very similar, but a closer look reveals that:

▪ In the lower right corner of figure 10-8 there is a large yellow tower (i.e., a class with only a few developers working on it. In figure 10-9 this tower is green—i.e., this class has not been changed much.

▪ The tall, red towers in both illustrations need to be examined more closely. They are large, have only one developer working on them, and are often changed.

Figure 10-9

Relationship between the number of changes made and class size depicted using Seerene (© http:// www.seerene.com/)

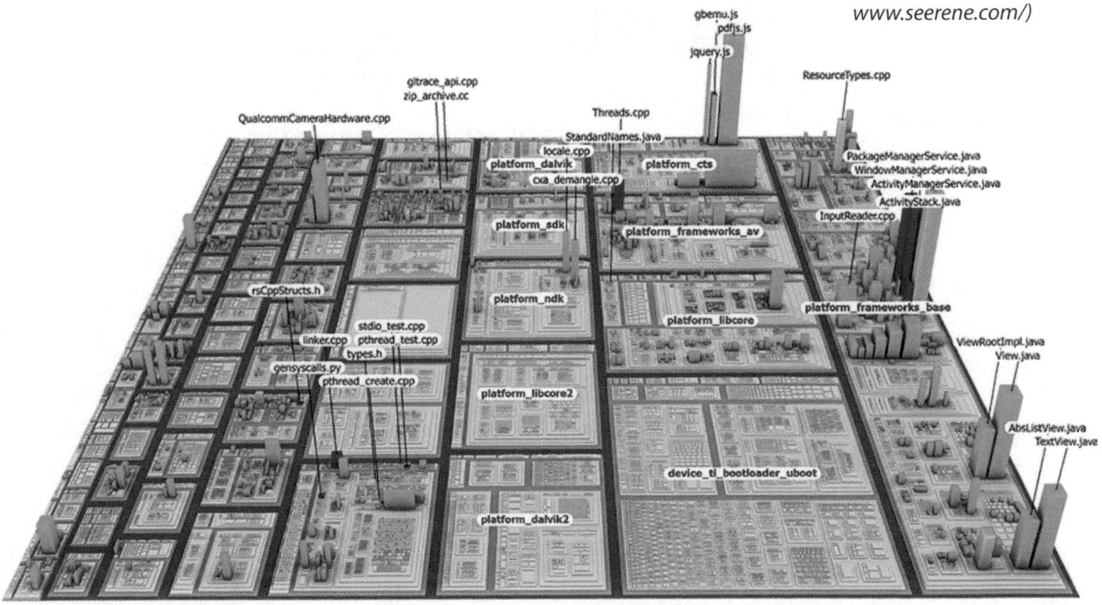

> **Keeping class sizes under control**
>
> Regularly measure the size of classes in your source code. Make sure that large classes are broken down.

10.4 Method Size and Complexity

The inner workings To evaluate the inner view of classes (i.e., the complexity a developer is confronted with when a class needs to be altered), you need to use the *number of lines per method* and *cyclomatic complexity* metrics (see fig. 10-10 and fig. 10-11).

Figure 10-10

Number of lines of code per method

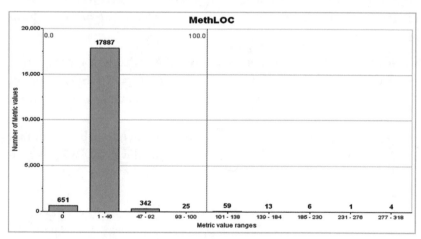

Figure 10-11

Cyclomatic complexity of methods

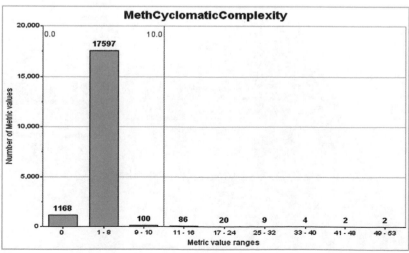

The metric *cyclomatic complexity* was introduced in 1976 by Thomas J. McCabe [McCabe 1976]. Cyclomatic complexity is defined as the number of a code snippet's linearly independent paths in a control flow graph. The McCabe metric resumes the principle of chunking (see Section 5.1.1), which states that having reached a certain level of complexity, a section of source code can no longer be completely understood by its developer. Additionally, this number provides us with the upper limit for the number of test cases necessary to achieve a complete branch overlap in the control flow graph [McCabe & Butler 1989].

Cyclomatic complexity = number of paths

The system evaluated in figure 10-11 has a maximum cyclical complexity value of 53. This is high, but is an exception compared to the majority of less complex methods. This is a typical value in systems developed by people who enjoyed good object-oriented schooling. Of course it would be better if these complex methods could be broken down to achieve a maximum value between 10 and 20. Each team should agree on a maximum value and check regularly that the source code adheres to it.

Typical values for cyclomatic complexity

The methods at the top of both evaluations should be investigated. Usually, the developers know these methods all too well and say things like, "Yeah, that's a terrible area" or, "That method is next on our refactoring list".

As with all metrics, cyclomatic complexity is merely an indicator. Methods with a high cyclomatic complexity should be inspected. They may contain a lot of complexity and splitting them into several methods would significantly increase their comprehensibility. However, it is also possible that the method in question consists of clearly structured, well-commented individual sections. In such a case, it is a matter of debate whether dividing the method into several smaller units would actually enable a better understanding of the algorithm. However, from a testability point of view and with regard to the complexity of the necessary test cases, decomposition seems like a wise idea.

Metrics don't represent the absolute truth

I once encountered a system that contained a method with a cyclomatic complexity of 637. This method was responsible for checking whether the account number entered on the web interface matched the bank's sort code. The banking association had published an algorithm for this purpose that was regularly updated as

Cyclomatic complexity 637

the banking landscape changed. Since the algorithm was provided in pseudocode as a long function, it was no surprise that the developers converted it into a method. The individual sections for the various sort-code numbers were easily recognizable thanks to blank lines and comments, so adding new banks and changing the logic for existing banks didn't cause any problems. A new block could be added or an existing block changed. However, bank mergers proved more complex for this over-long method. The thing to consider here was how often such modifications really occurred, and whether it was worth the effort. You should always consider whether there are other, more urgent issues that need refactoring.

> **Keeping the complexity of methods under control**
>
> Regularly measure the cyclomatic complexity of the methods in your source code. Make sure that complex methods are broken down, and that more than one person is familiar with complex algorithms.

10.5 Loose Coupling

For static programming languages, the degree of coupling can be relatively easily determined and measured using various tools. Coupling will be visible in graphical representations of the architecture but can also be measured in relation to individual building blocks (see fig. 10-12 and fig. 10-13).

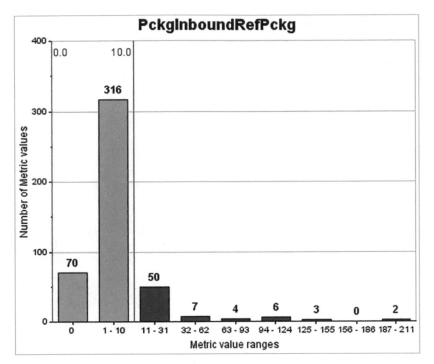

Figure 10-12
Number of inbound
relationships
for a package

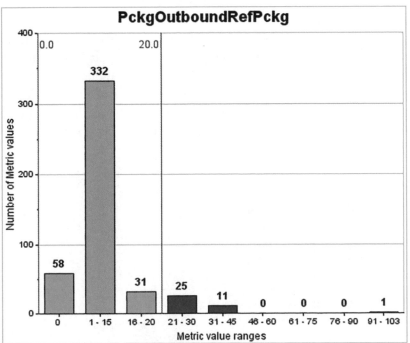

Figure 10-13
Number of outbound
relationships
for a package

Nodes of strong coupling

Building blocks that are used a lot and that in turn use many other building blocks are particularly interesting. These building blocks are involved in many of the system's processes and in many other places too. The same basic approach to metrics also applies here—i.e., you must look at all the conspicuous artifacts. Figure 10-14 shows a typical picture of classes that have strong coupling.

Figure 10-14

Classes with many inbound (dark blue) and outbound (light blue) relationships

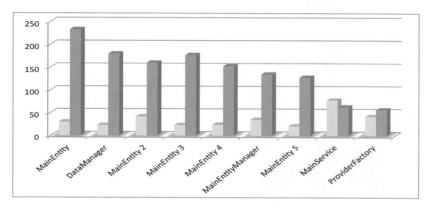

They are the same as the ones found in large classes—i.e., DB/file interface classes, central business objects, services, and central framework superclasses.

Superfluous coupling

However, just knowing that certain system classes have many relationships doesn't really help. We need clues that lead us to the places within the code where coupling is superfluous. A nice indicator for such places is the *Law of Demeter* (LoD) . This design rule says that classes should only be called by the methods of other classes that they know directly. Because the LoD can be formally defined it can be measured using analysis tools.

Figure 10-15

Violation of the Law of Demeter

```
public class A {
    private B b;
    public void testSomething(C c)
    {

        ☑  b.doSomething();
        ☑  c.doSomething();
        ☑  D d = c.getD();
        ☒  d.doSomething();
        ☒  c.getD().doSomething ();
        ☑  c.doSomethingOnD();
    }
}
```

Figure 10-15 depicts class A, which violates the LoD in two places (shown in red). LoD states that class A is allowed to work with all classes that it has as an attribute, that it receives as a parameter, or that it creates itself.

In the first green-highlighted line, A calls methods from class B—i.e., a method of one of its attributes. In the second and third green lines, it calls methods from class C. Since an object from class C is passed as a parameter, this is also OK. The first three lines correspond to the LoD and the corresponding rule: "Only talk to your closest friends".

Just talking to friends

However, as soon as class A starts calling methods on variable d, it is violating the LoD. Class D is not a direct neighbor of class A, so A shouldn't be using it. The LoD is violated here according to the rule: "Don't message your delegate object's objects". Hiding the usage of class D in the second red line doesn't make things any better either.

Leave distant contacts in peace

The correct way to deal with the fact that class A wants to do something to an object of class D is found in the final green line. Here, class A calls a method with the parameter c, which in turn does something with D. This means that A delegates the call to class C. This decouples class A from class D. Strictly speaking, it doesn't know if C modifies the object of class D and, if it does, what it does to it. While designing C, the task would be to name and offer the service doSomethingOnD() so that it is technically meaningful and does not mention D at all. Maybe the implementation of C will be changed sometime and the call doSomethingOnD() will be implemented in a completely different way. This implementation corresponds to another LoD guideline: "If you delegate, delegate fully!"

Delegation reduces coupling

Let us imagine that class D is also implemented in such a way that further classes are attached to it. As usual in object-oriented systems, we have a large network of objects. If we were to allow class A to traverse this object network using getX(), it would have to know all the classes along the way and traversing the object network would create a lot of coupling. By letting its neighbor (class C) modify something about D, class A follows the LoD principle: "Tell, don't ask!"

Avoid traversing object networks

> **Monitoring coupling between building blocks**
>
> Measure coupling regularly. Check the areas of your system where coupling is constantly growing. Let the *Law of Demeter* guide you to the areas in the code that need improvement.

Loose coupling in layers

Most of the systems we see today use diverse coupling between building blocks. In a layered architecture, the upper layers are allowed to use all the underlying layers. Many systems can benefit from this if there is technical and domain-oriented layering. However, from the point of view of loose coupling, this limitation is not sufficient. It is more important to restrict access so that even in the correct layering direction, not every building block can simply use any other building block.

> **Restrict coupling**
>
> Define clear rules that determine which building blocks are not allowed to couple. This will strengthen the cohesion of your building blocks.

Coupling with external source code

In addition to the coupling within an architecture, you have to look at the interface between your own source code and the external libraries and frameworks it uses. How strong is the coupling between your own source code and these external elements?

Figure 10-16 shows our analysis of the external libraries for a Java system. Because neither the source code nor the byte code of the external technology was parsed, external artifact packages are represented as dashed circles. Only the artifacts used in our own source code are shown. The relationships within the external technology are not displayed because we didn't grant the tool access to the appropriate structures.

Logging framework

The most important questions to ask when analyzing external technology are how likely it is the technology used will change, and how much this technology can be trusted. For example, the system shown in figure 10-16 uses SLF4J (Simple Logging Facade for Java). This is an abstraction layer used by various logger libraries and you can safely assume that it will continue to meet logging requirements in the future.

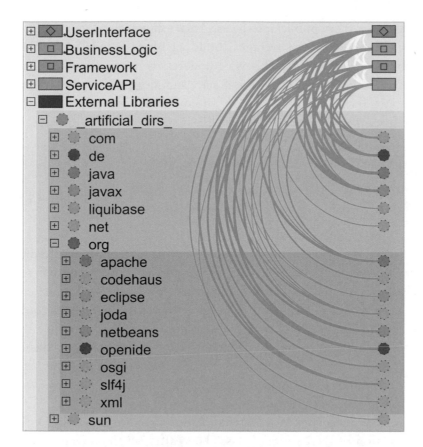

Figure 10-16

Use of external libraries[1]

Technology and/or external libraries and frameworks fulfill completely different roles, accompanied by differing levels of dependency. You will probably be more dependent on a user interface framework than on a logging framework. Even if the logger is used in almost all classes, the dependency is highly consistent and, with some effort, can be replaced with little complication. The user interface framework is (hopefully) only used by the user interface layer, but still represents a high level of dependency. This is because we use a range of very different user interfaces and interact with them. During your analysis, you have to consider the quality as well as the quantity of these links.

User interface frameworks

A reasonable way of dealing with an external library would be to encapsulate it within the building block that uses it. For example, the Hibernate implementations of a DAO should not use Hibernate

Encapsulating external access

---

1   The package node "de" is the typical root node in German software systems.

classes in their public interfaces. This follows the "separation of domain-oriented and technical building blocks" style of architecture (see Section 6.2). This way, updates to newer versions of the external libraries and frameworks are significantly simplified. When using external libraries, you are of course dependent on what the library offers as a public interface.

> **Coupling to external libraries and frameworks**
>
> Select libraries and frameworks according to their functionality and how much coupling you would have to introduce to use them

Implicit coupling   By using the available tools, you can (unfortunately) only determine cases of explicit coupling—i.e., places in the source code where a class uses another class or inherits from one. Implicit coupling cannot be analyzed automatically and is therefore much less convenient. Imagine you are to use a java container class interface that uses an iterator to pass on elements from a list and then display them in a list on the screen. Our initial tests show that the list is sorted alphabetically, which is exactly the kind of behavior we want to see at the user interface.

Some time later, a maintenance developer replaces the implementation of the container class. Thereafter, all the container class methods still work but the list is no longer displayed alphabetically. The maintenance developer was unaware of the container class requirement because the public interface only used the implicit knowledge given by the public interface tests. Unfortunately, this kind of implicit coupling cannot be discovered using tools.

Lazy Loading   Bad implicit coupling occurs if you use lazy loading. If you are
and databases   passed a lazy loaded object you require an active transaction. Without an active transaction the incompletely initialized object graph cannot be processed.

Databases are another form of implicit coupling that we are all familiar with. Over the years we have tried to modularize the software that works on databases, but all parts of our systems require data from one or more databases that are also used by a range of other applications. If you want to reduce coupling, you will have to look into using microservices and decomposing the relevant data sets.

10.6   Coupling and Class Size

Until now we have considered the size of building blocks and the coupling between them separately. Surprisingly, my evaluations have revealed an apparent connection between large classes and strong coupling. I say "apparent" because evaluating only 40 systems doesn't really produce statistically relevant results. These evaluations can therefore only be seen as an indication, even though they show clearly that systems with large classes also show strong coupling between those classes.

Each point in figure 10-17 represents a software system. The Y-axis plots the average number of executable lines of code per class and X-axis the size of the systems involved.

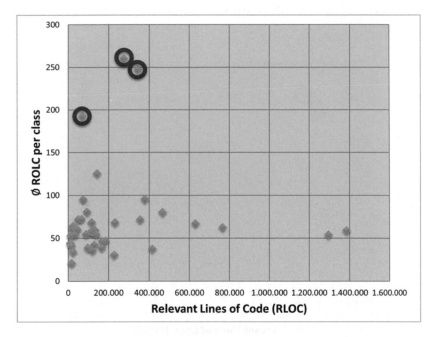

Figure 10-17

Average number of executable lines per class

Figure 10-17 shows that larger software systems do not automatically have bigger classes. On the contrary, the average class size doesn't increase compared to those in smaller systems. The typical size of the classes in the system we investigated was below 100 executable program lines.

Large systems have small classes

Only the three systems marked with a blue circle have larger classes than the other systems. The developers of these systems believed that large classes were not a problem, and that many smaller classes appeared more problematic. Apart from these three exceptions, we can assume that a system's developers have a similar idea of how large classes should really be. In larger software systems, the number of classes should increase while the average class size remains constant.

My guess was that systems with large classes should have fewer relationships per class. After all, classes had been merged and relationships eliminated. Figure 10-18 shows the average number of relationships per class in relation to system size.

Large classes → strong coupling

Like the average class size, there is also a limit for the number of relationships per class in large systems, and the average in most systems is about 11. Again, we found three outliers (indicated by the blue circles). These are the same three systems that already attracted our attention due to their particularly large classes.

Figure 10-18

Average number of relationships per class

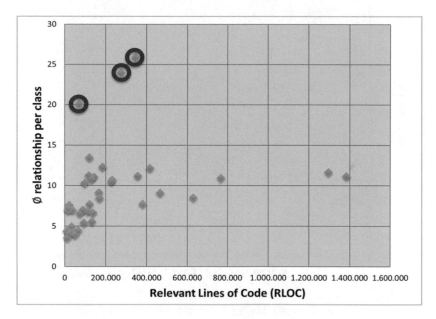

What makes these three systems different from the others? A closer look at the source code reveals that they all contain some very large classes. These large classes control major parts of the processes by calling many classes and passing the results on to other classes. In addition, they provide standard functionality, so they need to be known by many classes. The names of these classes ({*}Manager, for

Procedural design → large classes and strong coupling

example) indicate global responsibilities. In Section 10.1, we already showed that the term "manager" doesn't really help when designing a class with a single task. However, the source code of these manager classes clearly showed that they are not based on object-oriented design at all. The classes all have multiple static methods and pass data on to one another for further processing. This is a clear case of procedural development disguised as object-oriented programming.

Size and coupling can affect each other

Develop classes of comparable size and you will get a system with well-distributed coupling. This is a good first step towards modularity, although there is still a lot of work to do!

10.7 How Modular Are You?

Questions on modularity lead to surprising answers from some development teams. Happily, modularity is the basis for many class designs and the division of a system's building blocks.

One team I met had never heard of modularity, and this became particularly obvious in a discussion on how to resolve a cycle. The developer told me, "To resolve this cycle, I'll remove method X from the class A and move it into class B, then I'll move method Y from class A to class C, and the cycle is gone!" The developer was happy with this approach, while I didn't like it at all. This refactoring effort was completely decoupled from the question of whether or not the shifted methods matched the task of the target class. Although they were using Java, the developers weren't familiar with the basic idea of object orientation. They regarded classes simply as containers for methods, not as coherent units within the system. Please note, however, that this was an isolated case.

Classes are not containers for methods

Teams that design some parts of their systems as services often have a strong focus on modularity. Services should be perceived as units by their own and by other systems. For building blocks like this, the teams attach great importance to the public interface and to consistent design for a given task—i.e., a service.

Services strengthen modularity

> **Building blocks as services**
>
> Strengthen the modularity of your system by viewing its building blocks as services that are used via a public interface. This view will help you concentrate on a block's actual task.

Who doesn't match a pattern?

In systems built using a pattern language, the pattern elements give the development teams direct orientation regarding the responsibility a class should have. Such design rules are an important driver for modularity.

The other classes that aren't based on pattern elements are also interesting. These classes often have low modularity and several simultaneous responsibilities. At the end of the 1990s—a time when relatively few Java frameworks existed—we built our first productive Java-based systems. Back then, we always had a class called "Startup" that was responsible for initializing all the services during system startup and displaying the login window. In some cases, we integrated some of the required system-wide constants, file paths, and database accesses into this class. At first, this seemed the logical thing to do because some services had to be provided with this information at startup. Other classes, such as the user interfaces that were created by different classes later on, were able to retrieve this information from the startup class.

Startup and resources

The result was a startup class that knew many classes during the application launch and that was also queried by many other classes for the information it contained. Startup was usually involved in a large cycle and, from a modularity viewpoint, was tasked with starting up the system and managing resource information. Once we had grasped this architectural challenge, we chose a different design that divided the two tasks into separate classes. The startup class remained, but resource management was outsourced to a separate class.

> **Modularity of classes without patterns**
>
> Pay attention to classes for which no pattern element exists or appears to exist. These classes are usually worth discussing from the point of view of their modularity!

11 Real-World Case Studies

It goes without saying that you can only appreciate the full appeal of an architectural analysis if you examine your own system or at least participate in its examination. Of course, a book is no substitute for experience, but the following case studies should nevertheless give you a good idea of what system analysis is all about.

The companies involved have all given me their consent to publish the following case studies under the proviso that the domain identifiers for their systems are anonymized. The *Epsilon* system is the only exception.

Anonymous case studies

The Modularity Maturity Index (MMI) introduced in Section 4.5 makes it possible to compare the modularity of different systems. Figure 11-1 shows the MMI for the following six case studies.

MMI classification

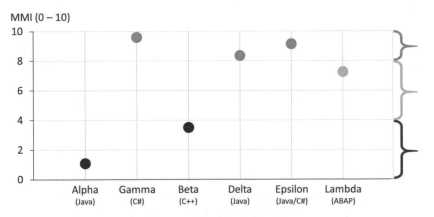

Figure 11-1

MMI for our six case studies

Even with this small number of systems, you can see that neither the size nor the programming language is a decisive factor in determining a system's MMI. It is much more important for the development teams to take modularity, pattern consistency, and hierarchization into account. This can only succeed if the developers and architects who maintain the system during the course of its lifetime undergo appropriate education and additional training.

Following their computer science studies, most developers can build smaller systems that are maintainable for as long as they remain small. Systems written by unexperienced developers are rarely structured in a way that makes them easy to extend, which is why they can't be easily converted into larger systems. It takes time for unexperienced developers to gain the knowledge they need to develop large systems, and this cannot be acquired without practical experience. The learning process is often painful for the developers and the organizations where they make their first attempts to build large systems. Alternatively, unexperienced developers can be assigned to work with an experienced developer/architect, allowing them to learn from their more accomplished colleagues. This phenomenon is clearly evident in the case studies that follow.

11.1 The Java System *Alpha*

The Aachen Company's *Alpha* system was first developed in the 1990s and has been continually developed over the years by various teams. *Alpha* was initially built using a functional programming language but was ported to Java in 1996. It has been used productively since 1993 and is regularly extended to include new functionality. For example, a SOAP interface was added in 2005 and extensive efforts were made to optimize performance in 2007. Additionally, the public interfaces were converted to use new technologies and older public interfaces were replaced.

A million Java LOC

When I analyzed *Alpha* in 2014, the development team had begun to find navigating the project exhausting. *Alpha* now has a million lines of Java code, making it large and quite complex. However, the maintenance team gave the impression that *Alpha*'s complexity could also be attributed to a lack of architecture. In the past, refactoring was repeatedly postponed due to time and budget restrictions. In recent years, more and more work had accumulated and the integration of new functions had become increasingly difficult. In this situation, which was wearying for everyone, management took the initiative and requested an architectural analysis.

Architecture documentation

At the beginning of the analysis, the developers showed me an architectural diagram to explain the system's architecture. Fig-

ure 11-2 shows an overview of the building blocks they used. The
illustration shows a kind of component diagram that includes the
communication technology that was used.

Don't be misled by the appearance of the diagram! The components J, K, L, N, P, and O make up just 12 percent of the system,
although they are displayed alongside M as rectangles of the same
size. The component M alone contains 50 per cent of the source
code, while the client components account for the remaining 38 per
cent. The components J, L, N, and P contain both client and server
elements, which is why they are not assigned to either category in
figure 11-2. The *Alpha* project has separate JARs for J, L, and O,
and the "remainder" of the system (client and server) must be delivered as one unit because the system contains no other separate components. This is a clear case of "uneven modules" (see Section 9.3).

Uneven modules

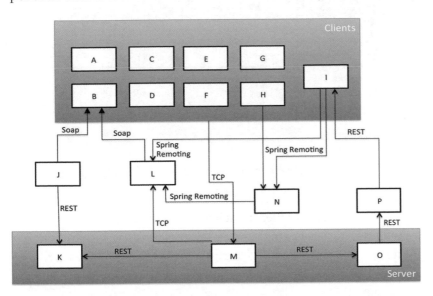

The system's developers and company management didn't like this
state of affairs at all, but it had nevertheless crept in over the years.
At the beginning of the development cycle in the early 1990s there
were few books or courses on software architecture, so awareness
of the subject was correspondingly low in most development teams.
Many of the systems that were developed at this time were built
without architectural concepts, and this is exactly what happened
to *Alpha*. Due to a lack of time and funding, the team was not able

Architecture was not
an issue

to use development and maintenance resources to develop a clear architecture. Note, however, that this is one of the most difficult tasks in maintaining a system (see Section 7.4.4).

Since *Alpha* is not split into projects, we imported it based on its package tree (see fig. 11-3).

Figure 11-3

The Alpha *package tree*

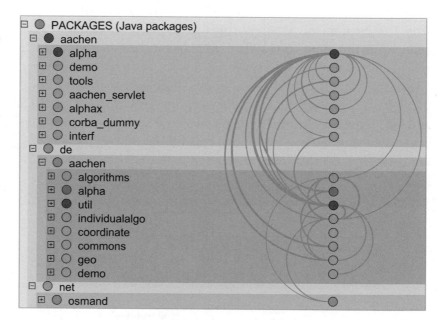

Target architecture ≠
Actual architecture

Three things show clearly that architecture guidelines were missing and that refactoring had not been tackled:

- There are two parallel branches in the package tree (with and without "de" as the first node). The older part of system (without the prefix "de") was never migrated to the new structure. (The package node "de" is the typical root node in German software systems.)

- The architectural ideas associated with figure 11-2 do not exist in the package tree. Even without anonymization, only three component names can be found in the sub-packages.

- In addition to the package node "alpha", which represents the name of the system, there are other nodes on the same level.

If the first investigation of a system's package or project structure reveals a situation like this, you can expect the subsequent architecture modeling to be complex. You will have to comb through the system package by package in order to create meaningful assignments to potential architectural artifacts. To some extent, you will also have to sort the classes into their correct architectural elements.

From an architectural point of view, *Alpha* violates the criterion of pattern consistency (see Section 5.2). The package tree doesn't provide a consistent pattern to help developers navigate the source code. Logically, this pattern is also missing in the architecture analysis.

Lack of pattern consistency

The cycle metrics are another criterion that quickly reveals how laborious the work will be. *Alpha* has 19 per cent classes in cycles, and the largest cycle consists of 370 classes spread over 43 packages. We didn't therefore expect to find a distinct and well-implemented pattern language (see Section 6.5). If a pattern language was used, it is worthwhile to model the patterns first and then use its layering scheme for the development of technical layers. This was not the case for *Alpha*, so we developed six technical layers from the package tree (see fig. 11-4). The class types BusinessObjects and TransferObjects reminded us of a pattern language.

Many classes in cycles

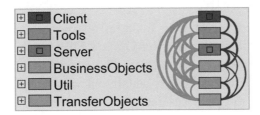

Figure 11-4

Technical layering in Alpha

Developing the technical layering took us one and a half days in total, compared to the half day a system of this size with clear architectural ideas would usually take. The main tasks were discussing the package and class assignments to individual layers, and analyzing the violations. After the initial assignment step, we later moved several classes to other layers while we investigated the violations. During the investigation of the violations we were able to develop and document many refactoring tasks. Figure 11-4 shows the result of our work and our discussions:

Technical layering as a starting point

■ The *Client layer* contains all classes (approx. 400,000 LOC) that form the various user interfaces. This also includes all classes that formulate requests and send them to the server.

- The *Tools layer* consists of various tools (approx. 180,000 LOC) that are only used by the developers and are therefore not part of the public client.

- The *Server layer* contains the system's core (approx. 300,000 LOC)—i.e., all classes that perform complex calculations. In addition, the server layer contains the public interface that the client layer is allowed to use to access it. Relationships in the opposite direction shouldn't exist.

- The *BusinessObjects layer* contains all classes (approx. 58,000 LOC) that represent real processes and values from the domain. These classes follow the J2EE pattern. In addition to the data parts, they can also have logic parts for processing. Business objects can be used by the server, but server access is prohibited for the business objects.

- The *Util layer* provides general functionality (about 53,000 LOC) that is not based on specific data classes. These are functions like the formatting of date objects or similar. The utility layer can be used by the layers above but must not have any dependencies of its own to other layers.

- The *TransferObjects layer* includes all classes (approx. 35,000 LOC) that follow the Transfer Objects J2EE pattern. These classes have the task of sending data back and forth between client and server. Transfer objects usually encapsulate a lot of data in a class and thus reduce communication effort. Typically, these classes do not have any logic parts and should therefore not have or need relationships to higher layers.

Overall, figure 11-4 shows that there are almost always relationships between layers that violate technical layering. Figure 11-4 may give the impression that there are a lot of violations, but the red relationships account for only 1.5 per cent of all relationships, while the other 98.5 per cent are on the correct side of the axis (shown in green).

Layer Violations →
Monolith
The remaining violations in figure 11-4 show why *Alpha* can only exist as a monolith. There are upward relationships between all other layers and the client layer. Two additional factors make a division of the server even more difficult. The first is that most of the transfer objects violate the JEE pattern that states that trans-

fer objects should only carry data. In fact, some of the transfer objects contain logic, and call business objects and other classes on the server. Secondly, access restrictions that some business objects should have been subjected to were ignored, allowing them to access server classes and classes on the Tools layer.

Furthermore, *Alpha* provides a public interface between the server and the client. Server classes that do not belong to the public interface must not be used directly under any circumstances. Figure 11-5 shows the Server layer with the Tools and Client layers that use the server above it. There are three building blocks in the server layer, but two of these shouldn't be used by the client layer, so we modeled them as private (indicated by the small "p"). The red arc on the left in figure 11-5 shows that access from the client layer violates the server public interface. Some of the elements on the Tools layer directly access the Server classes (illustrated by the yellow arc on the left). In contrast to the Client layer, and because the tools are only used internally, the Tools layer is allowed to access the server layer directly.

Public interface between client and server

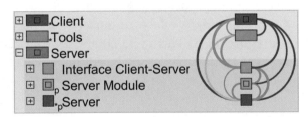

Figure 11-5

Public interface between client and server

One hundred and five classes from the client layer use 56 classes from the private part of the server. Based on this evaluation we developed some refactoring plans to clean up the public interface.

After working on the technical layering and the public interface, we subsequently dealt with splitting the domain. For systems of this size, it makes sense to split the domain in order to obtain independent domain-oriented building blocks. These independent building blocks can, if necessary, then run on their own servers and thus increase scalability. I deliberately did not use the term "microservices" because in order to implement this architectural style, the database would also have to be disassembled. Such a reconstruction is extremely complex for a system of this size and is therefore virtually impossible to achieve.

Domain splitting

Splitting *Alpha*'s domain was about as difficult as the technical layering. This was because we had to work our way through the source code package by package. In the end, we had modeled 26 domain-oriented building blocks and another building block called "Legacy". We were able to develop layering with 4 per cent validation remaining for 26 building blocks. We then defined a series of refactoring tasks that would further reduce the violations in the relationships.

The "Legacy" building block

What surprised me most during this analysis was the "Legacy" building block. As we began our domain-oriented modeling, some developers kept saying things like: "This code doesn't look familiar—does anyone know what it does?" One developer's answer was: "No, I think that's Legacy! That's what we do with the XY functionality in block Z." We collected all these parts of the system and found—to our surprise—that, over time, the developers had classified 13 per cent of the source code as "legacy". The loss of knowledge due to switching between generations of developers, the hope of reuse in the future, and the fear of breaking something led to *Alpha*'s developers never deleting dead code.

Class cycles

At the end of the study, we devoted ourselves to the large class cycle shown in figure 11-6. This cycle comprises 370 classes and covers 43 packages on five of the six layers (all except the Tools layer).

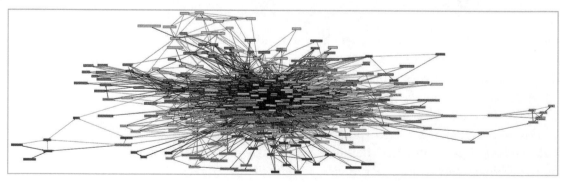

Figure 11-6

Class cycle involving 370 classes in the Alpha *system*

Examination of this class cycle at the technical layers level revealed that that business objects make up a major portion of it (see fig. 11-7).

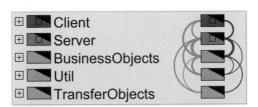

Figure 11-7

The Alpha *class cycle at layer level*

The red arc that connects the BusinessObjects layer to the Server layer represents calls from 47 business object classes to 27 server classes. All the other relationships represent calls between just one or two classes. If this strong relationship between the business objects and the server logic could be resolved, this cycle would be significantly reduced. At the same time, this cycle provides a good starting point for reducing leakage between layers.

Breaking the great class cycle

At the end of the analysis, we had identified the following tasks for improving *Alpha*'s architectural quality:

The next steps

1. Restructure the package tree based on the architecture

2. Repair the public interface between client and server

3. Resolve the large class cycle

4. Reduce the transfer objects and business objects to their original tasks

11.2 The C# System *Gamma*

The Goettingen Company's *Gamma* system was developed in spring 2014 by a four-person team using C#. It replaced an old application programmed in Visual Basic, which was no longer executable on later version of Windows. The legacy application and *Gamma* are designed as rich client applications that run on Windows PCs without a dedicated server component. Data is transferred to and from the central system in separate files, which are then processed on the client computer and imported into the local database.

The goals pursued by the company during the new development were technology change, better software quality, and better

C# replaces VB

usability for the user interface. The legacy application was not easy to maintain due to a lack of technological sustainability and poor internal quality, and the public interface was difficult to use for inexperienced users. In order to preserve the data transfer path from the central system and data import into the local database, the developers were not allowed to change the database structure used by *Gamma*'s predecessor.

25,000 C# LOC

To check the system's internal quality, we analyzed the system for half a day one year after it went live. The analysis was fast because *Gamma* is a small system with around 25,000 LOC. Furthermore, its architecture is in very good condition.

At its first reading, the *Gamma* system appeared highly uniform and well-structured at the namespace and directory levels (see fig. 11-8 and fig. 11-9).

Figure 11-8

Gamma's *namespace structure*

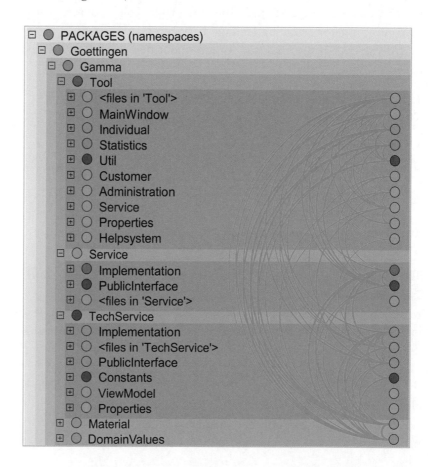

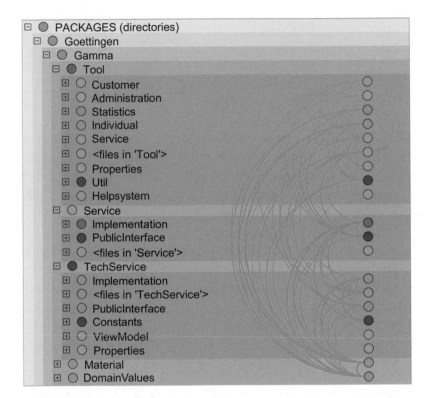

Figure 11-9

Gamma's *directory*

structure

Only one inconsistency can be found between figure 11-8 and figure 11-9. There is an extra namespace MainWindow below the Tool namespace that doesn't exist in the directories. The class that is sorted into the MainWindow namespace is still located directly below Tools in the directories. Since Visual Studio does not synchronize namespaces and directories, such discrepancies are common in C# systems (see Section 3.2). Since the *Gamma* namespaces corresponded exactly to the team's architectural vision, we chose them as the starting point for our architectural modeling.

In the namespace tree, the technical layering can be found in the namespace nodes directly below the Gamma node (see fig. 11-8). This provides confirmation of the development team's quality awareness—the technical layering pattern is precisely reproduced in the source code. In figure 11-8 you can already see that the technical layering shows no violations. We nevertheless created a technical layering view (see fig. 11-10) in order to enable the subsequent interface inspection step (see fig. 11-11).

Technical layering directly

in the tree

Figure 11-10

Technical layering

in Gamma

Below the Service and TechService layers shown in figure 11-8, you can see the PublicInterface and Implementation namespaces. A public interface is surprising in such a small system but can be explained by the developers' desire to prepare for the replacement of the existing database structure.

Public interfaces

in the tree

To model the public interface, we made all the namespaces and the files that lie directly in the Service and TechService namespaces private. In figure 11-11 this is indicated by the small "p" next to the corresponding namespace nodes. The red arcs to the left of the axis in figure 11-11 make it clear that there are interface violations. Classes from the Tool layer directly access classes in the Implementation namespace. In the current implementation, the interfaces of the Service and TechService layers are violated.

Figure 11-11

Interface violations in

Gamma's services

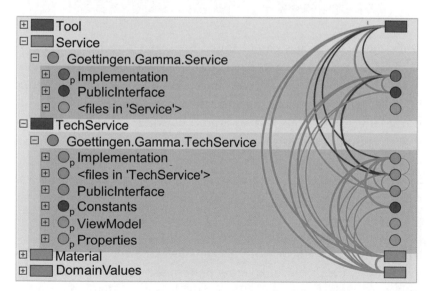

Interface violations

A closer look reveals that almost all violations between the Tool layer and both implementation namespaces are based on one pattern (see fig. 11-12 and fig. 11-13). The App class generates all service

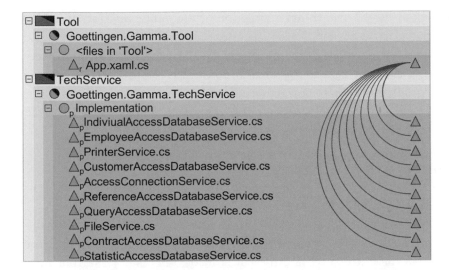

Figure 11-12

Violation of the public interface from Tool to TechService

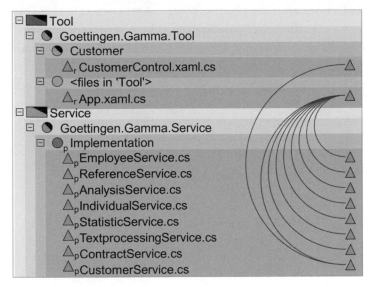

Figure 11-13

Violation of the public interface from Tool to Service

implementations from the Service and TechService layers and registers them with the ServiceRegistry.

Possible corrections for this violation could be:

- Use of dependency injection
- Generation of the service implementations locally on the Service and TechService layers using two factory classes in the public interface between the layers

Figure 11-13 also shows a violation of the public interface in which the class CustomerControl accesses CustomerService directly and does not go through the interface. The CustomerControl mistakenly uses the type CustomerService and not ICustomerService—a simple typo that is easy to correct (see fig. 11-14).

```
public partial class  CustomerControl : UserControl, INotifyPropertyChanged {

    private ICustomerService _service = ServiceRegistry.getServiceInstance(
typeof(CustomerService)) as ICustomerService;

.......
```

Domain-oriented

divisions

Following technical layering, we devoted ourselves to the domain-oriented divisions in *Gamma*. In the namespace tree shown in figure 11-8 there are several namespaces below the Tool node that have domain names (for example, Customer, Administration, Statistics, and so on). In the other namespaces, which represent technical layers, this division does not exist. The modeling of the domain-oriented slices was therefore more complex than the technical layering. We had to assign the classes individually to the domain-oriented slices from the Service, TechService, Material, and DomainValue layers. The result is tidy domain layering with a violation between the Infrastructure and Individual domain slices (see fig. 11-15).

Figure 11-15

Domain-oriented layering

in Gamma

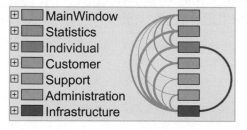

We assigned classes from all the technical namespaces to each of these domain-oriented slices. The individual namespaces are thus distributed over several domain-oriented modules (see fig. 11-16).

Domain-orientation

not in the namespace

structure

This domain-oriented view of the system was new to the developer, so we had a lively discussion about how to distribute the classes to the individual slices. Following the modeling step, the developer decided to introduce domain namespaces throughout the codebase to make this view of the architecture identifiable too.

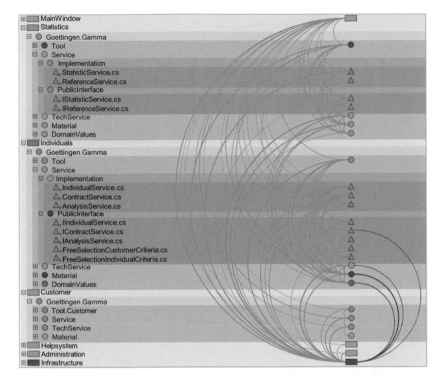

Figure 11-16

Distribution of

namespaces and classes to

the domain-oriented slices

We discussed the violations between the Infrastructure and Individual slices and found that the domain logic was wrongly migrated into the infrastructure. Here, personal data is prepared for file transfer. If the business logic is extracted into a service in the Individual layer, the relationship is reversed. Only the technical parts of the file transfer belong in the Infrastructure layer and should remain there.

For our final view of the architecture, we modeled the pattern language we found in *Gamma*. A part of the pattern language can already be seen in the technical layering shown in figure 11-10. The DomainValue, Material, TechService, and Service layers each contain one type of class from the *Gamma* pattern language, whereas the Tool technical layer contains a number of other patterns. These patterns from the GUI layer are often prescribed by the GUI framework used for development. In figure 11-17 we have made the GUI patterns visible in the sub-layers of the Tool layer.

Pattern language

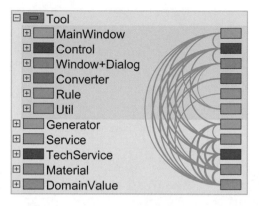

The Tool layer contains the Control, Window, Dialog, Converter, and Rule patterns (see fig. 11-17). There are also a number of utility classes. The classes for the patterns are distributed across the namespaces. If you now look at a pattern language layer, you will find that it contains classes from all the namespaces (see fig. 11-18). We made

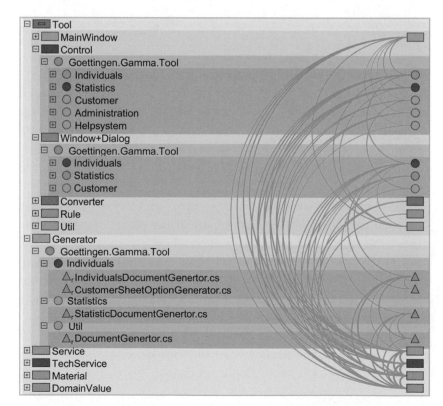

the assignments using regular expressions. For example, we added all classes that follow the **Control.cs pattern to the control layer. In addition, we found a number of classes with the suffix "Generator", which we also combined in a separate layer (see fig. 11-18).

During our discussion about the assignment of the individual classes to the pattern elements, the classes with the Window and Dialog extensions stood out. All classes that have one of these extensions constitute a window on the user interface and offer various interaction options. They all inherit from a .NET framework class called Window. This realization led us to assign all classes with these two extensions to the same pattern element layer (see fig. 11-19).

Repairing the pattern language

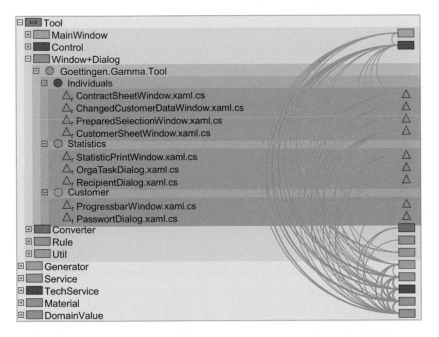

Figure 11-19

Gamma's *"Window+Dialog" classes*

This effect occurs time and again with pattern languages. For certain patterns, the definitions within the team are not always clear (What is a window? What is a dialog?). This leads to the creation of classes with yet more pattern names. Pattern languages can best deploy their guiding power for software system design if the patterns are clearly defined and the number of patterns remains manageable (see Chapter 8). In this case, the definitions for the Window and Dialog patterns were unclear. Following our analysis, the developer renamed all classes with the Dialog extension to Window.

Gamma doesn't have a single class cycle—a rare phenomenon in any software system. In this case, complete freedom from cycles at the class level is enabled by good use of the pattern language.

Gamma is a relatively small system. Nevertheless, our analysis gave the developer valuable hints on the current state of its architecture, and our discussions sharpened some of the existing architectural ideas. We found some minor errors in the source code but were able to define appropriate refactoring. Early investigation of a system is key in any case.

11.3 The C++ System *Beta*

The Bonn Company's *Beta* system has been in development for seven years as a research project involving several universities. *Beta* has passed through the hands of a number of developers, all of whom have added new algorithms for various complex computing procedures. In late 2013, the system's acceptance tests were due, prior to handover to a software development company that had been contracted to carry out system maintenance on the company's behalf. In order to estimate the maintenance effort, the company required an evaluation of the system's architecture.

613.000 C++ LOC

Beta was developed in C++ from the start and contains 613,000 LOC distributed over 1,056 classes in 936 h-files, 800 cpp-files, and 68 directories. The analysis took one day and was accompanied by two developers. The interesting thing about this analysis was that neither developer was one of the fathers of the system. They had only been on the team for three years and most of the system was already established when they started work on it. This allowed us to perform a highly concentrated analysis inside of one day (see Section 2.5).

Very coarse layers

The *Beta* directory tree shows four large layers: main, Application, Solvers, and Framework (see fig. 11-20), and a small number of relationships that contravene the layering model. However, there is no clear layering within the Application and Framework units. Since most systems don't use directories or packages to map layers, further analysis was necessary to reveal whether there was a problem here.

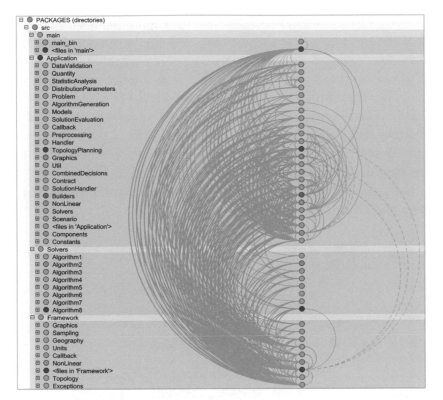

Figure 11-20

The Beta *directory structure*

Figure 11-20 shows a special feature of C++ systems (see Section 3.3). Besides the normal solid arcs representing relationships there are dashed arcs, which are displayed if there is a forward declaration for another class in the file of a class. These relationships are not represented as violations during layer modeling (see fig. 11-21) and are also ignored during the cycle analysis.

For our first model, we adopted the division into the four areas visible in the directory tree, as shown in figure 11-21. These are: main (8,835 LOC), Application (480,313 LOC), Solvers (50,251 LOC), and Framework (73,470 LOC).

Figure 11-21

Layering in Beta

Layer violations   These four building blocks, with their different tasks and the layering between them, were designed this way by the developers. Mapping the directories directly to the architecture is a good decision, as this enables the developers to find their way around more quickly.

The violations between the four layers can be resolved relatively easily. The two violations from Framework to Solvers (fig. 11-21, bottom right) and from Application to main (fig. 11-21, top right) are caused by the use of specific classes whose superclasses should be passed over. Figure 11-22 and figure 11-23 show the sections of the system that cause this violation. In these illustrations, all other files and directories are hidden.

Figure 11-22

Violation from Framework to Solvers

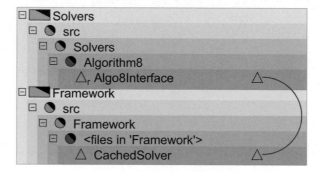

The CachedSolver class from Framework uses a solver class directly. The developers immediately recognized the solution for this violation when they looked into the source code. CachedSolver must go through a specially developed framework class to use the functionality behind Algo8interface.

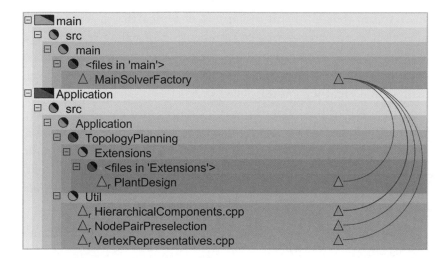

Figure 11-23

Violation from Application to main

The violation shown in figure 11-23 can also be easily resolved. The classes from Util in Application need to use a class from the framework layer instead of the MainSolverFactory from main. The declaration relationships from Framework to Application (see fig. 11-24) can also be removed by inserting and using corresponding abstract base classes in the Framework.

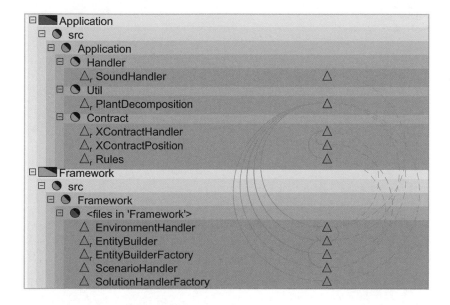

Figure 11-24

Declaration relationships from Framework to Application

Such speedy resolution of violations is typical for a situation in which the team has a strong comprehension of which relationships are allowed and which prohibited. A few violations have crept in overtime but these are easily resolved. The earlier development teams did a great job on this level.

The entire application in one layer

The result of this refactoring is a division of *Beta* into four layers that build on each other. However, if you examine this layering more closely, it becomes clear that the division is not based on the traditional technical layering model of user interface, business logic, and infrastructure (see Section 6.3.1). The structure chosen for *Beta* only separates three parts from the application:

1. Framework is a layer of its own that defines specifications for all areas of the application

2. The solver layer contains algorithms that are used in the application

3. main is used to start the application together with the Framework

Layering in Application and Framework?

Genuine technical layering should be found both in Application (see fig. 11-25) and Framework (see fig. 11-26).

Figure 11-25

Structures in Application

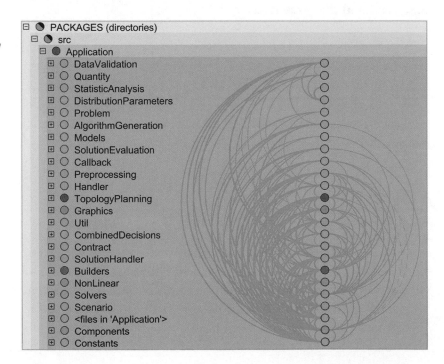

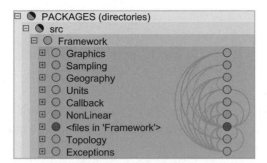

Figure 11-26

Structures in Framework

Figure 11-25 and figure 11-26 do not suggest any technical layering, and the development team didn't have any structures based on the directories in technical layers to hand.

However, during our discussion of the violations between `Framework`, `Solver`, `Application` and `main`, we had already noticed that the system's developers used a number of patterns. The various pattern elements allow technical layering that can only be found in some parts of the directories.

Pattern language as technical layering

Based on these patterns, we divided *Beta* into pattern layers (see fig. 11-27). Overall, we were able to assign 80 per cent of the source code to these patterns, which is a very good value for an initial structuring using patterns. This means that the developers actually live out these patterns and try to use them to build the system. In comparable experiments with other systems, we have usually only succeeded in assigning 50 per cent of the source code to a pattern.

In the course of our modeling, we grouped the patterns into coarse groups of similar patterns such as data processor, data, basis, and so on. This way, we were able to reduce the number of patterns (see fig. 11-27) and develop a proposal for technical layers. *Beta* is a system in which the pattern language can be used as a substitute for technical layering. The division into pattern groups breaks down the patterns into a manageable number that can be converted directly into technical layers.

Pattern groups

Figure 11-27

Layering according

to patterns

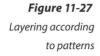

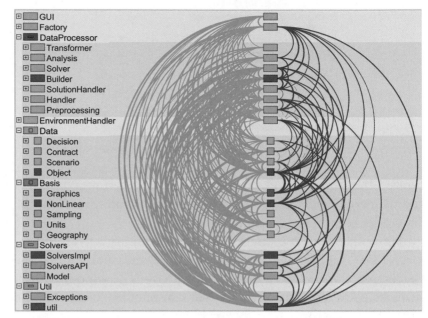

Due to time constraints we were unable to examine the violations between the patterns in detail. The number of correct (green) relationships shown in figure 11-27 clearly exceeds the number of bad (red) relationships. The red arcs make up only four per cent of the total number of relationships shown in figure 11-27. The pattern layering in *Beta* is obviously well executed.

Domain-oriented split
and public interfaces

A system as large as *Beta* should have a domain-oriented split with public interfaces between the building blocks. However, we found neither in the directory tree or the class names. Together with the developers, we modeled a domain-oriented split[1] for the application area. This view of the architecture was new for the developers, so—logically—no good domain-layered partitioning was possible. At this point, the *Beta* development team is facing a lot of work if they want to continue developing their application.

Class cycles

Finally, we looked at *Beta*'s cycles and metrics. At 23 per cent, the number of classes in cycles is high, but there is only one large (115-class) cycle in Application and a bunch of smaller cycles in other parts of the system (these involve 22, 7, 7, 6, 5, 5x4, 12x3,

---

1   We haven't included an illustration here because it is virtually impossible to effectively anonymize the domain-oriented structure of the system

and 17x2 classes). This result is surprising compared to other systems of this size. More than 15 per cent of classes in cycles usually indicates that there is at least one cycle that involves more than 300 classes. *Beta* is an exception. The relatively small number of cycles results from good use of pattern language.

Figure 11-28

The Application class cycle showing its 115 classes

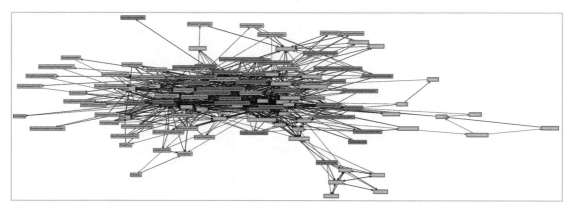

The largest class cycle (see fig. 11-28) is in Application. Since Application contains 78 per cent of the source code, this was to be expected. A cycle of this size cannot be resolved at class level due to the large number of classes involved.

Class cycle in the pattern language

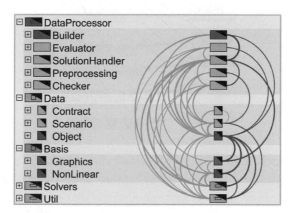

Figure 11-29

The Application class cycle sorted by pattern language

Figure 11-29 shows clearly which relationships should be removed first, namely: the ones between the technical pattern layers. We could define refactoring for the four red relationships between the lower pattern layers and the data processing layer, which would break the large cycle into several smaller, more easily manageable ones.

Class cycle in the framework

The largest cycle in Framework involves 22 classes. This cycle is interesting because only some of the classes are responsible for the coupled structure. In figure 11-30 the problematic relationships responsible for the cycle are marked in blue. The 12 blue and purple classes at the bottom and the three green classes at upper right are only loosely attached to the cycle, and are only involved at all because there is a relationship between the EntityConstraint and Solution classes.

Figure 11-30

Framework class cycle involving 22 classes

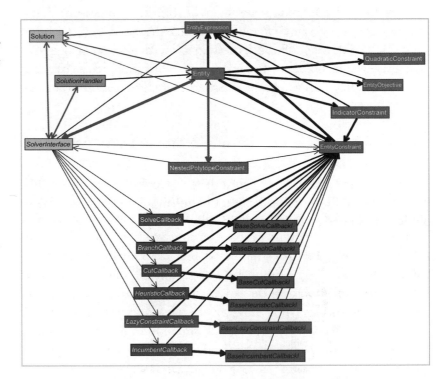

Reducing the cycle

The cycle shown in figure 11-30 will dissolve after a redesign of the collaboration between the Solution, SolutionHandler, Solver-Interface, Entity, EntityConstraint, EntityExpression and Nested-PolytapeConstraint classes. For these classes (see fig. 11-31), the development team must clarify the responsibilities and define which is allowed to use which others.

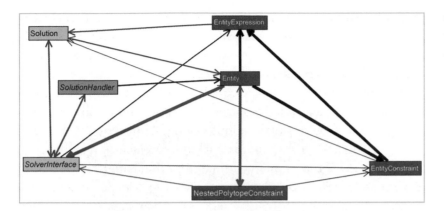

Figure 11-31

Central class cycle
in Framework

The following tasks for improving the architectural quality of *Beta*   *The next steps*
were discussed with the development team:

1. Change the directory structure from `Application` and `Framework` to match the rough pattern language layers

2. Resolve the class cycles in `Application` and `Framework`

3. Analyze and remove the violations between the patterns

4. Examine the remaining 20 per cent of the source code and assign it to existing or new patterns

5. Document the patterns in detail

11.4 The Java System *Delta*

The Dresden Company's *Delta* system was developed in Java at the beginning of the 2000s and has been in use ever since. It is used to calculate seasonal and geographical fluctuations in demand for consumer goods. *Delta* is a client-server application connected to an enterprise service bus (ESB) that enables it to exchange data with other applications. The *Delta* client was originally developed using JFace and the Standard Widget Toolkit (SWT).

At the time of our analysis, *Delta* was being converted into   *486.000 Java LOC*
a web application. The main focus of our analysis was therefore on the server components and the ways they interact with each other and with the client components. *Delta* comprises a total of 486,400 LOC, of which 242,600 belong to the server components and 225,700 to the legacy client.

Directory tree as a basis   At the start of our analysis we parsed the system using the package tree and obtained the following result:

Figure 11-32

The Delta *package tree*

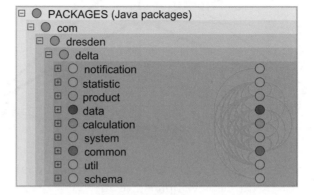

The system's developers were flummoxed by the representation of their system shown in figure 11-32. They had divided their system into several Eclipse projects and only ever considered the system's architecture at this level. In order to model *Delta*'s architecture based on the team's view we converted our analysis to mirror the structure in the directory tree.

Figure 11-33

The Delta *directory tree*

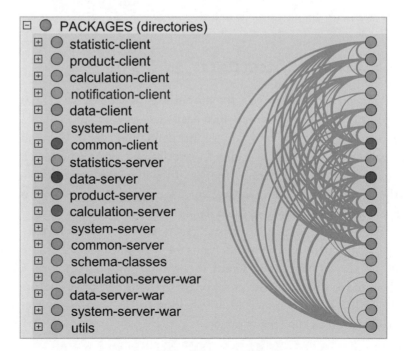

Figure 11-33 shows *Delta*'s structure with its various client and server projects as well as some domain-oriented divisions. The individual directories contain parts of the package trees, each of which begins with com.dresden.delta. Figure 11-33 shows that the development team already attaches importance to a layered architecture. This is a hierarchical tree without any cycles, and the client projects are all arranged above the server projects. The development team uses Maven to ensure that there are no cycles at this level. Using this basis, it was very easy to create a technical layer model (see fig. 11-34).

Good technical layering

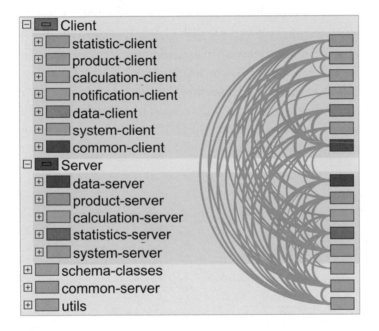

Figure 11-34

Delta's *technical layering*

Next, we examined the system's domain layering. In contrast to the technical layer model, the developers have not yet tested this view of their system using technology. Figure 11-35 and figure 11-36 illustrate the domain-oriented split—first in the server alone and then together with the client and server parts.

Domain-oriented slices

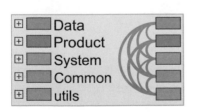

Figure 11-35 (left)

Domain-oriented layering in the Delta *server*

Figure 11-36 (right)

Domain-oriented layering with client and server

Different splits in client
and server

A comparison of figure 11-35 and figure 11-36 shows that by adding the client projects, several relationships become visible that contravene the planned server layering. These violations have two causes, which can be easily identified in figure 11-37.

1. On the one hand, figure 11-37 shows that various business clients, such as stammdaten-client (client master data) and auswertung-client (client evaluation), need services from stammdaten-server (master data server). These relationships are based on the requirements of the users for the development of the different clients. The individual clients in the *Delta* system require functionality from all server subsystems in order to perform their technical tasks.

2. On the other hand, common-client requires services from almost all other server projects. These relationships indicate that the public interface between Common and the server projects is technically successful, but not yet fully developed in a domain-oriented sense. Here, we need to check whether parts of the server functionalities required by common-client should be migrated to common-server.

Figure 11-37

Domain-oriented layering
with contained projects

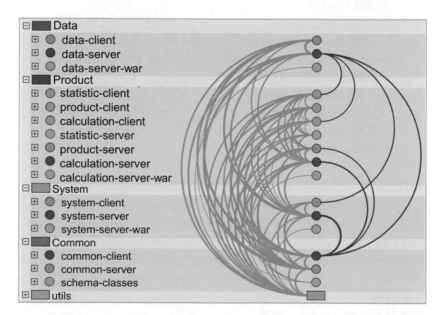

Since the clients are currently being redeveloped as web frontends and their layout will also change, we refrained from performing a detailed investigation of the violations at this point. Uniform domain-oriented layering in the server and client source code would reduce coupling in the system and should be considered during the new implementation as a web frontend.

During our discussions on the technical and domain-oriented layers, it became clear that the system already contained a number of patterns that allow further structuring of the source code. With the help of these patterns we were able to classify *Delta* using a pattern language (see fig. 11-38).

Pattern language

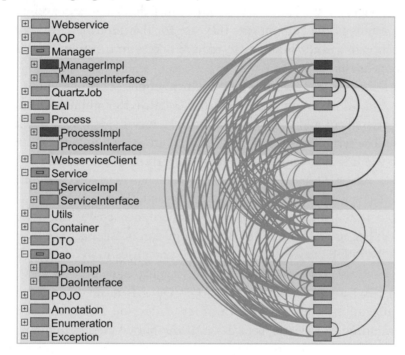

Figure 11-38

The Delta *Pattern language*

Altogether we were able to assign 80 per cent of the source code to these pattern layers which, as already mentioned in Section 11.3, is a very good value for an initial structure based on patterns.

Although the system's architecture has never been verified on the basis of these patterns, figure 11-38 shows surprisingly few red arcs. We were able to discuss and resolve all the violations during our discussions. In particular, the understanding of the "Manager" pattern was improved in contrast to "Service" and "Process".

Delta has a reasonable total of 16 patterns in its server-side source code. The use of patterns limits the design space and reduces design complexity, although too many patterns can lead to increased complexity and fuzziness in the design. We recommended that no additional patterns are built into the server-side source code during further development, and that the tasks and relationships within the existing patterns are clearly defined and used stringently.

In figure 11-38, the "p" next to the `ManagerImpl`, `ProcessImpl`, `ServiceImpl`, and `DaoImpl` layers indicates that we have also examined the system for public interfaces. Systems require public interfaces to create abstractions between components on which the other components can build. Other components don't need to know all the details of the components they use for the implementation of a functionality, and should only require access to a public interface that is as thin as possible.

Public interfaces

Delta has reached a size at which public interfaces need to develop slowly within the system. Usually, the public interface between client and server is written first, and this is true in *Delta*'s case. The system is divided into public interface and implementation areas below the Webservice, Manager, Process, Service, and DAO (Data Access Object) patterns. The client has access to the public interfaces while the implementation doesn't. This rule is correctly implemented throughout *Delta*, and there are separate nodes for the public interfaces and the implementation in the package tree.

Overall, however, the client source code uses more classes than the interface classes from the Web service, manager, process, service, and DAO areas. For example, DTOs (Data Transfer Objects) and Enumerations are also used. In order to develop *Delta* further we recommended a clear specification of the public interfaces between client/server and the individual domain-oriented modules, and making these visible in the structure of the system.

Class cycles

When we talked about class cycles at the end of the analysis, *Delta*'s developers made it clear that they look at cycles just as critically as we do. The only cycles they allow are between POJOs[2] and DTOs. *Delta*'s POJOs directly map the tables in the relational database and the developers have transferred the bidirectional relationships from the database directly into their POJOs and DTOs.

---

2 The acronym POJO stands for Plain Old Java Object and was coined by Martin Fowler. POJOs are classes developed purely in Java that do not contain any extra technology the way EJBs (Enterprise JavaBeans) do. In some cases, business objects and value objects are called POJOs if they are technology-free.

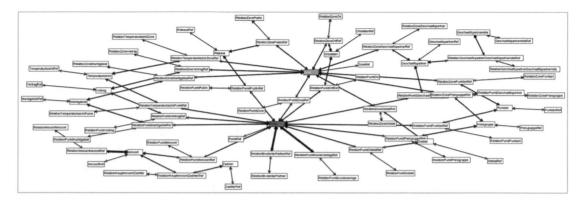

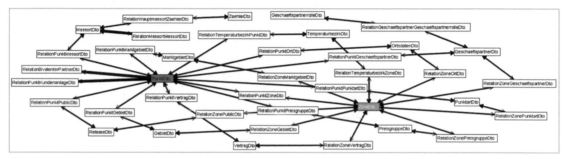

Figure 11-39 and figure 11-40 show *Delta*'s two class cycles. Seventy-eight POJO classes and 39 DTO classes in master data servers are each collected around two classes (shown in orange and green). These two classes are the system's business core classes, so their central position is not surprising. All relationships in these class cycles are bidirectional, as declared by the developers. The class cycles in the business objects (POJOs and DTOs) are independent of the rest of the system, just as we suggested in Section 9.1.1. Even if a cycle-free design for business objects is desirable in principle, it is irresponsible to rebuild the business core of a system just to avoid cycles.

Overall, *Delta*'s developers have done a good job and the amount of necessary refactoring is small:

1. Resolve the remaining violations in the pattern language

2. Assign the remaining 20 per cent of the source code to the pattern language

3. Rethink domain layering when re-implementing clients

Figure 11-39 (above)
POJO class cycle in the
master data server

Figure 11-40 (below)
DTO class cycle in the
master data server

The next steps

11.5 The Java System *Epsilon* (with C# Satellites)

246.000 Java LOC

The Essen Company's *Epsilon* system has been in development since 2009 and consists of a platform programmed in Java and several C# satellites. For this case study, we analyzed the Java platform and two of the satellites. The (larger) Java part of the system (246,000 LOC with 3,370 classes) has been in productive use since 2010. Java-*Epsilon* offers a range of services that combine various geographical maps with geographical motion data. In addition, Java-*Epsilon* contains several Java clients for desktop computers and a Java client for a video wall in a control station. The system's development is handled by a team of four people.

14.000 C# LOC

The two C# parts o the system we analyzed (10,000 and 4,000 LOC) allow working with cards on touch devices and are based on Java-*Epsilon* services. C#-*Epsilon* 1 and 2 communicate with the Java-*Epsilon* services via a REST interface using JSON. C#-*Epsilon* 1 and 2 went into production in summer 2015 and were each developed by two or three people. For the purposes of our analysis we considered the three systems separately.

11.5.1 Java-*Epsilon*

Domain-oriented components in a deployment structure

At its highest level, Java-*Epsilon* consists of three deployment components: client, server, and common (see fig. 11-41). Server and common together form the platform that Java-*Epsilon* offers to the outside world. The system's own clients and the two C# satellites we looked at are based on this platform. The three main components are subdivided into further subcomponents. The server consists of 15 Maven artifacts, common has 13 Eclipse projects, and the client contains another 39 Eclipse projects. For the sake of clarity, the client node shown in figure 11-41 is collapsed. Asked about *Epsilon*'s architecture, the developers referred to precisely this structure, bearing witness to an excellent match between the architecture and the project structure. The architecture's rules stipulate that server and client may only communicate with each other via the common layer, although server, client, and common contain domain-oriented components that build on each other without cycles.

In order to make this architecture information visible, we analyzed the system using the artifact/project structure rather than the
Java packages. Figure 11-41 shows that the two architecture specifications for Java-*Epsilon* have already been implemented, with both
the client and server parts working only in the common area. Client
and server do not know each other directly. Furthermore, there are
no cycles between the domain-oriented components.

Cycle-free, domain-oriented components

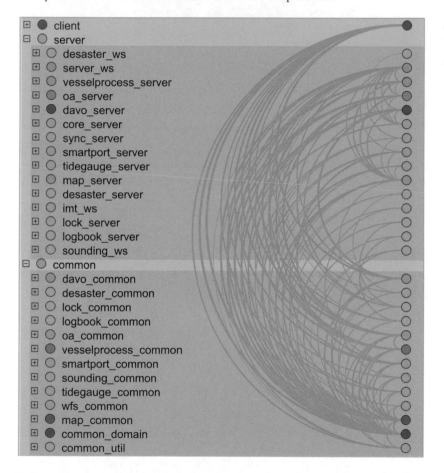

Figure 11-41

The Java-Epsilon component structure

Below the domain-oriented components there is a package tree that
has lost some clarity. In figure 11-42 you can see that the company
name has changed over the years and that both the old and new
names still exist in parallel within the package tree. The development team has not yet renamed all packages to reflect the new company name because this would mean that all applications based on

Violation of pattern consistency

the Java-*Epsilon* web services would have to be checked. However, the team considers this effort to be manageable (a maximum of two person-days), so renaming is scheduled.

Figure 11-42

A section of the Java-Epsilon package tree[3]

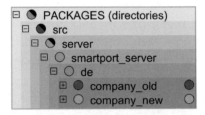

Layered domain   In addition to its successful client-server separation and cycle-free components, Java-*Epsilon* is also remarkable in that the second structure level is formed directly by domain-oriented components. In many systems you will find a mixture of domain and technology-based components on this level. In order to check how the domain name is distributed between client, server, and common, we began by modeling a division into domain-oriented slices (see Section 6.3.2).

Figure 11-43

Domain-oriented layering for Java-Epsilon

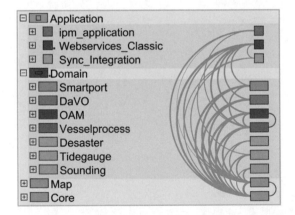

Figure 11-43 shows that the domain-oriented split has been well implemented. We modeled Application as the top layer. Here you can see the brackets for three different uses of the platform: as a desktop application, as web services, and for synchronization between various external services. Below Application is the application's actual business core. This Domain layer contains seven layers, each of which provides a specific domain name. Each of these

---

3 The package node "de" is the typical root node in German software systems.

layers contains client as well as server and common projects. Some of the Domain layers contain more than one of the domain-oriented project shown in figure 11-41. Finally, below the Domain layer there are two domain-oriented base layers, Core and Map. Core provides technical base classes, while Map contains technical base classes for the representation and use of maps.

Violations can be found in two places in figure 11-43: Core accesses Map in contravention of the layering, and Vesselprocess uses functionality from OAM. The violation between Core and Map can be resolved easily. Figure 11-44 shows that classes from Core-client need the class ServiceException (indicated by the red arc). The part of the system shown in figure 11-44 is filtered so that all classes and relationships that use ServiceException are displayed (indicated by the green arcs).

Violations of the domain-oriented layering

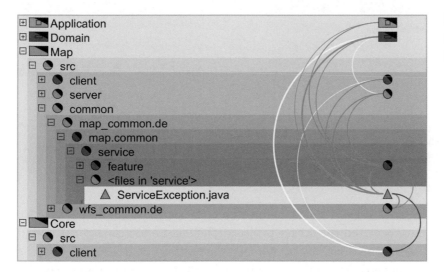

Figure 11-44

Violation from Core to Map

If you look at the relationships shown in figure 11-44, you can see that ServiceException actually belongs in the Core layer and can be moved there without causing any issues. Such a violation, where one or more exception classes are located in the wrong place, is a typical phenomenon in an initial analysis. The exception class was built and stored together with the classes with which it was originally developed. As the system architecture grows and more classes use the exception, the more such exception classes and auxiliary classes with constants and auxiliary methods have to move downward in the layer model.

The second upward relationship between Vesselprocess and OAM is more difficult to resolve than the violation between Core and Map. The class BerthBlockadeSyncService from Vesselprocess uses several other classes from the OAM layer (see fig. 11-45). In principle, BerthBlockadeSyncService could be moved to the OAM layer, although technically speaking it belongs more to Vesselprocess. Here, the development team has to discuss the design of the classes involved in order to find a solution.

Figure 11-45

Violation between

Vesselprocess and OAM

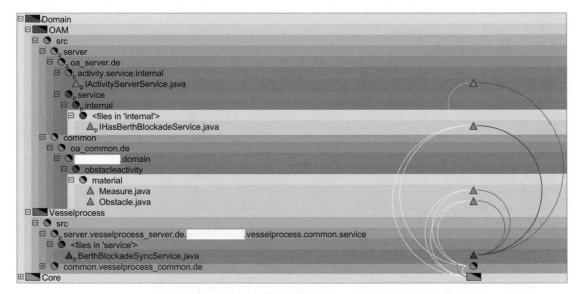

Public interfaces

of the domains

In figure 11-45, the "p" subscript (for "private") indicates that we have declared the server projects (packages and classes) as internal projects of their layers. We introduced this rule to ensure that the server projects only work with each other via common projects and do not call each other directly.

If we look back at figure 11-43, we can see that only three of the domain-oriented layers—Smartport, OAM, and Vesselprocess—have relationships to each other. The other four layers—DaVO, Desaster, Tidegauge, and Sounding—are independent of each other and do not call each other at all.

Smartport, OAM, and Vesselprocess use each other, so a model that prohibits access to the server projects from outside would reveal violations. Figure 11-46 shows Smartport and OAM's relationship to Vesselprocess. Apart from the violation we just investigated in figure 11-45, you can see that the developers followed the "private server projects" rule. Relationships from Smartport only go from the client project to the common and client projects in Vessel-process. So Smartport is independent on the server platform level. OAM and Vesselprocess, on the other hand, work more closely but do not violate the "private server" rule. In addition to the OAM-client relationships, there are other relationships between OAM-server and OAM–common to the common project in Vesselprocess.

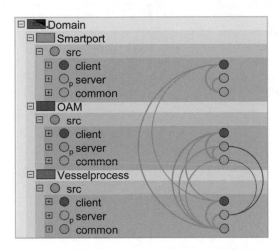

Figure 11-46

Cooperation between the domain layers

Next, we examined the technical layering below the separation of client, common and server. The package tree contains isolated nodes that are relevant to the technical layering. For example, there are packages with the names view, command, and tool, although most of the packages have domain-oriented names anyway. Java-*Epsilon* nevertheless has identifiable technical layering that is reflected in its pattern language.

Pattern language as technical layering

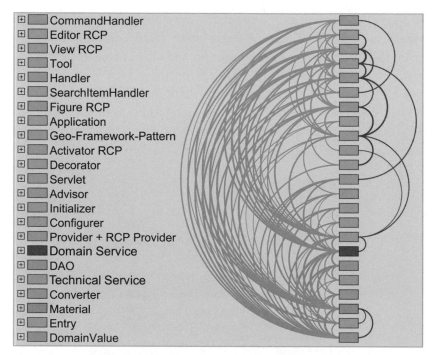

During our analysis, 80 per cent of the source code could be assigned to patterns[4], and violations of the pattern language account for only two per cent of all the relationships shown in figure 11-47. In my experience, such high values can only be achieved by a development team that is fully aware of its patterns and that lives and breathes them when programming.

Violations in the pattern

language

Our discussions enabled us to solve some of the pattern language violations. Some classes had ended up in the wrong pattern layer due to incorrect naming and, in some cases, classes from a pattern layer unintentionally used a parent pattern. For these cases we were able to define simple refactoring. We concentrated on the relatively few violations in the server and common parts of the system, as these need to be of particularly high quality to serve as a platform for further systems.

---

4   In figure 11-47 we have hidden four patterns—Extension, Factory, Adapter and Listener—that are perpendicular to the hierarchical patterns. These patterns are designed so that they can be used by all other patterns and can in turn have relationships to classes from the other patterns.

Some violations in the pattern language show effects that are typical for the use of frameworks:

Typical violations of the pattern language

- *Pattern doubling:* The Java-Epsilon development team's pattern language contains a "Domain Service" pattern, while various frameworks use the "Provider" pattern. During our discussions, we were unable to identify a real difference between these two patterns. Such pattern duplication reduces the clarity and simplicity of the architecture and should therefore be avoided. Since Java-Epsilon contains 537 domain services but only 46 providers, the Provider pattern should be omitted. The classes inherited from a framework provider should be called services.

- *Multiple use of a pattern name:* In figure 11-47 you can see three layers that all have the word "Handler" in their names ("CommandHandler", "SearchItemHandler", and "Handler"). The handler layer contains all classes that we could not identify by name as special handlers. In order to clarify the tasks and rules relating to the use of handler classes, the development team needs to examine the handler patterns and verify their usage.

- *Framework-based pattern variants:* When implementing tools for the clients, the development team used different user interface designs over the years. These variants are reflected in the Editor RCP, View RCP, Tool, Handler, and Figure RCP layers. The various Java-Epsilon clients were built using Eclipse RCP, and the development team chose the appropriate variant for each specific application context. To improve maintainability, it would make sense in the long run to consolidate these variants.

After analyzing the domain-oriented and technical layering, we evaluated the number and complexity of Java-*Epsilon*'s class cycles. The system has only one per cent classes in cycles. This is a great value for a system of this size. The 35 classes involved in cycles are divided into three triple cycles and 13 double cycles. In figure 11-48, the colors show that two of these cycles are located locally in a package. Only the uppermost triple cycle extends over two packages. The tasks of these classes must be discussed, and the team needs to either resolve or at least document them.

Minimum class cycles

Figure 11-48

Three-class cycles in Java-

Epsilon

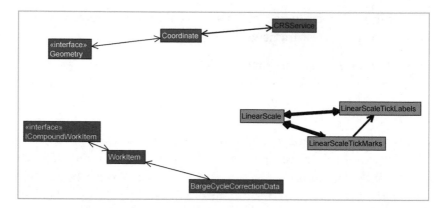

Next Steps To conclude our analysis, we prioritized the measures we had identified, starting with the least costly:

1. Resolve the violations between Core and Map

2. Resolve the violations between Vesselprocess and OAM at server platform level

3. Standardize the package tree to reflect the new company name

4. Unify the Provider and Domain Service patterns

5. Fix the remaining pattern language violations in the server and common parts

6. Analyze the triple cycles and resolve them if necessary

7. Check the different handler variants for uniform use of patterns

8. Analyze the client construction pattern variants

9. Examine the remaining 20 per cent of the source code that could not be sorted into the pattern language.

11.5.2 C#-Epsilon 1

This part of the system was developed as a prototype for a feasibility study and was expanded to create a production-ready system by September 2015. To make sure that the previously developed prototype classes have good architecture, the development team invested three hours investigating C#-*Epsilon 1* with me. Following input, the namespace tree of C#-*Epsilon 1* appeared as shown in figure 11-49.

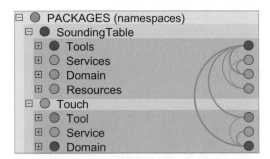

Figure 11-49

The C#-Epsilon 1

namespace tree

The namespace structure of C#-*Epsilon 1* clearly shows the technical layering. Its two-part structure consists of the SoundingTable application and the Touch framework but also shows the layered structures Tools, Services, Domain and Resources (sic) below these nodes. It is interesting to note that the developers named the framework namespaces in the singular—i.e., Tool, Service–while in the SoundingTable application, the corresponding namespaces are named in the plural. Such singular/plural variants occur time and again but can usually be quickly unified.

Technical layering

in the namespaces

Although the namespace tree is layered, the development team had other ideas for the architectural rules for the technical layers. To express these rules, we modeled the technical layering, and figure 11-50 shows the architecture as planned by the team. The same structure is reflected below the SoundingTable application and the Touch framework, with two components (Tool and Service) that must not know each other, and the underlying layers, which Tool and Service can access. Figure 11-50 shows a violation of the planned architecture in SoundingTable's Tool component, indicated by the red arc to Services.

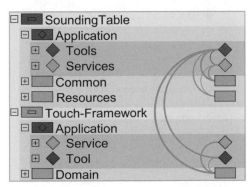

Figure 11-50

Technical layering

in C#-Epsilon 1

This violation is caused by the `ServiceLocator` class, which requires the `StartUp` class (see fig. 11-51). This incorrect reference can easily be resolved because `StartUp` has no further references in the Services part of the system. We therefore moved the `StartUp` class to `Tools`.

Figure 11-51

Violation Between Tools and Services in Application

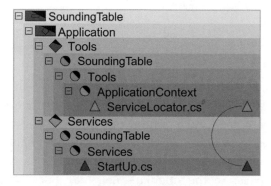

Domain-oriented layering

The domain namespaces are located below the technical namespace nodes. The development team's domain-oriented architectural concept is reflected in figure 11-52. There are two layers above the touch framework that provide basic domain-oriented services. The `Workplace` layer contains functionality for the touch device workstation and, building on this, the `Map` layer lays the foundations for working with maps. In the layer above, various smaller applications are available that work on the maps. The development team was pleased to see that they had built largely independent applications. Only the relationship between `Tide` and `Depth` violated this principle. In addition, there was a relationship between `Workplace` and `Export`.

Figure 11-52

Domain-oriented split in C#-Epsilon 1

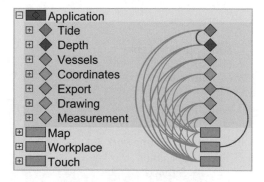

We examined the two five-class violations shown in figure 11-52 together. One of the developers immediately said, "Yes, exactly! We have always felt uncomfortable with these classes! They don't have a good design." In both cases, the development team decided to rethink the design of the classes involved.

Finally, we focused on the pattern language, which is well implemented in C#-*Epsilon 1*. There is an adequate number of patterns for the system's size and they are well hierarchized (see fig. 11-53). The violations in the pattern language are caused by five classes. These violations were immediately obvious to the development team and a lively discussion arose on how to solve them. The decisive question at the pattern level is not so much whether the basic design of the class, (i.e., its tasks) is correctly assigned, but much more whether the class is really appropriate to the pattern. How and why does this class violate the rules of the pattern type to which it is assigned?

Pattern language

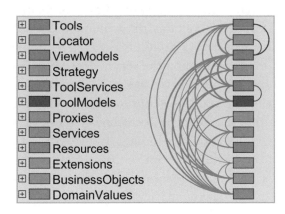

Figure 11-53

Pattern language

in C#-Epsilon 1

C#-*Epsilon 1* doesn't have a single class cycle—a rare phenomenon in today's software systems. In my opinion, the freedom from cycles at class level results from good use of pattern language.

C#-*Epsilon 1* is a relatively small system, but our analysis nevertheless gave the development team valuable hints on the current state of its architecture, and the discussions we had sharpened some of their architectural ideas. We also found some minor bugs in the source code and defined appropriate refactoring. As so often, an early investigation into the state of a system is always to be recommended.

11.5.3 C#-Epsilon 2

Like C#-*Epsilon 1*, the second C# part of *Epsilon* was developed as a prototype for a feasibility study and was expanded into a production-ready system by October 2015. Since C#-*Epsilon 2* is very small (4,000 LOC), two hours were sufficient to check the system's architecture. The parsed namespace tree is shown in figure 11-54.

Figure 11-54

The C#-Epsilon namespace tree

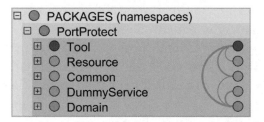

Technical layering in the namespaces

The namespace structure of C#-Epsilon 2 is technically layered using layers that result relatively automatically (see fig. 11-55). The layer name "TechnicalAdapter" embodies a fascinating part of our analysis, as this layer contains the Common namespace. In most rich-client architectures, Common is reserved as a container for the classes used by the client and the server. This layer ensures that the deployment of client and server has to be combined with the Common artifact. However, in C#-*Epsilon 2*, the Common node contains classes that are adapters to technical frameworks (Windows Presentation Foundation and a card framework). The developers told me that the name was born out of necessity. They simply had no other idea for how to separate these classes. Together we came up with the name TechnicalAdapter.

From an architectural point of view, this separation of the technical and domain-oriented classes is a very good idea (see Section 6.2). Making this separation pattern visible in the namespace tree is the icing on the cake when it comes to producing complete pattern consistency.

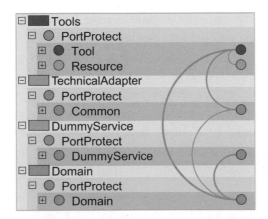

Figure 11-55

Technical layering

in C#-Epsilon 2

In order to refine the technical layering of C#-*Epsilon 2*, we then modeled the pattern language (see fig. 11-56).

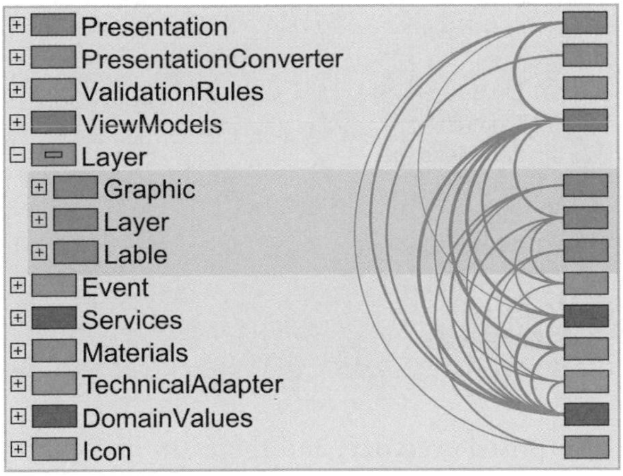

A T&M pattern language

Figure 11-56

C#-Epsilon 2's *pattern*

language

Since this pattern language is a T&M architecture (see Section 6.6.1), the major pattern elements DomainValues, Materials, and Services were easy to identify.

And then things got really exciting. I knew for certain from past C# analysis that we would find Converters and ViewModels, and the other pattern layers emerged later during our discussions. It quickly became clear that not all team members knew all the different patterns, so we were here able to significantly increase the team's understanding of the patterns. Overall, the pattern language in C#-*Epsilon 2* is well implemented using a reasonable number of patterns.

A first domain-oriented

layering

Finally, we turned to the domain-oriented architecture of *C#-Epsilon 2*. We found no domain-oriented architectural structures originating from the system's own namespaces, which is no surprise for such a small project. Nevertheless, the team had a concept involving four domain-oriented slices that were meant to build on each other. We modeled these four layers and assigned the classes manually to each layer. Figure 11-57 shows that parts of the namespaces have ended up in almost all the domain-oriented layers. Only the bottom layer contains classes from only the Tool namespace.

Figure 11-57

Domain-oriented layering

in C#-Epsilon 2

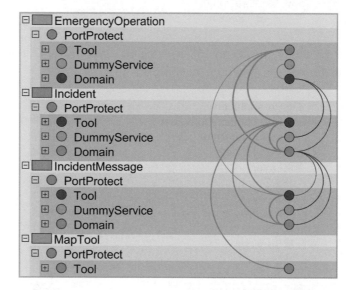

This result surprised everyone, and the team had expected a much fuzzier structure. Figure 11-57 shows that basic domain-oriented layering exists with only a few violations. These turned out to be caused by just two classes! This is a great result for an initial examination based on technical criteria.

Violation of the domain

In both cases the pattern is the same (see fig. 11-58 and fig. 11-59): a class (`IncidentId` and `IncidentMessageId`) that represents an ID for a material (business object) knows the ID of its parent (`EmergencyOperationId` and `IncidentId`), which is also a material (business object).

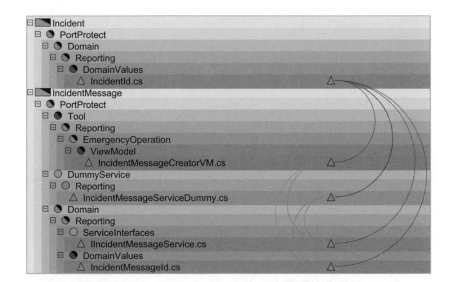

Figure 11-58

Violation involving

IncidentId

Due to these relationships, other classes from the corresponding domain-oriented layers are also dependent on the ID in the layer above. The longer-serving members of the development team saw the violation and immediately told me, "Yes, we've thought about whether that's a good idea before " and, "I think there was a reason, but I don't remember it anymore". Moments like this, when you realize you haven't documented important architectural decisions, are always frustrating. At this point, the team decided to either find the reason or remove the relationship direction. For the case that the reason was found, the team was ready to create documentation for the architectural decision involved.

Such a modification would significantly increase the testability of the individual domain layers. You could then test `IncidentMes`-`sages` independently of `Incident` and `EmergencyOperation`. `Incident` can only be tested together with `IncidentMessages` without having to include `EmergencyOperation`.

Figure 11-59

Violations involving

EmergencyOperationId

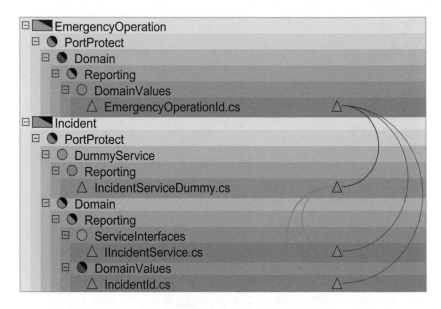

Like C#-Epsilon 1, C#-Epsilon 2 has no class cycles.

Like C#-Epsilon 1,

C#-Epsilon 2 has no class

cycles.

C#-*Epsilon 2* is a very small system. Our analysis was nevertheless valuable to the development team. We not only helped to sharpen the team's architectural vision and improve it for the future, we also helped a new member of the team gain insight into the patterns and structures in the source code much faster than would otherwise have been possible.

11.6 The ABAP system *Lambda*

The Luebeck Company's ABAP *Lambda* system is designed to administer insurance products. *Lambda*'s development began in 2002 as a replacement for a legacy system written in PL/1. *Lambda* has been in production since 2004 and has since been expanded and maintained by a team of 10 developers. To begin with, *Lambda* was developed using common ABAP artifacts (reports, function groups, and so on). Since 2011, the system's developers and architects have made great efforts to use the object-oriented capabilities of ABAP and build all additional functionality using classes and interfaces.

4 million ABAP LOC

Lambda today comprises a code base of 4 million LOC with 10,300 ABAP artifacts. Although ABAP requires more source code than Java, C#, or C++ to produce comparable functionality, *Lambda* is still a large system (>1 million LOC) according to common standards.

For a long time, the company's development team took particular care to produce high-quality source code. As an example, it uses the SAP Code Inspector—an integrated SAP tool that can be used to check source code artifacts for performance, security, syntax, and compliance with naming conventions. The tool can also produce statistical information about relationships or search for specific ABAP words (tokens) and, as a result, generate information, warnings, and error messages about various properties of the artifacts being inspected. In order to make the architecture visible and verifiable, the company began analyzing *Lambda* automatically every night using Sotograph. The initial architectural modeling was carried out together with *Lambda*'s architects.

As described in Section 3.4, ABAP has some unique features compared to the other object-oriented programming languages considered here. These include global namespaces, various non-object-oriented artifacts besides classes and interfaces, an integrated database, and integrated SAP functionality. In spite of these differences, you can nevertheless analyze the structures in ABAP systems in a similar way to those in Java, C#, or C++ systems.

Loading *Lambda* into Sotograph gave us the structure shown in figure 11-60. It shows the different packets that make up the system's base layer. These packets are domain-oriented building blocks, which contain sub-packets that in turn contain SAP artifacts. At the bottom of figure 11-60 you can see the "EXTERNAL_LIBRARY" node, which is where all the SAP artifacts that *Lambda* uses are mapped. These artifacts are not included in the 4 million LOC we counted, and are instead identified as virtual artifacts from the existing ABAP code.

Domain-oriented partitioning in the packet tree

At the top packet level shown in figure 11-60 there is no visible layering. This is not surprising, as the development team didn't provide for layering for the domain-oriented packets. For the domain-oriented packets, public interface compliance is key if one domain-oriented packet wants to use functionality from another.

A structure based on the domain is a typical phenomenon in ABAP systems. In contrast to Java, C#, or C++ systems, technical layering is never found on the first packet level and rarely in the packet structures contained therein. I think this is because technical layering in ABAP is expressed in terms of the various types of ABAP artifacts. The types and database tables are found at the bottom, on which function groups and reports are based, which in turn are used by transactions and Dynpros (an ABAP-specific interface technology).

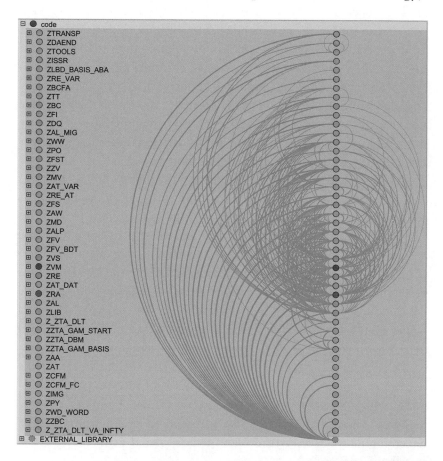

Figure 11-60

The Lambda *packet structure*

For the technical layering, we oriented ourselves using the names of the system's individual ABAP artifacts. We were able to distinguish between different ABAP artifacts such as reports, transactions, database tables, and so on, due to their type. We also found that *Lambda*'s architects did a good job with adding name extension to the classes and interfaces. For example, classes that have controller functionality are identified by the _CTR_ or _CONTRL extension.

Lambda's architects have developed their own pattern language (see Section 6.6), which provides a great deal of clarity in the system's architecture. Using these ABAP artifact types and naming conventions, we were able to model and examine *Lambda*'s technical layering within one day.

Figure 11-61 shows *Lambda*'s technical layering and SAP functionality without restrictions due to interfaces. At the top, we modeled two layers that contain all artifacts that are either obsolete or not transportable. Obsolete artifacts (indicated by the red arcs from the code to the "Obsolete Objects" layer) are those that the development team actually wanted to delete but couldn't because they are used by other artifacts. Non-transportable objects are artifacts that are in the $TMP or $XMPL packet in SAP. SAP has its own transport mechanism for transferring artifacts from the development system to the test or production environments. Artifacts that are stored in these packets should under no circumstances go into test or production. This is not a problem in itself, and only raises issues if other artifacts need these non-transportable objects. This is why we placed the "Non-transportable objects" layer above *Lambda*. All uses of these objects are shown as red arcs.

Technical layering

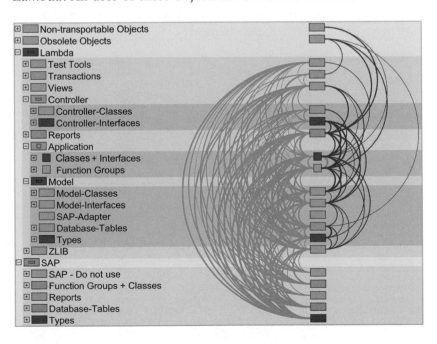

Figure 11-61

Technical layering

in Lambda

ABAP Pattern Language

Most of the relationships shown in figure 11-61 follow the layering planned by *Lambda*'s architects, and only three per cent of the relationships don't conform. Approximately a quarter of the relationships are based on reports and function groups that were not designed according to object-oriented principles. During our analysis, we examined a number of these layer violations. Function groups are often used in ABAP in a way that makes them architecturally distinct from object-oriented classes. Function groups are containers for function modules, each of which offers its own functionality. However, function groups can also offer functions and variables that are used by multiple function modules. This enables you to easily create large function groups that, in *Lambda*, contain up to 40,000 lines of code. We are still in discussion with *Lambda*'s architects about how to build a meaningful representation of the function groups and the function modules they contain using an appropriate tool (such as Sotograph).

Public interfaces

The structure shown in figure 11-61 strongly suggests that *Lambda*'s technical layering requires the use of public interfaces. For example, it is obvious that in the Model layer the interface models from outside the layer and not the model classes should be used. The situation is similar for the database tables and various SAP functionalities that *Lambda* uses.

Figure 11-62

Public interface violations

in Lambda

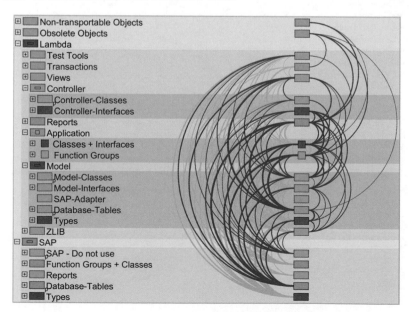

In figure 11-62 the many red arcs (i.e., violations) on the left of the central axis have become visible because we declared different sub-layers as private (indicated by the "p" subscript). In this illustration, we have grayed out the green (permitted) arcs to make the violations easier to see.

The model shown in figure 11-62 represents the architects' vision for the system's future architecture. Ideally, they would like to use the model classes to write a capsule for all database accesses. The many red arcs to the database table layer in figure 11-62 show that they have not yet reached this stage. Eighty-nine per cent of the public interface violations in figure 11-62 are caused by the use of database tables defined in *Lambda* or SAP. This illustrates the strong integration of SAP applications with the database.

Domain-oriented split

Following technical layering, we analyzed the domain-oriented partitioning. It was important to the architects that the individual domain packets were addressed via clear public interfaces. For each domain packet, there should be one or more function groups that make the functionality accessible to other domain packets from the outside. These function groups are to be stored in a sub-packet specifically designed for this purpose, which makes its public interface character clear via naming conventions. This sub-packet thus forms a facade for other packets, so that the internals of the corresponding packet remain hidden. Since *Lambda* is a large system with many functional packets, we worked our way through the analysis from domain packet to domain packet—a structure that was already visible in the system's newer source code. However, many of the older areas still have to be converted to the new structure, which equates to a lot of work for someone.

Class cycles

As with all our other case studies, we finished up by taking a look at the system's class cycles. For a system as large as *Lambda*, which has been developed over many years, the number and size of the existing cycles is very small. The largest cycle comprises just 13 artifacts and less than two per cent of all artifacts are involved in cycles. The architects have obviously done a very good job with their specifications for class names and the resulting pattern language.

The next steps   The pending tasks for improving *Lambda*'s architecture are:

1. Dissolve the technical layering violations
2. Resolve the public interface violations in the technical layer model
3. Clearly structure the domain-oriented public interfaces
4. Discuss and introduce a database capsule if necessary

12 Conclusion: The Path Toward Sustainable Architecture

We are living in very interesting times! I like to compare our current knowledge of software architecture with the cathedral builders of the 12th century. Back then, visionaries began the construction of incredibly impressive buildings. Some of them are still standing, but others were never finished or collapsed soon after construction was completed. Structural analysis and knowledge of suitable materials developed over time and in parallel to the construction work. Our situation today is very similar. Nobody has to apply for building permits for software systems, even though a system failure can have dramatic consequences that are certainly comparable to those of a collapsed cathedral.

Architecture in the 12th century

In this book (and of course in many others too) you will find some first steps toward a type of standardization that a potential construction supervisor could review. We have provided you with plenty of tips on what you can do as a developer, architect, project manager, or manager to keep the level of technical debt in your projects low. The most important tasks to help you prepare for a review of your technical debt are summarized below. Using the keywords in the margin, you can use the index to navigate to the chapters that contain more detailed information on your chosen topic.

Building permits for software

- Schedule regular architecture discussions with all participants. Only those who know the architecture can preserve it. Ignorance leads to continual architectural erosion.

Architecture is a "Holschuld"

- Select the architectural style(s) that you would like to use with your teams. Make sure everyone knows the architectural style and its rules. Review your choices regularly.

Architectural styles prevent debt

Layered architecture   ■ Don't just rely on rough architectural styles, such as layered architecture. Use a pattern language that suits your needs. A pattern language regulates and structures the class level.

Pattern languages   ■ Monitor the use of your pattern language. Don't allow the creation of "annual growth rings" due to new patterns being added every year. Question the patterns provided by the frameworks you use. Make sure the framework patterns fit into your pattern language and that they don't dilute it.

Domain-oriented layering   ■ Make sure good domain-oriented design plays an important role in your organization. Good domain-oriented design is the foundation of long-lasting architecture. Keep domain-oriented and technical classes separate.

Microservices   ■ Plan to divide your domain-oriented modules into independent, autonomous units at an early stage. Use the possibilities offered by Domain-Driven Design (DDD) to embed this division in the domain and the domain language.

Automate testing   ■ Ensure that automated testing is the most natural thing in the world for your teams. Without automated testing, refactoring becomes a dangerous undertaking.

Architecture analysis and improvement   ■ Check your architecture regularly at different levels using appropriate analysis tools. Consider everything the tools find as indicators, not as the truth. Discuss your findings regularly with your team. This strengthens quality awareness within the team.

■ Start your architectural reviews as early as possible in the development process. The quality of the architecture is quickly set in stone at the beginning of a project or during the implementation of an extension. The earlier you start, the easier the repairs will be.

Training and Development   ■ Visit as many conferences as you can to keep up with the latest trends. Continuous engagement with the software development scene ensures that everyone involved remains alert and ready to improve their skills.

This entire book focuses on the sustainability of the internal structure of software systems, but the subject of software architecture itself of course encompasses much more. In addition to the topics covered in this book, software architects have to deal with a variety of other topics too. These include:

- Technical concepts such as distribution, integration, persistence, security, logging, scalability, exception and error handling, and much more besides.

- IT landscapes and their implementation using service-oriented architecture, messaging, and other communication models

- Business processes and their meaningful implementation in individual systems and IT landscapes

- Communication and documentation of the chosen architecture and architectural decisions within the teams and for all other stakeholders

- Architecture management that coordinates business objectives, business processes, applications, and hardware

- Collaboration within the company that includes everyone who is involved in architectural roles

There are a variety of excellent books and online sources that discuss these topics. Every day, new concepts and ideas are being developed that present new possibilities for all of us. Have fun analyzing and improving your architecture!

Appendix

A Analysis Tools

At the beginning of the current millennium, there were still no good tools available for analyzing software systems. At the time, system architecture was examined by reading source code in the development environment. This was time-consuming and incomplete, as it is impossible to read all the lines of a system's code and somehow keep track of the overall structure. Fortunately, as of about 2002, a number of tools began to appear that allow an in-depth analysis of a system's actual architecture in a professional environment.

Read the source code

This appendix provides an overview of some common analysis tools, presented using a set of criteria based on the three phases of architectural analysis (extraction, mapping, and analysis) defined in figure 2-3 (see Section 2.2). These criteria define which functionality a tool must offer in order to aid successful architectural analysis and improvement:

Criteria for tools

■ **Extraction of the actual architecture:**

1. The structures within the source code (elements such as classes, packages, and relationships) are parsed and displayed

2. The structures provided by the build artifacts are parsed and displayed

■ **Mapping the target architecture to the actual architecture:**

3. Modeling of architectural elements such as layers and subsystems is possible for any degree of nesting

4. Modeling of the public interfaces for all architectural elements

5. Assigning elements of the actual architecture (such as classes, packages, namespaces, and directories) to architectural elements such as layers and subsystems is possible using selections and regular expressions

6. Support for the parallel setup of multiple models for different views of the architecture

■ **Analysis of the actual architecture:**

7. Architectural violations can be inspected with graphical support at all levels right down to the source code

8. Filters can be set so that only partial aspects of the architecture are visible—for example, classes that cause a layer violation

9. Refactoring such as moving classes and packages or creating new packages

10. Evaluation of typical object-oriented metrics and complexity metrics

11. Definition of custom queries for inspection of any aspect of the actual architecture

12. The evolution of the architecture over time can be analyzed by comparing different source code states

This book only mentions tools that I have used myself in real-world customer workshops. I have come across other tools, too, that are great for long-term monitoring of architecture and quality development but are not yet suitable for the types of architectural improvement favored in this book. The Axivion Bauhaus Suite[1], Seerene[2], SonarQube[3], and TeamScale[4] are particularly exciting. Axivion's Bauhaus Suite is great for analyzing software in embedded systems. Seerene evaluates metrics from various sources and presents them as cities, making it very well suited to illustrating technical debt issues to management at an implementation level. SonarQube is an open-source dashboard that can be used to monitor metrics and architecture rules using onboard functionality and additional plug-ins. TeamScale provides comprehensive support for quality metrics and integrates well with development environments.

---

1 *www.axivion.com*
2 *www.seerene.com* (formerly SoftwareDiagnostics)
3 *www.sonarqube.com* (formerly Sonar)
4 *www.teamscale*.com

I would like to apologize to all the companies who develop tools that I have forgotten or only mention in passing. Furthermore, if I have missed anything or got anything wrong in my descriptions of the software I use, please let me know so I can get it right in the future.

A.1 Lattix

Lattix[5] analyzes software systems written in ActionScript, Ada, C/C++/Objective-C/Delphi Pascal, Excel, Fortran, Java, JavaScript, .NET, Oracle, SQL, and Sybase. Once imported, a system's structure is displayed as a Dependency Structure Matrix (DSM). The relationships between the individual components are displayed as numbers at the corresponding intersections. The rows of the matrix can be expanded and collapsed.

Dependency Structure Matrix

Lattix displays layered architectures so that relationships are only shown in the lines below the diagonal. All the relationships shown in the cells above the diagonal are layer violations. Lattix enables you to follow and analyze violations right down to the source code level (see fig. A-1).

Figure A-1

Dependency Structure Matrix in Lattix[6]

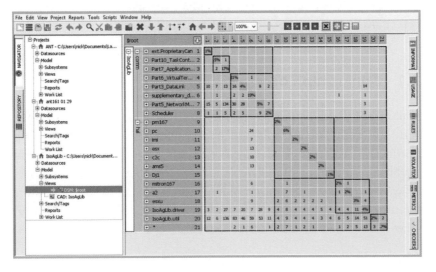

---

5 *www.lattix.com*

6 Illustration courtesy of *www.lattix.com.*

Conceptual Architecture   The architecture is modeled in the matrix or in a so-called Concep-
Diagram   tual Architecture Diagram (see fig. A-2), where rules can be created
and public interfaces defined for the various relationships involved.

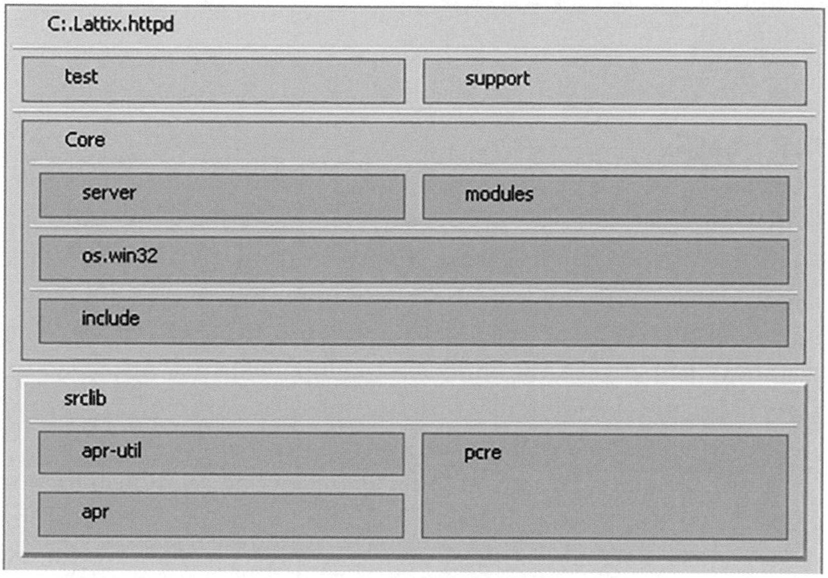

Figure A-2
Conceptual Architecture
Diagram in Lattix[7]

Lattix fulfills all the extraction, mapping, and analysis conditions
listed at the beginning of this chapter except #5 (regular expressions), #8 (custom filters), and #11 (custom queries).

A.2   Sonargraph Architect

Architecture view   Sonargraph Architect inspects the internal structure of Java software systems. Sonargraph Architect is hello2morrow's follow-up
product for the Sotograph /SotoArc platform (see Section A.3) and
enables architecture modeling in groups of layers, views, and sections, as well as the definition of additional public interfaces. Unlike
the other tools presented here, Sonargraph models an architectural
view rather than the source code structure (s. fig. A-3).

---

7   Illustration courtesy of *www.lattix.com*.

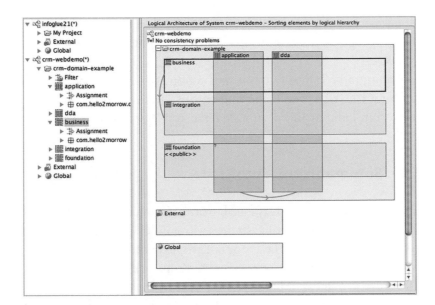

Figure A-3

Architecture view

Architectural violations can then be analyzed in the Sonargraph Explorer and displayed in the Exploration view (s. fig. A-4). Just like Sotograph, Sonargraph offers numerous options for filtering its views. Dependencies can be examined at any depth of abstraction. In the latest version, you can model the architecture directly on the source code, similar to Sotograph.

Exploration view

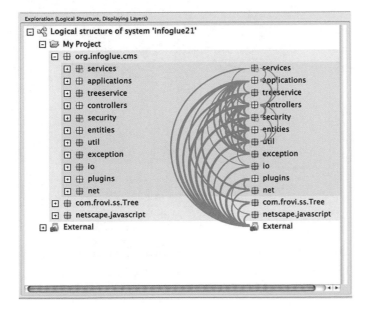

Figure A-4

The Sonargraph Exploration view

Alongside architectural analysis, Sonargraph also offers a variety of metrics, plus integration into your development environment or SonarQube.

Sonargraph fulfills all the extraction, mapping, and analysis conditions listed at the beginning of this chapter except #2 (structures from build artifacts) and #11 (custom queries).

A.3   Sotograph and SotoArc

Sotograph and SotoArc form a platform that enables the inspection of the internal structure of systems written in C/C++, Java, C#, PHP, ABAP, and TypeScript. The Sotoplatform also offers an interface for importing other programming languages using external parsers.

SotoArc   Figure A-5 shows SotoArc. This part of the platform models a software system's architecture and lets you inspect any violations. For more details on the options offered by SotoArc, see Section 2.3.

Figure A-5

SotoArc's graphical architecture modeling view

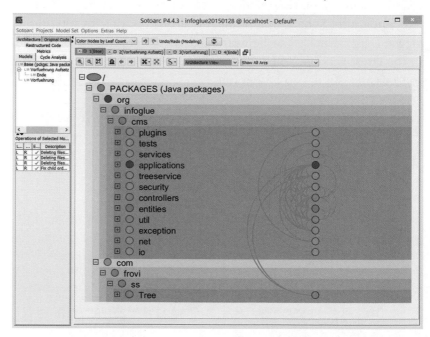

Sotograph   Sotograph is the second part of the Sotoplatform and is designed to evaluate and graph metrics for all architectural elements on various different levels. It also allows custom queries from the Sotograph database, which can be edited using an SQL variant. It also offers support for comparing multiple versions of a single system.

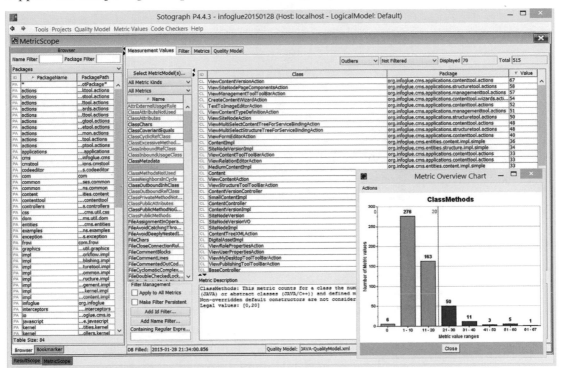

Sotograph and SotoArc fulfill all the extraction, mapping, and analysis criteria defined at the beginning of this chapter.

Figure A-6

Sotograph metric evaluation

A.4 Structure101

Structure101 analyzes software systems written in Java and C# natively, and additional languages can be imported via an interface using third-party parsers. Figure A-7 shows the tool's user interface, which can be used to analyze existing system structures. The main function of the tool's Levelized Structure Map is the visualization of classes within their packages and build artifacts.

Levelized Structure Matrix

Figure A-7

*Levelized Structure Map
in Structure*[8]

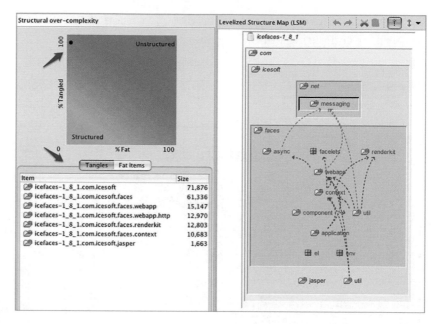

There are numerous filter options for viewing, and dependencies can be mapped at any depth of abstraction. For example, you can choose whether all dependencies should be displayed or only those between selected elements. Permitted dependencies are represented by solid arrows, while dashed arrows represent unwanted dependencies. You can also move elements within the graph to simulate refactoring.

Architecture diagram   In addition to working on the actual architecture extracted from the source code and build artifacts, Structure101 can be used to generate architectural diagrams (see fig. A-8). These diagrams can be used to model different views of the architecture. The elements of the individual architectural components can be custom defined using regular expressions and public interfaces can be individually specified. Structure101 can also evaluate a limited set of metrics.

---

8   Illustration courtesy of *www.structure101.com*

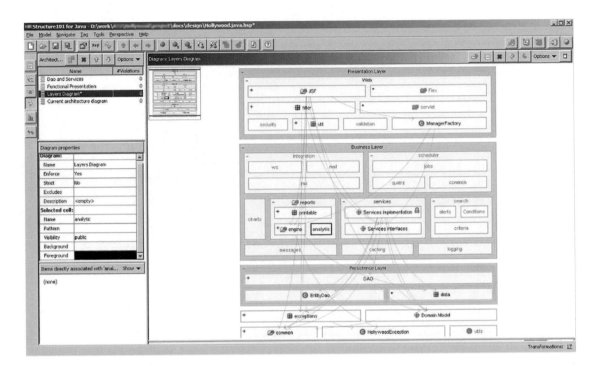

Structure101 fulfills most of the extraction, mapping, and analysis criteria defined at the beginning of the chapter. The only exceptions are #10 (metrics) and #11 (custom queries).

Figure A-8

Architecture Diagrams in Structure101

References

[Alexander 1982] Alexander, C.: A City is not a Tree. In: Kaplan, pp.; Kaplan, R. (edpp.): Humanscape – Environments for People, 1982, pp. 377-402.

[ANSI/IEEE 2000] ANSI/IEEE-Standard-1471: IEEE Recommended Practice for Architectural Description of Software-Intensive Systems – Description. ANSI/IEEE Computer Society, 2000.

[Bass et al. 2007] Bass, M.; Mikulovic, V.; Bass, L.; Herbsleb, J.; Cataldo, M.: Architectural Misalignment: An Experience Report. In: Proceedings of the 6th Working IEEE/IFIP Conference on Software Architecture, IEEE Computer Society, 2007, pp. 17-26.

[Bass et al. 2012] Bass, L.; Clements, P.; Kazman, R.: Software Architecture in Practice. Addison-Wesley, Reading, MA, 2012.

[Bäumer et al. 1997] Bäumer, D.; Gryczan, G.; Knoll, R.; Lilienthal, C.; Riehle, D.; Züllighoven, H.: Framework Development for Large Systempp. Communications of the ACM, 40 (1997), 10, pp. 52-59.

[Beck 2005] Beck, K.: Extreme Programming Explained: Embrace Change. 2nd ed., Pearson Education, Upper Saddle River, NJ, 2005.

[Becker-Pechau & Bennicke 2007] Becker-Pechau, P.; Bennicke, M.: Concepts of Modeling Architectural Module Views for Compliance Checks Based on Architectural Stylepp. In: Software Engineering and Application (SEA 2007), Cambridge, MA, 2007.

[Binder 1999] Binder, R. V.: Testing object-oriented systems: models, patterns, and toolpp. Addison Wesley Longmann Publishing Co., Boston, MA, 1999.

[Bischofberger et al. 2004] Bischofberger, W.; Kühl, J.; Löffler, pp.: Sotograph – A Pragmatic Approach to Source Code Architecture Conformance Checking. In: EWSA 2004, Springer-Verlag, Berlin, Heidelberg, 2004, pp. 1-9.

[Boisot & Child 1999] Boisot, M.; Child, J.: Organizations as Adaptive Systems in Complex Environments: The Case of China. Organization Science, 10 (1999), 3, pp. 237-252.

[Booch 2004] Booch, G.: Object-Oriented Analysis and Design with Applicationpp. Addison Wesley Longman Publishing Co., Boston, MA, 2004.

[Brooks 1986] Brooks, F. P.: No Silver Bullet – Essence and Accidents of Software Engineering. In: International Federation of Information Processing (IFIP)

Congress '86, Dublin, Ireland, Elsevier Science Publisher B.V., 1986, pp. 1069-1076.

[Buschmann et al. 2007] Buschmann, F.; Henney, K.; Schmidt, D. C.: Pattern-Oriented Software Architecture – On Patterns and Pattern Languagepp. John Wiley & Sons, 2007.

[Cunningham 1992] Cunningham, W.: The WyCash Portfolio Management System. Experience Report, OOPSLA '92, 1992.

[Darcy 2001] Darcy, D. P.: Software Complexity: Integrating the Task Complexity Model and Cognition. Joseph M. Katz Graduate School of Business, University of Pittsburgh, Pittsburgh, 2001.

[Darcy & Slaughter 2005] Darcy, D. P.; Slaughter, pp. A.: The Structural Complexity of Software: An Experimental Test. IEEE Transaction on Software Engineering, 31 (2005), 11, pp. 982-995.

[Davis 1984] Davis, J. pp.: Chunks: A Basis for Complexity Measurement. Information Processing & Management, 20 (1984), 1, pp. 119-127.

[Dijkstra 1968] Dijkstra, E. W.: The Structure of the T.H.E. Multiprogramming System. Communications of the ACM, 11 (1968), 5, pp. 341-346.

[Dijkstra 1976] Dijkstra, E. W.: A Discipline of Programming. Prentice Hall, Englewood Cliffs, NJ, 1976.

[Ebert 1995] Ebert, C.: Complexity traces: an instrument for software project management. In : Fenton, N. E.; Whitty, R.; Iizuka, Y. (edpp.): Software Quality: Assurance and Measurement – A worldwide Perspective. International Thomson Computer Press, London, 1995, pp. 166-176.

[Evans 2004] Evans, E.: Domain-Driven Design: Tackling Complexity in the heart of Software. Addison-Wesley, 2004.

[Feathers 2004] Feathers, M. C.: Working Effectively with Legacy Code. Pearson Education, Upper Saddle River, NJ, 2004.

[Fenton & Pfleegler 1997] Fenton, N. E.; Pfleegler, pp. L.: Software Metrics: A Rigorous & Practical Approach. PWS Publishing Company, Boston, 1997.

[Fielding 2000] Fielding, R. T.: Architectural Styles and the Design of Network-based Software Architecturepp. Dissertation University of California, Irvine, 2000.

[Floyd 1992] Floyd, C.: Software Development as Reality Construction. In: Floyd, C.; Züllighoven, H.; Budde, R.; Keil-Slawik, R. (edpp.):

Software Development and Reality Construction. Springer-Verlag, Berlin, 1992, pp. 86-100.

[Floyd 1993] Floyd, C.: STEPS – a methodical approach to PD. Communications of the ACM, 36 (1993), 6, pp. 83.

[Floyd et al. 1989] Floyd, C.; Reisin, F.-M.; Schmidt, G: STEPS to Software Development with Userpp. In: ESEC'89, University of Warwick, Coventry, UK, Springer-Verlag, 1989, pp. 48-64.

[Fowler 2001] Fowler, M.: Reducing Coupling. IEEE Software, 18 (2001), 4, pp. 102-104.

[Fowler 2002] Fowler, M.: Patterns of enterprise application architecture. Addison-Wesley, Boston, MA, 2002.

[Fowler & Lewis 2014] Fowler, M.; Lewis, J.: Microservices, *http://martinfowler.com/articles/microservicepp.html*, 2014.

[Fowler et al. 2001] Fowler, M.; Beck, K.; Bryant, J.; Opdyke, W.; Roberts, D.: Refactoring – Improving the Design of Existing Code. Addison-Wesley, Boston, MA, 2001.

[Gamma et al. 1994] Gamma, E.; Helm, R.; Johnson, R.; Vlissides, J.: Design Patterns, Elements of Reusable Object-Oriented Software. Addison-Wesley, 1994.

[Garlan 2000] Garlan, D.: Software architecture: a roadmap. In: Proceedings of the Conference on The Future of Software Engineering, ACM Press, Limerick, Ireland, 2000, pp. 91-101.

[Glass 2002] Glass, R. L.: Sorting out software complexity. Communications of the ACM, 45 (2002), 11, pp. 19-21.

[Henderson-Sellers 1996] Henderson-Sellers, B.: Object-oriented metrics: measures of complexity. Prentice-Hall, Inc., 1996.

[Hofmeister et al. 2000] Hofmeister, C.; Nord, R.; Soni, D.: Applied Software Architecture. Addison-Wesley, 2000.

[Horstmann 2006] Horstmann, C. pp.: Object Oriented Design and Patternpp. John Wiley & Sons, 2006.

[IEEE 1990] IEEE: IEEE Standard Glossary of Software Engineering Terminology. IEEE Computer Society, 1990.

[iSAQB 2019] Gharbi, M.; Koschel, A.; Rausch, A.: Software Architecture Fundamentals, dpunkt.verlag, 2019.

[Jacobson 1992] Jacobson, I.: Object-Oriented Software Engineering. Addison-Wesley, Reading, MA, 1992.

[Jacobson et al. 1999] Jacobson, I.; Booch, G.; Rumbaugh, J.: The Unified Software Development Procespp. Addison-Wesley, Reading, MA, 1999.

[Kim & Garlan 2006] Kim, J. pp.; Garlan, D.: Analyzing architectural styles with alloy. In: Proceedings of the ISSTA 2006 workshop on Role of software architecture for testing and analysis, ACM Press, Portland, Maine, 2006, pp. 70-80.

[Knodel & Popescu 2007] Knodel, J.; Popescu, D.: A Comparison of Static Architecture Compliance Checking Approachepp. In: Proceedings of the Sixth Working IEEE/IFIP Conference on Software Architecture (WICSA'07), IEEE Computer Society, 2007, pp. 12.

[Koschke & Simon 2003] Koschke, R.; Simon, D.: Hierarchical Reflexion Modelpp. In: Proceedings of the 10th Working Conference on Reverse Engineering, IEEE Computer Society, 2003, pp. 36.

[Kruchten 2004] Kruchten, P.: The Rational Unified Process: An Introduction. 3rd ed., Addison-Wesley, 2004.

[Lakos 1996] Lakos, J.: Large-scale C++ Software Design. Addison Wesley Longmann Publishing Co., Redwood City, CA, 1996.

[Larman 2004] Larman, C.: Applying UML and Patterns: An Introduction to Object-Oriented Analysis and Design and Iterative Development. 3rd ed., Prentice Hall PTR, 2004.

[Lehman 1980] Lehman, M. M.: Programs, Life Cycles, and Laws of Software Evolution. Proceedings of the IEEE, 68 (1980), 9, pp. 1060-1076.

[Lilienthal & Züllighoven 1997] Lilienthal, C.; Züllighoven, H.: Application-oriented usage quality: the tools and materials approach. Interactions, 4 (1997), 6, pp. 35-41.

[Lippert & Züllighoven 2002] Lippert, M.; Züllighoven, H.: Using extreme programming to manage high-risk projects successfully. In: Software quality and software testing in internet timepp. Springer-Verlag, New York, 2002, pp. 85-100.

[Martin 2000] Martin, R. C.: Principle and Patterns, 2000; *http://www. objectmentor.com/resources/articles/Principles_and_Patternpp.pdf.*

[Martin 2013] Martin, R. C. : Agile Software Development, Principles, Patterns, and Practicepp. Prentice Hall International, Upper Saddle River, NJ, 2013.

[Mayrhauser & Vans 1997] Mayrhauser, A. v.; Vans, A. M.: Program understanding behavior during debugging of large scale software. In: Papers presented at the 7th workshop on Empirical studies of programmerpp. ACM Press, Alexandria, VA, United States, 1997, pp. 157-179.

[McBride 2007] McBride, M. R.: The software architect. Communications of the ACM, 50 (2007), 5, pp. 75-81.

[McCabe 1976] McCabe, T.: A Complexity Measure. IEEE Transaction on Software Engineering, SE-2 (1976), 4, pp. 308-320.

[McCabe & Butler 1989] McCabe, T.; Butler, C. W.: Design Complexity Measurement and Testing. Communications of the ACM, 32 (1989), 12, pp. 1415-1425.

[Melton & Tempero 2006] Melton, H.; Tempero, E.: An Empirical Study of Cycles among Classes in Java. Department of Computer Science, University of Auckland, Nr. UoA-SE-2006-1, 2006.

[Meyer 1995] Meyer, B.: Object success: a manager's guide to object orientation, its impact on the corporation, and its use for reengineering the software procespp. Prentice-Hall, Inc., 1995.

[Miller 1956] Miller, G. A.: The magical number seven plus minus two: Some limits on our capacity for processing informationpp. Psychological Review 63, 1956, pp. 81-97.

[Murphy et al. 2001] Murphy, G. C.; Notkin, D.; Sullivan, K. J.: Software Reflexion Models: Bridging the Gap between Design and Implementation. IEEE Transaction on Software Engineering, 27 (2001), 4, pp. 364-380.

[Myers 1978] Myers, G. J.: Composite/Structured Design. Van Nostrand Reinhold, New York, 1978.

[Noak 2007] Noak, A.: Unified Quality Measures for Clusterings, Layouts, and Orderings of Graphs, and Their Application as Software Design Criteria. Dissertation, Fakultät für Mathematik, Naturwissenschaften und Informatik, Brandenburgische Technische Universität Cottbus, Cottbus, 2007.

[Norman 1982] Norman, D. A.: Learning and Memory. W. H. Freeman & Co, ACM Press, 1982.

[Parnas 1972] Parnas, D. L.: On the Criteria to be Used in Decomposing Systems into Modulepp. Communications of the ACM, 15 (1972), 12, pp. 1053-1058.

[Parnas 1974] Parnas, D. L.: On a "Buzzword": Hierarchical Structure. In: IFIP Congress 74, North-Holland Publishing Company, 1974, pp. 336-339.

[Parnas 1979] Parnas, D. L.: Designing Software for Ease of Extension and Contraction. In: Hoffmann, D. M.; Weiss, D. M. (edpp.): Software fundamentals: Collected Papers by David L. Parnas, Pearson, Saddle River, 1979, pp. 269-286.

[Parnas 1994] Parnas, D. L.: Software Aging. In: 16th International Conference on Software Engineering, Sorento, Italy, IEEE Press, 1994, pp. 279-287.

[Parnas et al. 1985] Parnas, D. L.; Clements, P.; Weiss, D. M.: The Modular Structure of Complex Systempp. IEEE Transaction on Software Engineering, SE-11 (1985), 3, pp. 259-266.

[Reussner & Hasselbring 2008] Reussner, R.; Hasselbring, W. (Hrsg.): Handbuch der Software-Architektur. dpunkt.verlag, Heidelberg, 2008.

[Riehle & Züllighoven 1995] Riehle, D.; Züllighoven, H.: A pattern language for tool construction and integration based on the tools and materials metaphor. In: Pattern languages of program design. ACM Press/Addison-Wesley Publishing Co., 1995, pp. 9-42.

[Riel 1996] Riel, A. J.: Object-Oriented Design Heuristicpp. Addison-Wesley Longman Publishing Co., 1996.

[Storey et al. 1999] Storey, M.-A. D.; Fracchia, F. D.; Mueller, H. A. Cognitive Design Elements to Support the Construction of a Mental Model during Software Exploration. Journal of Software Systems, 44 (1999), 3, pp. 171-185.

[Voss et al. 2006] Voß, M.; Hess, A.; Humm, B.: Towards a framework for large scale quality architecture. In: Perspectives in Software Quality– 2nd International Conference on the Quality of Software Architectures, 2006, pp. 52-58.

[Wallnau et al. 1996] Wallnau, K.; Clements, P.; Morris, E.; Krut, R.: The Gadfly: An Approach to Architectural-Level System Comprehension. In: Proceedings of the 4th International Workshop on Program Comprehension (WPC '96), IEEE Computer Society, 1996, pp. 178.

[Wirfs-Brock & McKean 2002] Wirfs-Brock, R.; McKean, A.: Object Design: Roles, Responsibilities, and Collaborationpp. Pearson Education, 2002.

[Woodfield 1979] Woodfield, pp. N.: An experiment on unit increase in problem complexity. IEEE Transactions on Software Engineering, SE-5 (1979), 2, pp. 76-79.

[Zimmermann & Nagappan 2006] Zimmermann, T.; Nagappan, N.: Predicting Subsystem Failures using Dependency Graph Complexitiepp. Microsoft Research, Nr. MSR-TR-2006-126, 2006.

[Züllighoven 2005] Züllighoven, H.: Object-Oriented Construction Handbook. Morgan Kaufmann Publishers, San Francisco, 2005.

Index

Mahbouba Gharbi · Arne Koschel ·
Andreas Rausch

Software Architecture Fundamentals

A Study Guide for the Certified Professional
for Software Architecture® – Foundation Level
iSAQB compliant

2019
232 pages, paperback
€ 36,90 (D)
US $ 39,95

ISBN:
Print   978-3-86490-625-1
PDF   978-3-96088-644-0
ePub   978-3-96088-645-7
mobi   978-3-96088-646-4

This book gives you all the basic know-how you
need to begin designing scalable system software
architectures. It goes into detail on all the most
important terms and concepts and how they relate
to other IT practices.

Following on from the basics, it describes the
techniques and methods required for the planning, documentation, and quality management of
software architectures. It details the role, the tasks,
and the work environment of a software architect,
as well as looking at how the job itself is embedded in company and project structures.

The book is designed for self-study and covers
the curriculum for the Certified Professional for
Software Architecture – Foundation Level (CPSA-
F) exam as defined by the International Software
Architecture Qualification Board (iSAQB).

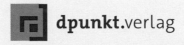